COSTING COMMUNITY

THEORY AND PRACTICE

Costing Community Care:

Theory and Practice

EDITED BY ANN NETTEN AND JENNIFER BEECHAM

PSSRU
UNIVERSITY OF KENT
AT CANTERBURY ■■■■

First published in Great Britain in 1993

Arena
Ashgate Publishing Ltd
Gower House
Croft Road
Aldershot
Hants GU11 3HR
England

Ashgate Publishing Company
Old Post Road
Brookfield
Vermont 05036
U.S.A.

Reprinted 1993

A CIP catalogue record for this book is available from the British Library

ISBN 1 85742 098 5 (Hardback)
ISBN 1 85742 102 7 (Paperback)

Typeset at the PSSRU, University of Kent at Canterbury

Printed in Great Britain at the University Press, Cambridge

Contents

Part III: The Application of Costs

Acknowledgements

This volume of essays grew from a series of workshops held in the Personal Social Services Research Unit so there are very few members of the Unit who have not contributed in one way or another. Particular contributions are acknowledged at the end of individual chapters. Our special thanks, however, must go to members of the Directorate (particularly Martin Knapp) for their cooperation and encouragement throughout the last year. All authors deserve a grateful mention for working so hard and for meeting our tight deadlines: Caroline Allen, Andrew Bebbington, David Challis, John Chesterman, Bleddyn Davies, Catherine Drury, Andrew Fenyo, Eriko Gould, Aiden Kelly, Martin Knapp, Paul McCrone, and Karen Traske. In addition, we would like to thank Charlotte Salter for her comments on early draft chapters, Deborah Sillifant for her organisational and secretarial support, Nick Brawn for the beautiful diagrams, and last but not least Jane Dennett for undertaking the desk-top publishing and providing invaluable advice and support.

Ann Netten and Jennifer Beecham
August 1992

List of Contributors

Caroline Allen, Junior Research Fellow, Institute of Social and Economic Research, University of West Indies, Barbados, formerly Research Associate, PSSRU.

Andrew Bebbington, Assistant Director, PSSRU.

Jennifer Beecham, Research Fellow, PSSRU.

David Challis, Assistant Director, PSSRU and Reader in Social Work and Social Care.

John Chesterman, Research Fellow, PSSRU.

Bleddyn Davies, Director, PSSRU and Professor of Social Policy.

Catherine Drury, Senior Practitioner, Medway/Swale Aftercare Project, Royal Philanthropic Society, formerly Research Associate, PSSRU.

Andrew Fenyo, Research Officer, PSSRU.

Eriko Gould, Research Associate, PSSRU.

Aidan Kelly, Senior Research Fellow, PSSRU.

Martin Knapp, Deputy Director, PSSRU and Professor of the Economics of Social Care.

Paul McCrone, Research Associate, PSSRU.

Ann Netten, Research Fellow, PSSRU.

Karen Traske, Research Associate, PSSRU.

Foreword

The publication of this book is extremely timely. Personal social services are undergoing the most radical changes for more than a generation. The Government's community care reforms, heralded by its White Papers and by the *National Health Service and Community Care Act 1990*, present local authorities with formidable challenges. Under the new approach to service planning and delivery, maximising the delivery of care within available resources will require not only different kinds of cost information but greater skill in cost analysis. Local government managers, and indeed central government administrators, seeking a better understanding of what cost information will be required, how it can be generated and how it can be applied to important issues of policy and practice need look no further than this book.

In the social services area the collection and analysis of cost information has too often been seen as at best a necessary chore and at worst a threat to 'sensible' care policies. Cost analysis has been something that can be left to backroom or 'ivory tower' accountants, statisticians and economists. This attitude always was bad management. If it were continued in the new 'internal market' it would be a recipe for short-changing clients, staff and the taxpayer. Appropriate cost information and analysis is simply too central to good policy-making and practice to be left only to specialists. A recurring theme of the essays in this book is that cost analysis does not make decisions but it can make decisions better informed. Put bluntly, policy-makers and managers who do not insist on good cost analysis, or do not use it when it is provided, will make more bad decisions than they should.

All social service managers should aim to be smart consumers of cost information. This does not mean that they have to become cost 'experts'. It does mean that they should have a good grasp of the uses of cost information and should have sufficient understanding of the basic principles of costing to be able to distinguish between good and poor cost analyses. The value of this book is that it brings together a clear exposition of the basic principles of costing, practical guidance on how to carry out costings, and illustrations of the application of cost information in tackling important social care problems. The advice and illustrations are based on extensive hands-on experience:

the Personal Social Services Research Unit at the University of Kent has unique expertise in producing comprehensive costings of community care and comparing costs with outcomes.

I recommend this book to personal social service policy-makers, managers and planners throughout local government and to their peers in the Department of Health. For all those concerned with maximising client welfare it should prove a cost-effective purchase!

Clive H. Smee
Chief Economic Adviser, Department of Health
September 1992

1 Costing Community Care: The Role of this Book

Martin Knapp, Ann Netten and Jennifer Beecham

1 The need for cost information

Cost information of some sort has long been available to policy-makers. For many years, local authority accountants and treasurers have been guided by their own codes of professional excellence, and their professional association, the Chartered Institute of Public Finance and Accountancy (CIPFA), has published standardised local authority accounts. Until relatively recently, it seemed as if these accounts were annually pored over by treasurers but annually ignored by all but the most senior or diligent of social services employees. Cost information has long been available, but little used.

For traditional (top-down, supply-led, single-agency) public expenditure planning, the cost information contained in agency accounts was probably adequate in design and quantity to satisfy most needs. However, the systems and incentives promoted by the *National Health Service and Community Care Act 1990* require a rather different approach to service planning and delivery. Ideally, as the Act, its antecedent White Papers and its later guidance and implementation documents make plain, health and social care decision-making will be bottom-up, needs-led and multiple-agency, with innovations encouraged by financial and other incentives, and system implications couched in terms of social and not merely public expenditures. The nature and intensity of the cost information requirements of the 1990s will be rather different from those of previous decades.

Since its establishment in 1974, the Personal Social Services Research Unit (PSSRU) at the University of Kent at Canterbury, has devoted much of its research activity to the resource implications of social care, locating that research within the *production of welfare* framework which links needs, resources and outcomes. For many years, therefore, costs have been part of the process of evaluating extant services or specific innovations.

In 1991-92, a series of workshops was held in the PSSRU to share experiences and expertise in the field of costing. This volume has developed from these workshops, although authors have put a considerable amount of effort into developing their papers into chapters. Together the following chapters span the four principal activities that require cost information in 'the new world order': policy formation and planning; purchasing; providing; and policy and practice evaluation.

1.1 Policy-making and planning

One of the requirements to be introduced as a result of the 1990 Act is the development of community care plans, jointly drawn up by local and health authorities, agreed with central government, and published for wider consideration. Any plan which is to have a chance of succeeding must be affordable, and the context for the new community care plans will help to encourage individual public authorities to define 'affordability' less narrowly than before. One of criticisms of the community care arrangements of the 1980s, as voiced by the Audit Commission, Griffiths and others, was that perverse incentives within the system encouraged authorities to try to minimise their own costs while simultaneously increasing everyone else's. Community care planning will require information on population needs and preferences, the services to meet those needs, and the costs of providing those services to *all* provider agencies.

1.2 Purchasing

In addition to policy-makers, purchasers throughout organisations charged with ensuring efficiency in community care will require cost information. In contrast to providers, who will need to construct cost information, the main focus for purchasers will be evaluating cost information and prices in negotiating contracts and in purchasing 'in-house' services. Moreover, case management itself will have its own costs needs, for the community care White Paper (Cm 849, 1989) advises local authorities to devolve budgetary responsibilities down to case managers or case management teams. Wherever they are in the organisation, those who are using costs need to understand how to rate the quality of the information they are receiving.

1.3 Providing

On the other side of the purchaser/provider divide, providers need costs information both to secure funding and to set prices. Voluntary organisations have long had to identify the resource implications of proposals to secure funding from local authorities and other agencies. Contracting requirements will accelerate these needs. Moreover, any grant calculation and allocation requires detailed cost data of statutory agencies. For example, in many local social services authorities the work necessary to draw up bids for the Mental Illness Specific Grant funds represented the first detailed costing of social care services for many years.

In addition to bidding for grants, providers will need to price their services for sale, to clients and their relatives, to public authorities, or to budget-holding case managers. Establishing the costs incurred in providing the services is only one stage in this process, but it is an essential one if the aim of achieving value for money in the provision of social care is to be accomplished.

1.4 Evaluating policy and practice

Needs-based planning, preparing community care plans, and purchasing and providing services are relatively new sources of demand for costs information. Demands for costs data of somewhat greater vintage derive from the need to evaluate the resource implications of different, and especially new, policies and practices; from the occasional calculation of the social costs of a condition such as dementia; and in the perennial performance reviews required for public probity, now often built around 'value-for-money audits' and 'efficiency scrutinies'.

The number of people needing to use or construct costs information has grown enormously in recent years. If these people are to be successful in their various endeavours it is vital that the information they use in both constructing and using costs is valid. Basic textbooks in economics and accounting can provide a good grounding in the principles of costing, but putting the principles into practice is another matter. The PSSRU has amassed a great deal of experience in costs research over the past eighteen years, and in the process has had to face practical problems and devise pragmatic solutions. This book aims to help bridge the gap between theory and practice in costing community care, but it does not pretend to provide all the answers. The costing of social care is a developing area of work, one which will need to continue to develop, and rapidly, if it is to keep pace with changes in service delivery and growth in demand for information.

2 The organisation of this book

This book is divided into three sections covering the principles of constructing costs, the principles of using costs, and illustrations of the policy and practice value of costing community care services. There is necessarily some repetition: for example, fundamental concepts such as the principle of opportunity costing, the importance of costing comprehensively and comparing like with like recur throughout the book. Such reiteration of important axioms is regarded as essential in an area which cannot be an exact science and in which most practical applications will come with caveats and reservations.

The first section of the book will be of most interest to those involved in the construction of the costs of community care. Those using cost information will also find it helpful in assessing the value and inevitable limitations on the information they are given.

Chapter 2 provides essential background reading for all users of this book. It describes the basic theory of costing and endeavours to demystify economic terminology. Throughout this book an economic approach to costing is taken as the most appropriate means to tackle the types of problem identified above. While accountancy and related disciplines have much to offer when financial accountability is the primary concern, the economic concept of opportunity cost is more appropriate when addressing issues of policy choice, practice and research. The concept of opportunity cost is defined and the implications of this approach to costing social care are explored.

Chapter 3 builds on the issues of theory raised by the previous chapter and translates the costing process into practice. The authors distinguish four key stages in costing, identify the practical issues that arise, and offer pragmatic solutions which draw on experience gained during the evaluation of the Care in the Community demonstration programme. In this demonstration programme the contribution of the informal sector to care was minimal. This is unusual in the provision of community care, where the contribution of the informal sector is a key element, often acknowledged but rarely costed. Chapter 4 examines the particular difficulties associated with costing informal care and describes an approach to the problems involved.

Throughout the first section the point is constantly reiterated that *how* you cost depends on *why* you are costing. The second section of the book, devoted to principles of using cost information, begins with a chapter which details the importance of the four costing rules that should be applied whenever cost information is being used. The chapter draws on practical examples in research and distinguishes between cost-effectiveness, cost-benefit and cost-utility analyses.

Chapter 6 discusses the methodological issues that arise when using official data sources to construct unit costs. The advantages of easy availability and extensive coverage of services have to be balanced by the problems of validity and reliability. Nevertheless, the authors identify the value of these data in today's cost-conscious climate.

It was noted above that providers need to have cost information in order to price services. Chapter 7 explores the problems involved for local authorities in pricing services to budget-holders and charging final consumers for services. The chapter discusses the objectives of pricing and charging and identifies some of the issues when costing services in order to set a price.

Those involved in formulating policy will find Chapter 8 of particular interest. The chapter presents a sophisticated analysis which considers the possibilities of linking needs-based planning to care manager choices, and identifies the importance of understanding the long-run resource implications of choices between different modes of care.

The final section provides four case studies which demonstrate the variety of uses to which costs data can be put, the strength of costs analysis as a research and policy tool, and the practical importance of the four rules, identified in Chapter 5. Chapter 9 describes in some detail the costing of a single centre which provided a number of services to people infected with AIDS and HIV. This provides an illustration of how to cost outputs: an exercise that is going to be increasingly important to managers of small facilities.

PSSRU case management experiments have been very influential in the development of the current reforms. The arguments in favour of this approach to community care were particularly powerful because the evaluations provided a detailed comparison of the resource implications of different modes of care. Chapter 10 describes the specific difficulties and issues involved in costing the case management projects and the key causes of variation in the costs of community care.

Variations in costs of care are also explored in Chapter 11, which demon-strates the use of the cost function approach in examining the costs of mental health services. The authors examine the association between costs and client characteristics, needs and outcomes, and point to possible differences between the various public and independent sectors in the efficiency of care delivery.

A similar cost function approach is employed in Chapter 12, which describes the costs of providing intermediate treatment and associated support services to young offenders. Variations in costs between users are linked to characteristics, needs, criminal charges, and relations with family. These linkages help in the prediction of the future costs of alternative sentencing patterns.

Finally, Chapter 13 discusses the role of costs research undertaken by the PSSRU and puts this in the context of the changing climate of social care over the last two decades.

3 Conclusion

The rapidly-growing demand for information about costs in the field of community care will be familiar to most readers of this book. Cost information is not always easy to gather or to employ in practice, and one aim of this book is to link the theoretical requirements of costing exercises with pragmatic solutions to guide applications. The examples throughout the book demonstrate that costing is not straightforward – for example, how a cost is estimated depends fundamentally on the purpose of the costing. But with sound underpinning principles, appropriate design and a modicum of determination, costing is certainly feasible and generally enlightening.

Part I:
The Costing Process

2 Background Theory*

Martin Knapp

In the last twenty years it has been rare to find a public policy or practice proposal which has not had to answer a series of 'But what does it cost?' questions. The oil price rises of the 1970s, and the economic problems they created, brought a halt to the years of rapid expenditure growth, and ever since the UK and most other developed countries have enjoyed roller-coaster economic fortunes. A couple of years of economic growth might encourage governments to spend more on social care, but it does not take long for a downturn in macro-economic fortunes to force a reversal upon public, private and voluntary sector spending. It is hardly surprising, therefore, that social care providers are cost-conscious.

The cost constraint on social care has been the subject of considerable criticism, but – as the previous chapter argued – all too little research. It is still possible to find people – probably few of whom will read this book – who believe that social care should be beyond the vicissitudes of national economic well-being. To these people the villains of the piece are the short-sighted politician, the penny-pinching accountant and the hard-headed economist. The incontrovertible fact that there are not and never have been enough resources to meet all of society's wants or needs will have been overlooked by these cost-sceptics. It is the scarcity of resources which forces society to make choices, and costs are among the factors often taken into account in choosing, for few social care activities are costless. Politicians, accountants and economists do not always behave as one would wish, but to criticise them for being concerned with costs is naive and perverse.

If we want to make the best use of scarce resources, if we want to deploy available social care services in such a way as to maximise their effectiveness or their success, or to distribute them in accordance with agreed criteria of fairness or justice, then we need to take a careful look at the cost implications of policy designs and practice decisions. Allocating resources in one way immediately implies the rejection of an alternative allocation, and this is the key to understanding the meaning of cost and its measurement. This chapter concentrates on some aspects of theory, beginning with the concept of opportunity cost, which will be illustrated with examples from across the social care spectrum, and then examines the basic links between costs and outcomes. Total, average and marginal costs will be introduced and illustrated. The next chapter will then describe how these theoretical constructs allow the computation of costs for practice, research and other purposes.

1 Opportunity costs

'What does it cost to provide community care for a frail elderly person living alone?' This apparently straightforward and unambiguous question might be answered with an apparently straightforward and unambiguous answer, such as '£100 per week'. But this and other similar questions deceive by their simplicity, for this answer is probably not picking up the *real* cost of care.

Daniel Defoe's tale of *Robinson Crusoe* can be used to illustrate what is meant by the 'real' cost. Suppose that Crusoe, on that eventful Friday when he first saw the footprints in the sand, had found not a fit, athletic man but instead a frail elderly man, shipwrecked on the island 40 years before. Crusoe would not have thanked us for giving him '£100 per week' to care for the elderly man, for money was of no use to him on his desert island. Much more useful would have been a gourd of goat's milk or a net of fish for, in caring for the man, Crusoe would have to give up the time he would otherwise have spent milking or fishing. The cost to Crusoe of providing the care could not be reckoned in pounds sterling but in terms of what he had lost by not using his time and energy in an alternative pursuit (milking and fishing). Of course, Defoe's hero did not find a frail, elderly man, but this distortion of a familiar story well illustrates the concept of opportunity cost. In general, the cost of a resource or service cannot be reckoned merely by reference to its price, but must be gauged in terms of what is given up. Many care resources and services are not bought and sold in the market, and those that are have prices that are frequently influenced by market distortions. The concept of opportunity cost is intuitively appealing and indispensable in the study of efficient and equitable allocations.

Robinson Crusoe had given up his milking and fishing in order to provide care, which had thus cost him the milk and fish he had not been able to collect. A little nearer home, we can imagine a social services department having to decide whether to build a multipurpose day centre or, using the same resources, to employ a small team of four child care workers. The cost to the social services department of the day centre is thus four social workers, and the cost of a social worker is a quarter of a day centre. We are expressing the cost in terms of the value of alternatives or opportunities that have been missed. The cost of using a resource in a particular service or mode of care, therefore, is not (necessarily) the money cost or price of the resource, but is the benefit forgone (the opportunity lost) by losing its best alternative use. Our need for cost information stems from our need to choose between alternatives. Resource inputs are scarce and we have to decide how best to employ them. Services are scarce, and we thus face the problem of choosing between alternative claims, wants or needs. Scarcity implies choice, and the act of choice gives us our definition of cost.

The social services department which chose to provide a day centre had not just rejected the child care team, but had rejected the benefits accruing from their work with abused or neglected children. In principle, therefore, to measure costs we must be able to measure benefits or outcomes. In practice, we will frequently use money to measure the opportunity cost, because money is a convenient yardstick against which to measure benefits. (It would be absurdly impractical to draw up a long list of alternative uses of a particular resource.) The money paid for a marketed resource will be a valid measure of opportunity cost if it reflects the value that the user places on it, and this will be the case if markets are, in the economist's terminology, 'perfect'. When market distortions are evident, the money price will need to be adjusted in order to give us an opportunity cost measure. Where a market simply does not exist, a *shadow price* must be found. In fact, there are four circumstances in which opportunity costs are different from market prices. These are where market prices: do not exist; are not stable; are distorted by market imperfections; or are difficult to apportion because inputs are shared.

1.1 Non-marketed items

A contentious practice of economists is their occasional desire to put monetary values on non-marketed items. The valuation of what we might call *intangibles* is inescapable, for every resource allocation decision makes an implicit valuation or trade-off of the costs and effects of the alternatives. It is important to make those valuations explicit. Three approaches to the valuation of intangibles have been suggested. The *human capital* approach uses earnings as a basis for valuing effects. The alleviation of some medical problem or physical disability which allows someone to return to work could be valued in terms of the extent of the growth of national productivity which resulted, roughly approximated by the future stream of earnings. As most social care clients do not and will not join the workforce there is little scope for employing this approach. *Implicit valuation* methods are based on the behaviour of either clients or decision-makers (including social work professionals) who, in their daily activities and decisions, make implicit valuations of resources and services. This second approach seeks to make these valuations explicit, and has proved popular and helpful in some health care studies. The third approach is based on clients' explicit judgements, based on their *willingness-to-pay* – their observed trade-offs between resources or states of welfare, or elicited through carefully-designed questions. Once again the very characteristics of social care clients might militate against the employment of this willingness-to-pay method. (Drummond, 1981, pp.134-140, describes these approaches in more detail.)

1.2 Price stability

Even if market prices exist and are good approximations to social opportunity costs, a complication may arise if the service or policy being evaluated is sufficiently large to alter those prices. Do we take the initial or final price as the measure of opportunity cost? For example, if all local authorities decided to double the proportions of children in care who were boarded out with families, they would likely find that the supply price of foster families would increase (the amount needed in payment or compensation before a foster home will be offered). Which boarding-out allowance is to be used as a measure of the cost of foster care? Is it the pre-expansion rate or the higher post-expansion rate? The solution is to take a combination of the two (with the exact formula being determined by considering the consumer and producer surpluses associated with the policy change, which need not detain us here). Of course, small-scale projects or procedures are unlikely to alter prices in this way. The point to stress is that prices cannot always be assumed to remain unaffected by the decisions under consideration.

1.3 Price distortions

If markets work in the wonderfully unfettered way assumed by Adam Smith, market prices and *social opportunity costs* will be identical. Generally, there will be differences between them, albeit often too modest to worry us. The two will deviate whenever there are market imperfections, such as monopoly power, indirect taxation and unemployment. Consider these three sources of deviation.

- If resources are supplied by a *monopolist*, or some group with market power, then price and social cost will generally differ. To get a closer approximation to social opportunity cost, observed prices can be adjusted in accordance with the nature of the production: if the resources would not otherwise have been used then their shadow price (the estimate of opportunity cost) is set equal to the marginal cost of production (see below for the definition of marginal cost). If, on the other hand, the resources are diverted from some other use, then the shadow price is set equal to the value in the next best use, equal to the demand price in the market. If some but not all of the resources have been diverted from other uses, then a suitable weighted sum of the marginal cost and the demand price is employed.

- *Indirect taxation*, where the only aim is the raising of revenue (a good example being VAT), will similarly distort prices so that they do not reflect the real social value of the goods, services or resources. If the resources would not otherwise have been produced or used then the shadow price is the supply price (the marginal cost of production), while diverted resources are set at the demand price (including the taxes). Combinations of the two are used accordingly. If, on the other hand, the taxation is imposed to reduce unwanted by-products such as pollution, or to redistribute income, then market prices need not be adjusted.
- A third source of market distortion is *unemployment*. Staff who would otherwise have been unemployed may have a zero shadow price. In fact, it might be more accurate to set the price equal to the value of forgone leisure and the costs of travelling to and from work, which implies a shadow price somewhere above zero. A further complication is that one must consider the government's macro-economic policies, for if the present unemployment level is that which is necessary for 'policy optimisation', then employing an otherwise unemployed person may create unemployment elsewhere, so that the shadow price is equal to the wage which is paid.

Whether it is necessary to make these adjustments is open to debate. Drummond (1980) advises that it is probably unnecessary to adjust prices when the item concerned is not important in the overall evaluation, when the deviation from the social opportunity cost value is small, or when the time and trouble of making the adjustment is excessive. This is not a counsel of indolence but simply recognises that the costs of conducting a proper costing might well exceed the benefits. An examination of most cost studies by economists in the health and social care fields will reveal that Drummond's advice is heeded.

1.4 Joint costs

Many resources are shared between a number of uses and users. Family centres may provide services for the under-fives and for children on supervision orders, act as the base for a social work team, provide day care services for elderly people, and may have residential facilities. An old people's home may offer day care to non-residents, house an office for a local care management team, and provide occasional respite care. How then are the costs of running a family centre or old people's home allocated between the different uses? How do we apportion the costs of, say, a residential children's homes to the individual children living within it? This problem can be addressed in two ways. The first is to study how resources are allocated within family centres, residential homes or wherever and to apportion overall budgets to component services and clients. Later in the book there are illustrations of how this can be done for intermediate treatment facilities (see Chapter 12) and a centre supporting people with HIV or AIDS (see Chapter 9). The second way to allocate joint costs is to estimate a cost function, a multivariate statistical route to 'average' apportionments across a reasonably homogeneous sample. Again there is an illustration later in the book, with an application to old people's homes in Chapter 5.

1.5 Private and social costs

The cost to Robinson Crusoe of caring for a frail elderly man could perhaps be reckoned in goat's milk and fish. Barring the total collapse of the British economy, we would be unlikely to express the national costs of social care in such terms. Thus the cost of providing a particular service will depend on the alternative services that could be provided from the same resources, and there is no reason to suppose that those alternatives will remain unchanged over time or between locations.

The distinction between private costs and social costs can be introduced at this point. Consider first the expenditures or accounting costs of social care. We might ask the head of a local authority old people's home for the annual cost of running the home. Consulting the financial accounts, she would be able to list expenditures on staff, provisions, laundry, electricity, gas, and so on. The same question posed to the director of social services might produce a larger figure, with expenditure on those field social workers, occupational therapy and chiropody services which support old people's homes' residents being added to the head of home's list, even though it might not be easy to calculate the exact costs themselves. These services do not appear in the accounts of the home but are financed by the social services department and thus need to be included when estimating the private costs to the social services department. Asking the Secretary of State for Health the same question could mean the addition of the cost of GP and nurse visits to the home. The government's list of expenditures covers more of the services received by residents and is closer to the social accounting cost of care. In many uses of cost information, particularly when considering the social implications of a care policy, it will be sensible to include a comprehensive listing of the costs to all agencies and individuals. This could mean including the costs borne by clients themselves and by their relatives.

The same distinction between the private and social costs of care arises with the opportunity cost concept. Whose opportunity costs should we be monitoring? Ideally we need to be looking at the full range of resources employed in a care activity, whether or not directly costed to the providing agency, and to measure their opportunity costs to society as a whole. That is, we should be looking at the alternative uses of resources not just to their employers, but to society. There are likely to be constraints on the range of alternatives possible in any particular case, so that the opportunity cost in the short term may be different from the opportunity cost over a longer period in which more alternatives may present themselves. This raises the related question of local autonomy and responsibility. In the short term, there may be few incentives for social services departments to consider the wider, social, implications of their decisions. In principle, all of the resources employed in social care need to be costed, whether or not they are provided by the public sector, and the method of costing should reflect the social nature of social care. To ignore social opportunity costs could mean the misallocation of resources between, for example, the public and private sectors, between formal and informal carers, between local authorities and the health service, or between different regions. A situation in which it would be justifiable to measure the private opportunity cost to, say, a social services department rather than to society as a whole would be when the latter is difficult or impossible to value. A good private opportunity cost measure would be preferable to an uncertain or arbitrary social opportunity cost.

The adoption of an opportunity costing approach to social care thus has the following implications:

- The opportunity cost of employing a particular resource cannot be measured without knowing (or hypothesising) the alternative employments available.
- Costs are forgone benefits.
- Opportunity costs are context-specific.
- Opportunity costs and accounting costs (expenditures) are generally different.
- Some apparently costly items or resources are actually costless.
- Some apparently free items or resources have non-zero costs.

Public sector accounts are designed for budgeting and financial probity, and it is therefore not surprising that they provide an inadequate basis for opportunity costing. The following examples illustrate this problem.

2 Examples of opportunity costing

2.1 Running a private old people's home

Consider a private old people's home which opened in 1985, and is likely to remain in service for many years to come. Because the private care agency already owns the building, the capital expenditure appears in its accounts as an estimated depreciation allowance or debt charge, the exact amount being a function of the original construction cost and the method of depreciation accounting employed. This is generally different from the opportunity cost of using the building as an old people's home. We need to place a value on the best alternative use of the building, which may be its private value as a small hotel, or its social value as a pre-fostering unit. Consider, for example, the former option: the opportunity cost of running an old people's home is the forgone revenue from hotel guests. Alternatively, consider the amount that the private care agency would need to pay out to rent a building for use as a home. This too would provide a better indication of the opportunity cost than would the depreciation costs. The opportunity cost of using the building, therefore, needs bear no relationship to the annual depreciation allowance computed by the accountant, nor to the original cost of construction or purchase.

The other resources employed in residential care similarly need to be costed in accordance with the principles of opportunity costing. It is helpful to distinguish staff costs and other running costs (call them 'living costs'). In many cases, the (market) price paid for these resources will reflect their opportunity costs. For example, the social value of the provisions purchased for the home will be roughly the same as the price paid for them since, at the margin, members of society will not pay any more for these provisions than their value to them. Thus, most living costs can be obtained with relative ease from the accounts of the home. Staff costs also appear in these accounts, but we have to be sure that the amount paid for individual staff members reflects the social valuation of their best alternative employment. This may be a reasonable assumption for regular, paid staff, but for volunteer staff, for example, the calculation of opportunity cost will be difficult. Expenditure by residents on personal items should also be included.

Consider now the costing of a new old people's home. This raises different practical issues, particularly estimating the cost of the land on which the home is to be built and the cost of design and construction. Again, it is important not to assume that publicly-owned land, or land already held freehold, is a free resource. The land may not be on offer for commercial use, but it will still usually have some alternative use which bestows positive benefits upon the owner and/or society. A vacant plot of land may, of course, bestow social benefits simply by remaining vacant.

The second component – the cost of designing and actually constructing the home – raises the question of the alternative uses of the funds which would be allocated to construction. This is a complicated issue and it is not necessary to try to summarise the arguments here. It is sufficient to note that we are interested in the social value of the next 'unit' of investment in the private sector, the so-called 'shadow price of capital'. Again, the amount spent is not necessarily the same as the true social opportunity cost.

2.2 Foster family care of children

In most countries, child care policy now lays greater emphasis on family care as an alternative to residential provision. The relative expansion of foster care services as an alternative to congregate residential care is common. What does it cost? Chapter 5 discusses the comprehensive and comparative costs of residential and foster care, but here we consider the costs of care to the foster families. The costs to foster families can be broken into three categories, following the framework suggested by Culley et al. (1976).

- *Direct costs*, which are the out-of-pocket expenses incurred in raising a foster child. These are likely to be higher than the costs of raising a child in their 'birth' family because of the felt need to compensate for deprivation or to continue a material standard of living enjoyed in a residential home. In the UK, these direct costs are estimated annually by the National Foster Care Association.

- *Indirect costs*, which are the opportunity costs to families of forgoing work or leisure. Implicit in many policy approaches (local and central, and stretching back many decades) is the assumed female caring role creating what some might see as an exploitable pool of labour recruitable at low cost for fostering. Low wage rates in many labour markets, particularly for women, reduce the opportunity cost of paid work outside the home. Homeworking, including fostering, therefore imposes low indirect costs on families and lowers the supply price. Of course, indirect costs of this kind arise for *all* children, fostered or not, although different children will make different demands on parents.

- *Non-economic costs* include consequences of caring such as stress or the effort family members put into raising children that does not result in forgone opportunities. The psychic costs of fostering would be included here. These non-economic costs are likely to be higher for children with special needs or characteristics (hyperactivity, delinquency, enuresis and so on) and for 'inclusive fostering', which encourages the involvement of the foster child's birth parents to the full.

There are direct, indirect and non-economic costs associated with each and every foster placement, but the important policy datum is the amount needed to compensate a family for such costs. The compensation might be rather smaller than the direct and indirect costs because of the joy associated with bringing up children. These benefits will be greater for some families than others and may also be related to the characteristics of the children fostered. This is one reason why some families currently foster but the majority do not. That some families currently offering foster homes are prepared to accept boarding-out payments which are below full costs should not be an excuse for complacency nor a reason to maintain boarding-out payments at their present level. There can be few local authorities which have a more than sufficient supply of potential foster families or which would not benefit from having a wider choice of families to match with the needs of children in care.

2.3 Volunteers

Volunteering within the social care sector is vast: Lynn and Davis Smith (1991) found that 24 per cent of all current volunteers in a national household sample had volunteered in the health and social welfare area, 14 per cent for groups supporting elderly people, and 19 per cent for groups working with children and young people. The efforts of volunteers reduce the burden on public expenditure. Consider, however, the opportunity cost to a volunteer. This cost will lie somewhere between zero, for a volunteer who forgoes no leisure of any value and who would not have been employed or actively engaged elsewhere, and the value that could have been obtained in paid employment. The value of paid employment includes the wage plus the non-pecuniary or long-term benefits of employment – the accumulated expertise that will improve career prospects and/or increase future earning capacity – and the 'psychic benefits' of work which generate job satisfaction. There might also be out-of-pocket expenses incurred in volunteering, such as travel and telephone costs, having a bigger car for taking elderly people to and from day centres, or a larger house so as to provide informal child-minding (Knapp, 1990). Thus, Davies and Challis (1986) argued that the negotiated payments in a care scheme with *paid* volunteers might reflect not only the marginal valuations of volunteers' leisure, but also their perceptions of the 'psychic benefits and costs' of helping elderly people. One in ten of the volunteers in the Kent Community Care Scheme was motivated by a desire to acquire the experience which could then be useful in getting a care job. The voluntary activity in these cases was a form of investment in human capital, so that a valuation based on forgone leisure would overvalue the cost of voluntary activity. (See also Chapter 9 below for broader discussion of volunteering costs, and Chapter 4 on the associated issue of costing informal care.)

3 Costs and outputs

It would be expected that the cost or expenditure per resident week in a nursing home would be higher in London than elsewhere because of the higher cost of employing staff. Cost might also be higher in a home accommodating more dependent residents, or one with a lower percentage of available places actually occupied. At numerous times in the chapters which follow, the relationship between cost and output will be examined. What are the basic parameters of that relationship?

The distinction is often and usefully made between final and intermediate outcomes, although different terms may be used by different people. Final outcomes measure the changes in user or carer well-being consequent upon the receipt of services, relative to the changes that would have arisen if nothing had been provided. Intermediate outcomes, by contrast, measure workload or throughput: the number of users supported, the quality of care offered to them, and so on (Knapp, 1984, Chap. 3). Because of the multiplicity, complexity and intangibility of final outcomes, the remainder of this chapter will concentrate on a simple intermediate outcome measure – the number of service users. This is merely a convenient simplifying assumption which does not alter the general argument. The cost-outcome relationship is fundamental to examinations of cost not only because of the obvious importance of the association between the resources employed and their impact on the lives of users and carers, but also because it introduces a number of concepts which will be needed later in the book.

3.1 Fixed and variable costs

Fixed costs arise no matter how many outcomes are produced. Variable costs vary with outcome and disappear the moment production ceases. Fixed costs are inescapable, variable costs escapable. The *fixed costs* of a children's home would be the benefits forgone by not using the building in some alternative way. The *variable costs* would be the opportunity costs of the staff, provisions, clothing and laundry. Of course, the adjectives 'fixed' and 'variable' are very much dependent on the time period under examination. For example, within a few months of closure, the children's home might be converted into a residence for elderly people. The fixed costs have thus 'disappeared' or have become variable costs.

3.2 Time horizons

It is helpful to distinguish three time horizons. The most immediate marks the limit to the *short-run* period within which decisions and plans are constrained by the fixity of certain resources. In the short run, certain (durable) inputs cannot be immediately added to or removed from the stock of employed resources. The dominant planning question in the short run is how best to employ existing fixed resources (such as buildings), by applying varying amounts of resources like labour and consumables. In the *long run*, the employment of any resources, no matter how durable or specialised, can be varied by the producer. If children's homes can be converted to old people's homes within two months of closure, then the long-run period might be two months away. Long-run planning means the producer must decide what new capital equipment and buildings to select and what existing 'fixed' resources to dispense with. Finally, we can distinguish a *very long-run* period within which the state of knowledge and technology, which were previously taken as given, can be improved or influenced. Current decisions pertinent to the very long run would thus cover the allocation of resources to research and development, and the search for improved or alternative services.

These three time periods do not correspond to fixed periods of calendar time. They are theoretical constructions which correspond to sets of planning questions and decisions. However, the costs of providing a service will differ in character between the three periods. In the short run, we can distinguish components of cost which are attached to fixed inputs (the fixed costs) and components attached to variable inputs (the variable costs). In contrast, long-run costs are all variable, but only within the confines of existing knowledge. These differences between the short run and the long run are important in the examination of cost-outcome relationships (see, for example, Davies and Knapp, 1978, pp.13-17). Very long-run costs must again all be variable, but in this case the extent of the variation is greater and unpredictable.

3.3 Total and average costs

The *total cost* of an activity is the sum of all expenditures (or the sum of all opportunity costs) during some specified period. The *average cost* is simply total cost divided by the number of units produced or delivered. Returning to the distinction between fixed and variable resources, we can then further distinguish: total fixed cost, total variable cost, and their sum, total cost. Corresponding to these are the average fixed costs, equal to total fixed cost divided by the level of outcome or scale of operation, average variable cost and their sum, average costs. These cost-outcome relationships are illustrated in Figures 1 and 2. When average costs are falling there exist economies of scale, and when they are rising there are diseconomies of scale. The initial economies are due to two factors: the sharply falling average fixed cost (as the fixed cost of running a building is shared between an increasing number of residents), and the falling average variable cost (due, for example, to economies in staffing). Diseconomies arise because beyond a certain occupancy level it becomes increasingly difficult for staff to cope with the larger numbers of residents given the lay-out and scale of the home. Evidence to support this shape of cost-outcome relationship is offered in Chapter 5, where some of the sources of economies and diseconomies are examined.

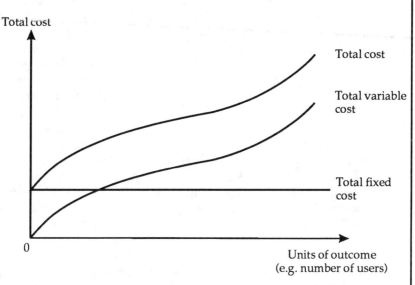

Figure 1
Total cost curves

Total cost

Total cost

Total variable cost

Total fixed cost

0

Units of outcome
(e.g. number of users)

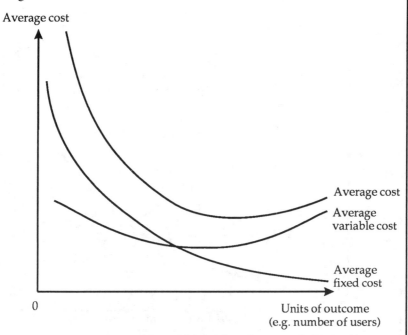

Figure 2
Average cost curves

Average cost

Average cost

Average variable cost

Average fixed cost

0

Units of outcome
(e.g. number of users)

3.4 Marginal costs

We have seen how the cost of providing residential care is a function of outcome. A great many decisions – indeed, the vast majority – concern whether to produce a little more or a little less. Should a care manager take on another family despite an already high caseload? Should a meals-on-wheels round be expanded to take in another few clients? The information needed for decisions such as these is the cost of an additional unit of outcome. That additional unit is often referred to as the marginal unit of outcome, and the cost of its production is the *marginal cost*.

The main problem with marginal costs is that they are not directly observable. Financial accounts provide total and average cost information, although rarely in a form which immediately allows one to readily calculate the marginal costs. Generally, calculation requires cost and outcome data over a number of years or from a number of similar care establishments, and the employment of a statistical technique such as multiple regression analysis. The locus of all marginal cost-outcome points is the marginal cost curve, which thus shows how the cost of extra units of producing outcomes or delivering services varies with outcome (see Figure 3). The point of intersection of the marginal and average cost curves is exactly at the cost-minimising

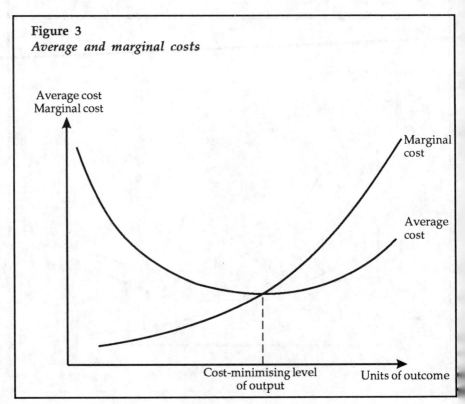

Figure 3
Average and marginal costs

Average cost
Marginal cost

Marginal cost

Average cost

Cost-minimising level
of output

Units of outcome

level of outcome, for when average costs are falling, marginal cost must be less than average, or else costs would not fall. Contrariwise, when average costs are rising it must be the case that marginal is greater than average cost.

3.5 Long-run cost curves

Each of the cost schedules described above was drawn on the assumption of a short-run planning horizon: at least one resource input was assumed fixed. In the long run all inputs are variable so that the outcomes can be expanded or contracted in number, not only by altering the variable inputs (the amounts of the staff and other resources), but also by employing more or less of the previously fixed input. This could mean expanding the building or adding further buildings. The total, average and marginal cost curves previously derived are thus all *short-run cost curves* which correspond to a particular quantity of the fixed input. They show how total, average and marginal costs vary as more or fewer staff and other resources are combined with the fixed amount of building capital. *Long-run cost curves*, which are plotted on the assumption that the quantities of all inputs can be varied, have similar shapes and properties to the corresponding short-run curves. It is unnecessary to describe these long-run curves here, although any micro-economics textbook will offer an account. In the very long run, cost schedules, to all intents and purposes, are indeterminate since technical progress and the acquisition of knowledge are too unpredictable to allow us to make assumptions about cost-outcome relationships.

4 Conclusion

Cost considerations have always been important in the planning of social care services, and their importance can hardly have been more pressing or more widely acknowledged than in recent years. Nevertheless, the 'cost of care' remains one of the most oversimplified and under-studied concepts in the lexicon of social care planning. A steadily-growing demand for cost information in recent years has elicited barely a trickle of cost research, some of which is peculiarly partial and misleadingly myopic, though nearly always undertaken with the best of intentions. In this chapter, we have set out the basic theoretical principles of cost definition, interpretation and measurement. Most fundamental is the need to distinguish costs from prices, both as constructs and in their usage. The two are often the same, but an opportunity costing approach will highlight the deviations.

As is well known, social care services are delivered most commonly in combinations. An elderly person may be attending a day centre, receiving regular visits from a social worker or health visitor, benefiting perhaps from housing subsidies, and occasionally seeing a GP. A child in care may be the focus of work from a local authority's education, health and social services departments. The cost of a care intervention should range as far as do the services used (or reserved) for a client, and one of the most serious inadequacies of the cost data presently available for social services is their incompleteness. In fact, this is not a criticism of the data themselves but of the naive way in which they are employed. The need for comprehensively-measured costs will be illustrated throughout this book.

Most cost statistics are available only at a highly aggregated level. Where possible we need to break them down to a disaggregated level. For many evaluative purposes we should be asking for whom (or for which type of client) and in what circumstances is one particular care plan more cost-effective than another. Moving away from grand generalisation and focusing on individual children, elderly people or other clients, we can more usefully relate resources to needs and produce benefits from costs.

Note

* Parts of this chapter are adapted from Chapters 2 and 4 of *The Economics of Social Care* (Knapp, 1984).

References

Culley, J.D., Settles, B.H. and Van Name, J.B. (1976) *Understanding and Measuring the Costs of Foster Family Care*, Bureau of Economic and Business Research, University of Delaware, Newark, Delaware.

Davies, B.P. and Challis, D.J. (1986) *Matching Resources to Needs in Community Care*, Gower, Aldershot.

Davies, B.P. and Knapp, M.R.J. (1978) Hotel and dependency costs of residents in old people's homes, *Journal of Social Policy*, 7, 1-22.

Drummond, M.F. (1980) *Principles of Economic Appraisal in Health Care*, Oxford University Press, Oxford.

Drummond, M. (1981) Welfare economics and cost benefit analysis in health care, *Scottish Journal of Political Economy*, 28, 125-45.

Knapp, M.R.J. (1984) *The Economics of Social Care*, Macmillan, London.

Knapp, M.R.J. (1990) *Time is Money: The Costs of Volunteering in Britain Today*, The 1990 Aves Lecture, Volunteer Centre UK, Berkhamsted.

Lynn, P. and Davis Smith, J. (1991) *The 1991 National Survey of Voluntary Activity in the UK*, Volunteer Centre UK, Berkhamsted.

3 Costing Services: Ideals and Reality

Caroline Allen and Jennifer Beecham

The previous chapter described the theoretical basis of costing. This chapter focuses on the problems encountered in putting this theory into practice. The ideal is to produce a costing which is both valid, in that it measures with accuracy what it is supposed to measure, and theoretically correct. While it is usually possible to follow theoretical principles (see Chapter 2), for pragmatic reasons it is usually more difficult to achieve accuracy. Indeed, initially some obstacles may seem insurmountable. This chapter shows that it is possible to clear these obstacles and to take short-cuts without breaking the economic rules of the game.

The methodology for calculating costs of care services described in this chapter is based on that developed for the evaluation of the Care in the Community demonstration programme (Knapp et al., 1992). This large evaluation involved the calculation of the costs of care packages for 390 clients, based on service receipt data collected nine months after discharge from long-stay hospitals in 28 areas of England. Clients in the study used an extensive range of services. Each service used by every client had to be costed. The multi-site focus of the evaluation meant that a balance had to be achieved between the need for costings which had national relevance and the need to reflect with accuracy the local idiosyncrasies of services. Although the methodology focuses on a particular study, the range and variety of services costed provides a sound basis for identifying key issues for a wide range of costing exercises.

1 The principles of costing

Chapter 1 suggests that there are diverse demands for cost information but, regardless of the how costs data are to be used, certain features should be incorporated into any costing exercise. The aim is for a truthful or valid representation of cost, which is at the same time reliable in the sense that the measure used yields the same result whenever it is applied to similar data (Kirk and Miller, 1986, p.19). The following principles, derived from economic theory, provide guidelines for the costing exercise. Service costs should be *inclusive* of all service elements, and take into account *cost differences*. They should be calculated as the *long-run marginal cost* of an *appropriate service unit*. There are also issues of *time* to be examined.

The calculation of costs must be inclusive, encompassing the cost implications of all elements of a service. Some service planners may primarily or initially be interested in the cost to their own agencies. Thus the amount of social services finance routed to a voluntary sector day care unit shows the cost of that service to the social services department but does not necessarily give the total (or comprehensive) service cost. Health authority funding, central government grants and private fundraising may also play a part. Current policy initiatives encourage the involvement in community care of a variety of different agencies which may provide a similar service at lower cost. Concentrating on the 'in-house' costs may also lead to overall inefficiency in service provision.

Unless costs are defined and measured comprehensively, one treatment mode may appear to be less costly than another when in reality that mode merely shifts costs into forms that have not been measured (Weisbrod et al., 1980, p.403).

Cost calculations should take account of cost differences. This chapter concentrates on those which are caused by input factors. Services in London, for example, are considerably more expensive than elsewhere in England (Derbyshire, 1987). Land and property values vary throughout the country and in some areas additional salary points are offered to encourage people to work there. Client characteristics, service outcomes and changes in client welfare also exert an influence on costs, but concern the use made of cost data so are discussed in later sections of the book (see Chapters 5, 10, 11 and 12) and are not examined further here.

Use of long-run marginal costs (see Chapter 2) allows examination of the difference which the option under study will make to the available resources. Short-run marginal costs are inappropriate for most costing tasks as they only include revenue costs and do not take account of the full costs of creating new services. But knowledge about the present time is more certain than knowledge of the future, so the convention is to use short-run *average* costs which include both revenue and capital elements as an approximation for long-run marginal costs. This is based on the widely-held assumption that, in the long run, relative prices will remain stable although absolute price levels may change (see also Jones et al., 1980; Mangen et al., 1983; Davies and Challis, 1986; Wright, 1987).

Once calculated, long-run marginal costs should be disaggregated to an appropriate unit of measurement to get as close to client-level data as possible.

Clients use services in discrete units; for example, hospital service use is counted by the number of in-patient days or out-patient attendances. More complex analyses allow more detailed levels of disaggregation, such as ward-level hospital costs (Haycox and Wright, 1984; Knapp et al., 1990) or disaggregation of residential care costs, in recognition of residents' dependency levels (Chapter 5 in this book).

The final guiding principle for costing concerns timeliness. The year chosen to calculate the costs data should be as up-to-date as possible to enhance the validity and utility of the results. Ideally, service costs information should apply to the time period in which the policy is to be implemented or the service used. Too much delay between policy and the presentation of costs data may mean that intervening variables, such as inflation, render costs data less valid. If different service costs rise by equal (proportionate) amounts, the problem of out-of-date information is less serious, especially if purchasing budgets rise equally. However, costs may change in relation to each other. For example, the annual inflation rate for health services in 1990-91 was 7.4 per cent but was slightly higher at 8.8 per cent for personal social services. For the period 1986-1989, however, the health services annual inflation rates were the higher. Data based on inaccurate information about relative costs is invalid. Decisions based on such data are likely to lead to inefficiency.

2 Ideals, reality and acceptable compromises

The principles described above and the economist's concept of opportunity costs underlie the methodology for costing services and should guide the search for practical solutions to costing problems. Reality presents two main obstacles to achieving an ideal costing: the scarcity of resources, including time, with which to undertake costing; and the lack or inaccessibility of data. The desire for quick results, presented concisely, to be provided within a limited budget counteracts efforts to achieve perfection. Compromises may be necessary, but these should be made on the basis of the principles set out above.

The level of detail required for the collection of cost information depends crucially on the objectives of the study. Illustrations of this can be seen throughout this book. Chapter 9, for example, describes the costs of a day activity unit, a study which required a very different level of disaggregation to that required for services used by clients in the Care in the Community evaluation. Moreover, if an exercise is focused at national policies then detailed information on regional variations is unnecessary (unless, of course, regional variations are the topic under study). One important focus of the Care in the Community evaluation was to examine the costs (and effects) of clients' packages of care. In this study variations in the costs of care packages associated with client characteristics, needs, outcomes and so forth were of interest. The decision to use nationally-representative peripatetic staff costs removed the influence of other possible 'confounding' variables, such as differences in salary scales, allowing valid national comparisons to be made.

In translating cost principles into practice, the degree of effort expended in picking up cost differences should depend on an estimate of the size of those differences. Employment costs for a health service worker of a certain profession on a certain grade will not vary throughout the country (except where regional weighting applies). However, building costs are likely to vary considerably with local land and property prices. Linked to this point, the degree of effort expended in pursuing costs data should be roughly proportional to the benefit of the data in terms of meeting the objectives of the exercise. Thus, where a service is likely to make up a large proportion of the total cost of care packages, more effort should be made to achieve accuracy. In the Care in the Community evaluation, therefore, particular attention was paid to accommodation costs, which account for a high proportion of total costs, and those associated with innovative or specialised services which were fundamental to the objectives of the programme.

The next section discusses a general approach to costing services and suggests a classification of services which determines the use of one of two methodologies. These methodologies are explained in sections 4 and 5 using the Care in the Community costings to highlight problems and solutions.

3 Practice

A building-block approach to the process of costing services can be depicted as a model comprising four stages (see Figure 1). These stages can be summarised as service description, identification of activities and service unit, identification of cost implications, and estimation of total and unit costs.

3.1 *Stage one: Identify and describe the elements of the service*

Before costing can begin, a detailed description of the service is required. This should encompass elements such as: the building used; the number, grade and hours of staff in different professions and roles; provision of other elements such as food and travel; and the number of clients provided for, or caseload. The description should cover all elements of the service, including those provided by another agency and elements which appear to have no cost relevance.

This description allows services to be divided into two categories for which different costing methodologies can be identified. First, *facility-based services* include services where groups of clients visit a building in which the service is provided, for example, residential- or hospital-based services and day care.

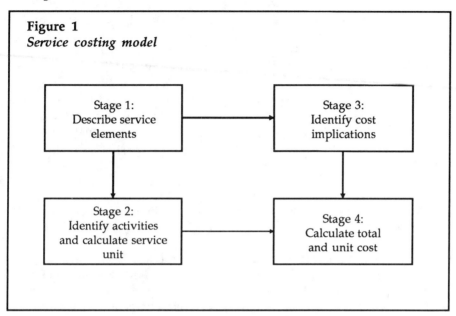

Figure 1
Service costing model

Second, *peripatetic services* are usually delivered by a single member of staff to individual clients or groups of clients. Clients may be seen either at an office or clinic, but staff also have the flexibility to travel to see clients in their own homes or at other locations. Examples of peripatetic services are social work or community nursing.

3.2 Stage two: Calculate a constant and relevant service unit to which a cost can be attached

Routinely-prepared expenditure accounts usually span one year and there may be times when it is most useful to present costs information annually. This is perhaps appropriate for a regional comparison of social work costs or when examining a policy shift in provision of care. It is often easier, however, to understand the cost consequences of policy and practice if data are presented in smaller units. Moreover, clients rarely use the whole of a service for a year; they use services in smaller units, perhaps seeing a social worker for 20 minutes a week, or attending day facilities for three days each week. For a social worker, therefore, it is useful to calculate the cost per minute, so that this unit can be multiplied by the number of minutes used by each client per week or per appointment. In contrast, there can be very few purposes for which it would be useful to represent the costs of day care per minute. A cost per session or hour would be more appropriate.

The choice of a unit of measurement for each service and the method by which it is calculated is an integral part of the costing exercise, and more details are given below. The unit should be relevant to the service and calculated by examining the resource implications of the different activities undertaken by the service. It should also be relevant to the objectives of the exercise and take into account the nature of the available data. The unit should remain constant for each type of service, although elements of the costs may be calculated separately. Thus, a home help visit may be costed as the number of minutes but the travel costs may be more easily expressed as a cost per visit.

3.3 Stage three: Identify and collect the information on the cost implications of the service elements

For each type of resource there are different cost implications. Thus, a building in which a service is located is usually intended to last longer than one year; there has been a long-term investment of resources. The running costs associated with use of that building, on the other hand, are recurrent expenditure, usually presented annually. Provider agencies can be approached for building valuations and facility accounts which provide the basis for costing. Staff time presents different problems. The cost of employing a member of staff includes their salary, but also additional costs such as the employer's national insurance contributions. Travel may be a staff-related cost but could also be provided for clients. At this stage *hidden costs* are also identified, such as costs to the clients of using a service (a charge or personal expenditure) and direct management costs. Following this identification task, the relevant data must be collected.

Obtaining access to this information is not always easy and plenty of time should be allowed for gathering it. In addition, specific data may not be readily available for some of these items, so information that allows an estimate should be collected. An accurate description of the service is vital to the estimation of costs where accounts are not available. Price indices are useful for such estimates or when data are obtained for a different year to that used to calculate service costs. The Department of Employment provides earnings indices for public administration, education and the health service. The Central Statistical Office regularly publishes the *Retail Price Index*, although this is not the index to use for many purposes. The Chartered Institute of Public Finance Accountants (CIPFA) publishes a variety of local authority statistics and the Housing and Construction Statistics (Department of the Environment) include price indices for output in the construction industry.

3.4 Stage four: Calculate the unit cost for the service

The service description and the collection of cost information allow the total cost of the service to be calculated. This final stage is complex and is explained in detail in the following sections on methodology. The aim is to calculate a relevant unit cost for each service which reflects the long-run marginal costs of an appropriate unit of service. This can be achieved by dividing the total cost of the service by the unit of measurement calculated at stage 2. In each of the methodologies below, practical solutions developed for the Care in the Community evaluation are used to explain how problems can be overcome. Hidden costs are discussed in the final section.

4 Costing facility-based services

Box 1 identifies the main groups of service elements which comprise a facility-based service and the data requirements that allow a cost to be attached to each service. The text below discusses in some detail the cost calculations for buildings and other *capital expenditure* and continues by examining *revenue cost* implications using routinely-produced annual accounts.

Box 1
Costing facility-based services

Service elements	Information required
Building: location and size Equipment, furniture and fittings	Valuation of capital
Building-related expenses: power, rates, maintenance	Expenditure accounts
Full staff complement: professions and grades	Salary-related costs and expenditure accounts
Other service-related expenses: food, stationery, transport	Expenditure accounts
Ex-budget services: other agency-funded resources, direct management, client-borne costs	Salary-related costs and expenditure accounts

---

4.1 Capital costs

Many community services are based in a building which is visited by clients. To estimate the long-run marginal (opportunity) costs of these services, the

cost implications of these buildings must be included in the total costs. Further-
more, it is desirable that they be calculated in a way that allows these costs
to be counted alongside revenue costs so that the total costs of a service can
be presented in one figure. Capital costs should be *annuitised* over the lifespan
of the buildings. The convention for calculating the opportunity costs of
capital is to assume that the best alterative use would be to invest the resources
to earn interest over the lifespan of the building, commonly estimated at 60
years. (Shorter periods, such as five or ten years, can be used for equipment,
aids and adaptations which reflects their shorter life expectancy.) Thus the
value of the resources includes interest which could have been earned had
the money not been tied up in buildings or equipment. The opportunity cost
of capital, therefore, is often calculated as the constant stream of cash payments, or *annuity*, which will deplete the lump sum over the lifetime of the
capital (Bromwich, 1976). Annuitisation necessitates the choice of an
appropriate value for the resources 'tied up' and an appropriate rate of
interest. The value of a building may be estimated as the actual building costs
(obtained from the provider agency) suitably inflated or the 'new-build'
replacement cost. The rate of interest should be that which is applicable in
the market where the resources would be invested. For example, in calculating
the costs of public services, the real (inflation-adjusted) rate of return on
public sector investments is appropriate. The Treasury currently estimates
this at 6 per cent (H.M. Treasury, 1989). Using standard interest rate tables,
the annuity generated by (the replacement costs of a building estimated at)
£1 million can be calculated as £61,876. This represents the annual opportunity
cost of the capital investment in that building.

[margin note: Cost to Central Gov.]

There are, of course, cases where this approach cannot be used. For example,
when costing private sector residential or nursing homes, valuations for
buildings and other capital-intensive items are rarely available. In these cases
convention suggests that the fee (for shelter and care) is set at a level that
covers both revenue and capital costs. Given the public policy focus of the
evaluation and the likely proximity of the fee (as a market price) to the real
cost, this is an acceptable compromise. Similarly, when costing privately-
rented accommodation, it is often inappropriate to ask residents or landlords
for the value of a property. Again, convention suggests that the rent (fee for
shelter) covers the cost implications of the original capital investment.

Domestic accommodation sits a little uneasily in the category of facility-
based services for, although a building is provided, the services related to
that facility are limited and there are no facility-based accounts. Public sector-
rented properties, for example, provide shelter for many clients of care services
but the calculations are complex and costs need to be built up from a variety
of sources, including the resident's level of living expenses (see section 6).
To calculate the opportunity cost of the building the local authority Valuation
Officer can provide information on the value of different-sized properties in
the area. In addition, public sector housing is subsidised by the local authority.

These revenue or recurrent costs are included here as they are the direct result of provision of the building or the capital element of the service. Housing accounts are difficult to obtain and even more difficult to disaggregate to 'facility' level. CIPFA housing statistics suggest that the housing departments' subsidy costs include: supervision and management; repairs and maintenance; debt management; and some miscellaneous expenditure. The cost of these subsidies per household can be calculated from these data. Similar subsidy costs apply for housing association-owned properties where information on national allowances can be obtained from the associations.

4.2 Revenue costs

To calculate the revenue costs for residential care when it is provided by the public sector (health authorities or social services departments) and the voluntary sector, routinely-produced annual income and expenditure accounts provide the starting point. To these accounting costs are added those borne by other agencies – a form of hidden costs. Examples for residential care may be GP services, district nursing visits, or forgone local taxes (such as rates, community charge or council tax). These are 'forgone' because the residents do not pay this amount, so the local authority must bear the cost of not receiving them. It also may be necessary to remove items from the revenue accounts. For example, amounts paid in rent for the property are removed as the cost implications of capital investment have already been costed; double counting is as great a sin as incomplete costings! Similarly, any expenditure on structural alterations is treated as capital rather than revenue, whereas expenditure on recurring maintenance is a revenue cost. Staff attached to outreach or day care services for non-residents are not resource inputs to the residential service but the costs of another service that is based in the same building (see Chapter 2 for a discussion on joint costs). Expenditure on these services should also be removed from the revenue accounts.

Following these procedures and adding the resident's personal consumption costs, which are the resident-borne costs of using that facility, the revenue costs per annum can be calculated. The annuitised capital cost of the facility is added to obtain the total long-run marginal cost per annum. The choice of a unit to which costs are attached depends on the function of the facility. Thus, for short-term or relief care a resident-day may be appropriate. For long-term residential care a resident-week may be more useful. Both should be calculated by taking into account the number of residents. For a facility that has recently opened, however, the current occup- ancy rate may not reflect the facility's long-term level of provision so it may be more appropriate to use the number of places which will eventually be filled. Either of these figures is then multiplied by the number of weeks per year the facility is open (there are actually 52.143 weeks per year). This is the divisor with which the *unit cost* is calculated.

Two other types of service are considered in this section. Day activity facilities and hospital-based services are important features of community care in terms of provision, use and costs. Like residential services they exhibit tremendous interfacility variation in objectives, services provided, client characteristics and so forth and therefore warrant individual facility-based costing exercises.

Day activity services provide an important element in care packages but despite being called by a variety of names (for example, day care, social club, or drop-in centre) these labels rarely describe the service. Some facilities cater for a particular client group, others are open to everyone; some are based in a special building, others are provided in village halls or community centres; the service may be available each day of the week or for just one or two sessions; staff/client ratios vary with the function each facility performs and the clients served. Each of these is a potential *cost-raising factor* so the service should be described accurately and a unit of measurement appropriate to the service and to the purpose of the costing exercise chosen.

Costs of these facility-based day services are calculated using the same methodology as residential services. When costing day care, however, special attention is paid to the level of resources which come from another budget, such as sessional workers or income generated from fundraising, otherwise total costs are easily underestimated. It may be necessary to contact relevant personnel to clarify both accounting information and other agency resources which are used.

Hospitals also show a wide variation in purpose and scale. They may range in size from more than 650 beds to perhaps 50, providing services in acute or long-term care and any combination of in-, out-, day-patient and accident and emergency services. Since 1987-88, hospital expenditure data are provided by specialty categories, for example, psychiatric care or surgical specialties. Specialty costs, however, include only direct patient treatment services and exclude support services such as maintenance, estate management, power and catering. Information from individual hospital expenditure accounts allows costs to be more easily allocated to each of the service units; per day for in- and day-patient services and per attendance for out-patient and accident and emergency services. Following the principle of calculating comprehensive costs, those borne by other agencies – such as social work provided by local authorities – should also be included. Capital costs are calculated as described above.

The importance of accurate recognition of the cost implications of these facility-based services cannot be overestimated as these services are costly to provide. For example, in 1989-90 adult residential services still absorbed nearly 30 per cent of the personal social services gross current expenditure (Department of Health, 1991). In addition, the type of accommodation (and therefore the cost) affects the other range of services a client might receive. Thus, residents of a nursing home would be unlikely to receive home help visits as domestic services are provided within the residential service. People living in private households rarely receive waking night cover from professional staff, but may use several other peripatetic services.

5 Costing peripatetic staff

As with facility-based services, when calculating the costs of peripatetic staff pragmatic decisions must be made about the level of detail required with the focus of the exercise in mind. The methodology set out below describes a building-block approach to costing peripatetic staff, illustrated with national data. The methodology can be used for a range of staff groups, such as field social workers, community nurses, chiropodists and home helps. A methodology for costing general practitioner services is included at the end of this section as an example of the *top-down approach* to costing peripatetic staff.

Having identified the elements of the service (stage one), a cost can be allocated cumulatively using the information described in Box 2 (stage three) to obtain a unit cost. The elements to be included are salary-related costs and office and service-related expenses (overheads).

Box 2
Costing peripatetic services

Service elements	Information required
Staff: profession, grade, hours	Salary-related costs (salary scales, regional weighting, NI and superannuation rates, travel and subsistence payments)
Office/clinic: location, size	Valuation of capital
Building-related expenses: power, rates, maintenance	Expenditure accounts
Service-related expenses: supervision and clerical support	Salary-related costs and expenditure accounts

---

5.1 Salary-related costs

Many staff groups have nationally-applicable pay and conditions and it is often difficult to identify precise pay scale points for different staff members. The decision to use national-level data on *pay scales* can short-cut a number of research tasks without losing too much detail. While it is true that in some professions more difficult cases are given to more experienced staff, other sources of variability were felt to be more important in the evaluation used to illustrate these methodologies. If the costing exercise is focused on one local authority the following methodology can still be used, but local working conditions should be substituted for the national-level data.

Although using national-level data may make the task more manageable, it does not solve all the problems of calculating these service costs. Most categories of employees are paid on a variety of scales, each with incremental points. Professional organisations can provide information on appropriate grades or indicate how many members of staff are in each grade. The average pay in each grade is multiplied by the number of whole-time equivalent staff in that grade. Dividing the total pay by the total number of whole-time equivalent staff gives a weighted average pay. Where salary information is not available for the appropriate year, figures can be inflated using the previously-mentioned earnings indices. The appropriate *regional weighting* is added to the average pay and then the percentage rate for employer's *national insurance* and *superannuation contributions* for each professional group.

Although staff do not always travel to provide care for clients, the payment of *travel and subsistence expenses* is a cost to the employer of providing the service and therefore is included when calculating the cost of the service. This approach, used in the Care in the Community evaluation, spreads the cost of travel evenly throughout the cost of the service, and the time taken travelling is added to contact or appointment time. An alternative approach would be to calculate the cost of travel per visit separately, perhaps the relevant bus fares, and add this to the cost of each visit.

In the Care in the Community evaluation, two methods were used to calculate travel and subsistence expenses. For nursing staff a proportion of costs was added, equal to the percentage of travel and subsistence costs over other nursing costs (pay plus salary-related costs). This was averaged over all relevant community health service areas. For some other categories of staff this information was not available and a cost was built up from information on methods of payment for travel and subsistence. For example, the major part of travel expenses payments are made on mileage or distance travelled. Data on the average distance each type of professional travels were multiplied by the mileage allowances. It was assumed, in the absence of more accurate data, that the means of transport was a car, and half the staff were regular (essential) users and half were standard (casual) users.

5.2 Overheads

Many care professionals have an office or clinic base which has capital and revenue cost implications. In addition, staff are supported by clerical and supervision services. Together these constitute *overhead costs* which are an important element of the cost of providing services. In the Care in the Community costs work, the overhead costs for health authority staff were calculated by adding a percentage to the salary-related costs. This percentage was based on the input of general services (including items such as clerical services, personnel and maintenance of health centres) to the total revenue cost of the community health services after these general services costs were excluded. Direct credits were not removed from the total revenue costs as they included, for example, patient charges which are a cost of the service. These figures were taken from the health authority financial statements for community services and averaged over all relevant districts. Capital costs associated with health authority staff were included in the total service costs by adding a percentage based on the annuitised cost of capital as a proportion of revenue costs.

An alternative method of calculating the capital cost implications of offices or clinics for peripatetic staff is to use the methodology described for facility-based services taking into account the fact that many of the offices are shared. This method might be more appropriate where data on local working conditions are used. Here, an appropriate size of office space is attributed to each staff member and multiplied by the average value of office space for that year. Running costs for the building, such as power and light, can be apportioned from the revenue accounts.

The most appropriate unit to which the costs of peripatetic staff can be attached is one minute. This allows building-related costs to be calculated over a whole year, as most premises function throughout the year, and salary-related costs to be divided by the official length of the working year for each professional. The working year can be based on contracted hours, thus allowing for holidays and statutory days leave, or may also include an estimation for sick leave and other absences. The most basic unit cost, therefore, is a cost per minute which can be multiplied up in recognition of service receipt data or the objectives of the exercise.

In the Care in the Community evaluation, client-level service receipt data were collected with the aim of calculating how much care each client received from each service or professional in a week, although adjusted for less frequently-used services. For example, where a client saw a social worker once during a thirteen week period for 30 minutes, the social worker's contact time per week was calculated as 30 minutes/13 weeks=2.31 minutes. If a domiciliary visit was made, travel time might take an extra 20 minutes. The length of time spent on providing care would then be 50 minutes, or 3.85 minutes per week. If several clients were seen on one visit, the time spent providing care was divided by the number of clients seen.

If cost per minute is not appropriate for the work undertaken, then a relevant unit can be calculated from activity data. For example, if the only information available is on face-to-face contact, this may underestimate the total cost of providing social work support. Other dimensions of workload activity may be: time spent on non-direct client-based activities such as case conferences, writing reports or advocacy; time spent travelling to appointments; time spent attending meetings; and time spent on general administration. The OPCS study (Dunnel and Dobbs, 1983) provides useful data on the time implications of nurse's activities as well as methods of travel and office allocations. There is little information on the cost implications of such activities for local authority staff and there is an urgent need for research in this area.

5.3 Top-down approach

For some professionals, such as those employed by Family Health Services Authorities (formerly Family Practitioner Committees), it is more difficult to build up an average cost per minute using the above procedures because of the complexity of payment for these professionals. General practitioner services provide a useful illustration as their income (as non-fundholders) largely depends on the amount and type of work done. There are different fees for different types of service, such as the removal of stitches or for the provision of contraceptive services. There are higher capitation fees for patients aged over 65 than for patients under 65. There are different fixed payments depending on seniority, or whether the GP is on study leave. GPs are also directly reimbursed for some practice expenses including some staff, premises, improvements to premises, drugs and dispensing. Direct reimbursement varies widely with the nature and location of the practice. A pragmatic solution to this complex problem is to take the total cost of general medical practitioner services for the appropriate year and to divide the cost by the number of practitioners.

Similarly, data on the time implications of general practitioner activities is not easy to collect so, for the Care in the Community evaluation, global estimates on the likely length of appointments were derived from the Butler and Calnan (1987) study on GP workloads. From their figures it was calculated that GPs spend 9.3 minutes on the care of a patient they see in surgery, and 27.1 minutes for a home visit, including time spent on administration, reading, writing and training. These figures compare well with the DHSS estimates (DHSS, 1987). Using the calculated cost per minute and these activity data, a unit cost per surgery or domiciliary appointment was obtained.

The methodologies described above result in the calculation of comprehensive service costs. Two important areas of hidden costs – client living expenses and managing agency costs – have been alluded to rather than explicitly examined and are discussed in the next section.

6 Hidden costs

The methodologies describe the calculation of costs for either facility-based or peripatetic services and identify some hidden costs. For example, the full description of a social services day care centre will reveal some service elements (costs) that are 'hidden' if only the facility accounts are considered, such as sessional staff funded by the health authority. Similarly, calculation of the long-run marginal costs recognises the cost implications of buildings which do not always appear in revenue accounts. In practice, costs are only hidden in relation to the starting point of the costing process and are, theoretically, defined as indirect costs (see Chapter 2). Over and above the costs considered above are two important 'knock-on' costs of providing services. These are the cost consequences to clients who use the service and those which fall to the agency providing management services.

6.1 Client living expenses

The client-borne costs of services have been mentioned in earlier sections. However, it is particularly important to take into account the costs of clients' living expenses when comparing different modes of care that include residential services. The calculations are complex as these costs vary with the type of accommodation in which that person lives. There is, for example, a great deal of variation in the extent to which living expenses are met from the accommodation budget. In residential homes the fee paid includes provision of food, furnishings, domestic and social care as well as shelter. The resident retains only a small allowance ('pocket money') for personal expenditure. In other specialised accommodation and care settings (hostels, for example) some elements of residents' income are paid to the providing agency for shelter and care and some are available to the resident for personal expenditure. In these facilities, personal expenditure may have to cover food or other living expenses. In non-specialised or domestic settings (private households) the amount of money available to the client after paying for shelter is larger, but they will often have to pay other household expenses, such as for heat, light and leisure. To ignore the client-borne costs of living expenses would be to underestimate the total costs of care. This is of particular importance in comparative evaluations as the level of underestimation will vary for each setting.

The calculations become even more complex where the client lives with family or friends. The precise amounts of expenditure or income may be unclear as the allocation of income within the household is unknown. The most practical assumption to make is that total household income is divided evenly between household members. When estimating household expenditure the *Family Expenditure Survey* provides data on average expenditure patterns for the whole country. This should only be used where more accurate, client-based, data are not available. Where clients income comes mainly from social security benefits, national expenditure data are rarely appropriate as the income levels are set too high. In these cases benefit levels for the relevant year should be used as an estimate of living costs.

6.2 *Managing agency costs*

The direct overhead elements of services, covering personnel and the cost implications of buildings, were discussed earlier, but what other overheads should be included in the cost calculations? Should the costs of administrative sections of a social services department (for example, the finance department, the director or policy and planning groups) be included? There obviously must be a practical limit to any service costing exercise. These administrative sections may have an important support function for, say, a social worker, but the cost of this support will be only a small proportion of the cost of providing a social work visit. The benefit of such a time-consuming allocation of resources would be small for the type of exercise which has formed the basis for this chapter. Moreover, with a public policy focus, the assumption is that, in the long run, the input from these sections into individual services is unlikely to change as a result of an expansion of the service. Current moves toward the purchaser/provider split may make such costs more explicit thus facilitating their future inclusion at the service level.

There are two exceptions to this approach: first, where there is a specific input into a particular client's care package, perhaps where an assistant director chairs a meeting or authorises an unusual course of action; and second, where a middle-management arrangement has been set up to oversee a particular service. For example, a new post might have been created (costed as peripatetic services) or a resource centre developed (costed as a facility-based service) which provides centrally-based services. It is often difficult to apportion these costs in any other way than allocating them equally across service users. Chapter 10 discusses these issues further with reference to case management.

7 Conclusion

This chapter has explored the practical implications of applying economic theory and principles when costing services. The main limitations are: scarcity of resources to undertake costing; the lack or inaccessibility of data; and, occasionally, the seemingly impenetrable barrier of the technical language used by economists. These barriers can be overcome, acceptable compromises made and balances found which do not impinge upon the validity of the results. We do not suggest the methodologies described above are perfect or complete, as such work can always be developed and expanded. However, the example used in this chapter is a good compromise between economic ideals and constraints imposed by the real world. Discussion of the issues at stake and the description of the methodologies should enable readers to develop optimum strategies in relation to the particular costing exercise they face.

Readers of this chapter should leave it with two axioms fixed clearly in their minds: consistency and clarity. Consistency ensures that principles adopted at the beginning of the exercise are used throughout. Clarity – of purpose, methodology and goals – ensures that activities undertaken can be replicated under similar circumstances, thus increasing the scope and validity of costs research.

References

Bromwich, M. (1976) *The Economics of Capital Budgeting*, Penguin, Harmondsworth.

Butler, J. and Calnan, M. (1987) *Too Many Doctors?*, Gower, Aldershot.

Davies, B.P. and Challis, D.J. (1986) *Matching Resources to Needs in Community Care*, Gower, Aldershot.

Department of Health and Social Security (1987) *General Medical Practitioners' Workload*, report prepared for Doctors and Dentists' Review Body, 1985-86, HMSO, London.

Department of Health (1991) Memorandum laid before the Health Committee, House of Commons Paper 408, HMSO, London.

Derbyshire, M. (1987) Statistical rationale for grant related expenditure assessment (GREA) concerning personal social services, *Journal of the Royal Statistical Society*, 150, 309-33.

Dunnel, K. and Dobbs, J. (1983) *Nurses Working in the Comunity*, Office of Population Censuses and Surveys, Social Survey Division, HMSO, London.

Haycox, A. and Wright, K.G. (1984) Public sector costs of caring for mentally handicapped persons in a large hospital, Discussion Paper 1, Centre for Health Economics, University of York.

H.M. Treasury (1989) Discount rates in the public sector, Press Office circular 32/89, 5 April.

Jones, R., Goldberg, G. and Hughes, B. (1980) A comparison of two different services treating schizophrenia: a cost-benefit approach, *Psychological Medicine*, 10, 493-505.

Kirk, J. and Miller, M.L. (1986) Reliability and validity in qualitative research, *Qualitive Research Methods*, Vol. 1, Sage Publications, Beverly Hills, California.

Knapp, M.R.J., Beecham, J., Anderson, J., Dayson, D., Leff, J., Margolius. O., O'Driscoll, C. and Wills, W. (1990) Predicting the community costs of closing psychiatric hospitals, *British Journal of Pyschiatry*, 157, 661-70.

Knapp, M.R.J., Cambridge, P., Thomason, C., Beecham, J.K., Allen, C.F. and Darton, R.A. (1992) *Care in the Community: Challenge and Demonstration*, Gower/Avebury, Aldershot.

Mangen, S.P., Paykel. E.S., Griffith, J.H., Burchall, A. and Mancini, P. (1983) Cost-effectiveness of community psychiatric nurse or out-patient psychiatrist care of neurotic patients, *Psychological Medicine*, 13, 407-16.

Weisbrod, B.A., Stein, M. and Test, L.I. (1980) Alternatives to mental hospital treatment. II. Economic benefit – cost analysis, *Archives of General Psychiatry*, 37, 400-405.

Wright, K.G. (1987) *Cost-Effectiveness in Community Care*, Centre for Health Economics, University of York.

4 Costing Informal Care*

Ann Netten

The fundamental importance of the contribution of unpaid, informal carers to the mixed economy of welfare has been widely acknowledged by policy-makers (Griffiths, 1988; Cm 849, 1989). Much work has been done on who does the caring, experiences of the caring process, and particular problems associated with conditions such as dementia (Finch and Groves, 1983; Qureshi and Walker, 1989; Ungerson, 1987; Levin et al., 1989).

As Parker (1991) points out, a major reason for the increased interest in informal care is cost. In particular, the increasing numbers of very elderly people in the population are leading to higher levels of demand for services (Netten, 1991a). Policies aimed at diverting people from residential-based care to caring for them in their own homes will probably reduce the costs to the health and social services. Almost certainly, however, they will increase the cost to the informal sector. Recognition of this fact is implicit in the increased policy emphasis on supporting carers (Cm 849, 1989).

Any thorough evaluation of a community-based initiative or ongoing programme therefore needs to address both the contribution of and the impact on the informal sector. Frequently these issues are discussed in terms of the stress on carers (Charnley, 1989), needs for services (Twigg et al., 1990), equity (Finch and Groves, 1983) or concerns about the future supply of carers (Phillipson and Walker, 1986). Underlying each of these is the issue of the opportunity cost of informal care, both to carers and to society as a whole. Studies of the costs of informal care have tended to focus on the financial consequences of caring for individual carers (for example, Glendinning, 1992). Here the intention is to examine the theoretical and practical implications of estimating the comprehensive opportunity costs of caring.

In this chapter, therefore, the theoretical issues in the costing of this unpaid contribution are identified and the methodological implications of estimating costs to society or to individual carers are identified. Some of the practical problems that can arise are put in the context of costing the informal care input from the principal carer in a study of elderly people receiving community-based social care in ten local authorities (Davies et al., 1990). Before it is possible to cost anything, however, it is of vital importance to be clear what it is that is being costed: exactly what is meant by informal unpaid care?

1 Defining informal care

In Chapter 2 the prospect of Robinson Crusoe encountering a frail elderly man was cited as an example to illustrate the true meaning of opportunity cost. If, however, such a hypothetical elderly man possessed skills such as basket-making, and knowledge and experience of living off the land, it is quite feasible that he would have enhanced rather than reduced the productive capacity of the island economy. There would have been a change in the mode of production but no net cost. It is important to be clear about this distinction between disability and people who have disabilities because all too often the assumption is made that elderly and disabled people represent an economic burden.

It is, therefore, the effect of disability that needs to be costed and here it is helpful to use the social production of welfare approach (Netten and Davies, 1990; Netten, 1991b) to define this effect. In this framework the household is depicted as a productive unit with the household members aiming to derive welfare from time and goods by producing *commodities* such as housework and nutrition. The ability of the household to produce these is subject to a number of restrictions among which is concern for the welfare of other household and family members.

Care inputs are required when disability results in an increased demand for commodities and/or a lowered productivity level from one person to the point where another member has to substitute for them or other changes need to be made in the way commodities are produced. For example, if someone breaks their leg the majority of their household chores will be taken over by another member of the household. A diagnosis of diabetes however, may result in no substitution but an increased amount of expenditure and work associated with the production of the commodity of nutrition.

Normally, the need for informal care caused by a short-term situation, such as illness, will be easily met by the household from its own resources. Long-term progressive disability that tends to occur in later life, however, can put intolerable burdens on a household which has limited resources. It is in such situations that members of other households become involved in producing commodities for the person with disabilities and the productive unit becomes the informal care network.

2 Types of cost

Using this framework in costing the impact of disability on an individual carer or on society, it is necessary to define what has been given up in order to change the way commodities are produced. Comprehensiveness is paramount in this process as costs are to a degree substitutable. For example, in ensuring that a person with disability has an adequate level of 'housework' a carer may pay for someone to do the cleaning or go to the elderly person's house and do it themselves. In the first case money has been given up; in the second, time.

The types of cost shown in Box 1 are used as examples of carer situations which have different cost implications. Obviously not all carers will incur all of these types of cost, but they help to specify what needs to be taken into consideration when costing care provided by informal carers.

Box 1
Types of costs of care

- direct financial expenditure on goods and services
- non-waged time
- waged time
- future costs
- accommodation

Having identified what has been given up it is necessary to put a value on it. Just as Robinson Crusoe would have to be repaid by a gourd of goat's milk or a net of fish, it is the result of what has been given up that needs to be valued. Benefit or pleasure gained from the time spent doing an activity (such as fishing) is defined as *direct utility*. *Indirect utility* is the benefit that results from the activity (a net of fish). As Chapter 3 explains, services are usually costed on the basis of lost indirect utility – the value of labour in terms of the wage rate and so on – as a financial cost can be attached to this. Similarly, in the following analysis, the lost indirect utility will be identified as the cost to carers.

Although the cost to the carer as well as the cost to society is discussed here, it is society's valuation that is used in both cases. The value that each person puts on his or her time (or money) will be individually determined. How carers feel about what they have given up can be explored through the relationship between the 'objective' opportunity cost, which uses prices determined in the market place, and subjective feelings, measured by such indicators as the Malaise Inventory (Rutter et al., 1970).

3 Direct financial expenditure

The financial costs of care include those goods and services which would not have been purchased in the absence of disability. These may include higher costs of heating, laundry, special foods and travel when visiting an elderly person in order to look after them. The cash valuation of these provides the estimate of indirect utility or opportunity cost.

There are two principal types of good – consumption goods and capital. Box 2 shows the cost equation[1] for informal care where this is the only type of cost incurred. Consumption goods are consumed or used up in the process of production. Actual expenditure on food, heating and laundry which is directly attributable to disability is often hard to establish. It requires detailed questions about expenditure patterns and a base-line for comparison, be it other households in similar circumstances without the disability in question, or speculations by the members of the household concerned about likely expenditure in the absence of disability. In particular, problems arise because disability can result in loss of income so, in households where there is disability, expenditure on such items as food and fuel will often be lower than in households where there is no disability.

Box 2

Where there is only a financial contribution made by the carer the cost equation is:

$$C = px + k$$

Where:
- C = opportunity cost of care
- px = expenditure on goods and services
- k = discounted weekly expenditure on capital goods

Baldwin (1985) investigated the financial consequences of disablement in children by comparing the expenditure patterns in families with disabled children with those in the same income bands in the *Family Expenditure Survey*. Where information about actual levels of expenditure is not forthcoming, it is necessary to draw on this type of study or to use other indicators such as the supplementary benefit payments which are paid for additional expenses such as heating or dietary needs. Chapter 10 describes a case study in which this type of approach was used.

'Capital' goods are manufactured goods that are used to produce commodities. In the household context, expenditure on capital goods might include adaptations such as ramps or aids such as button fasteners which increase a disabled person's productivity. In order to assess their cost, allowance should be made for the fact that they depreciate over time. Expenditure on a capital good therefore ought to be discounted over its expected life. There is no reason why the methodology for this should be any different than when estimating the opportunity costs of capital for services described in the previous chapter.

An alternative approach to the problem of assessing the cost of disability is the derivation of household equivalence scales. Equivalence scales are used to gauge the impact of, for example, an additional child on a family's standard of living. They are estimated on the basis of establishing how much additional expenditure would be required in order to bring a household up to the standard of living it would have had in the absence of the child. Jones and O'Donnell (1992) use the household production approach to examine the impact of disability on expenditure in households where there are younger adults with disabilities. They draw on approaches described by Deaton and Muellbauer (1980) distinguishing expenditure on items that are affected by disability and items that are not. The level or share of expenditure on those goods which are not affected by disability is used as a proxy for standard of living. While clearly potentially extremely useful, this type of approach is complex and often requires more in the way of reliable data than are available in practice. For example, transactions between households cannot be dealt with using *Family Expenditure Survey* data.

In estimating the social opportunity cost of care, financial transactions between individuals or households will be irrelevant. However, in the case of the costs to the carer, the transactions – both financial and in terms of goods – *will* be relevant. Indeed the carer may end up financially better off because of a caring relationship (Box 3).

Box 3
The cost equation for the carer, including financial transactions, thus becomes:

$$C_c = px + k - m$$

Where: C_c = the opportunity cost to the carer
  m = the financial contribution by the elderly person

---

4 Costing time

The bulk of the cost of informal care is in terms of a commitment of time so how this is costed is of fundamental importance. There are two distinct problems in costing time forgone: first, estimating the time spent because of care; and second, identifying how this time should be costed.

4.1 Estimating time spent on care

One difficulty that arises in identifying opportunity cost of time is that, given the relationship between, for example, an elderly person and carer prior to the onset of disability, a certain amount of time would have been spent together in the absence of disability. This time cannot be regarded as part of the opportunity cost. If it is assumed that only time spent on caring tasks is included, this may result in underestimating care inputs. For example, where mobility difficulties result in isolation, a vital element of the caring relationship is the social contact provided by the carer.

Where carers live in separate households it is sometimes possible to establish likely contact time in the absence of disability by discussing prior visiting patterns. There are difficulties, however; such patterns are likely to vary enormously depending on the relationship between the people concerned, gender, cultural norms and other factors.

Where a carer and an elderly person share a household, joint production also becomes an issue. Joint production occurs when more than one commodity is produced at the same time: for instance having a chat (social contact) while doing the housework. If there is no loss of productivity the case is clear: there is no measurable cost in terms of indirect utility as there has been no effective substitution. No time has been given up in order to produce the additional commodity of social contact. A cost is incurred if the distraction or irritation caused by this results in lost productivity (that is, less housework done). This can only be effectively costed if it is possible to ascertain how much extra time would be needed to achieve the same level of production. For the purposes of estimation it is often reasonable to assume that where carers and elderly people live in the same household, time spent on social interaction need not result in any specific substitution of time. Caring tasks, on the other hand, normally will result in time being given up. Moreover, carers often can be quite clear that considerations of safety, while not resulting in any specific tasks, mean they cannot leave an elderly person alone and thus have spent time in the company of the elderly person that otherwise would have been spent elsewhere.

In empirical studies another difficulty may emerge. Often the last visit made is not seen as typical but carers find it impossible to estimate what is typical. In the majority of cases, substituting time spent on caring during the last visit is a reasonable compromise, but this can result in no time apparently being spent on caring tasks despite carers identifying these as being under-taken for the elderly person.

In the study of ten local authorities (Davies et al., 1990), a number of carers identified tasks but not the amount of time spent on them. These cases were examined in detail. It emerged that the tasks concerned were: shopping, collecting pensions, accompanying the person out, medication, odd jobs about the house, laundry and gardening. It can be argued that because the carer would have to be shopping anyway, relatively little extra time would have to be spent on these activities (although this will clearly vary from case to case). Of the remaining tasks, only laundry and gardening resulted in an increased level of time being allocated by those carers who had specified total time spent caring. Analysis of these cases revealed that laundry and gardening each took about an hour per week.

4.2 Estimating the cost of time

In accordance with the principles of opportunity costing, it is desirable as far as possible to ascertain what would have been done with the time in the absence of disability. A basic assumption in economic theory is that people allocate their time in order to get as much benefit as they can. This is clearly restricted by a number of constraints: the length and distribution of hours in the working week, for example, and the need to earn income. It is helpful at this stage to categorise time spent by members of the household by type of activity. Box 4 illustrates a categorisation of time.

Box 4
Types of household activity

- market activity – such as work for pay
- leisure-pleasure activity – such as home/public entertainment
- meeting physiological needs – such as sleep, personal care
- 'productive' non-market activity – such as housework, gardening

---

Ideally the impact of each type of activity forgone would be costed separately but this presents both theoretical and practical problems. In the future it may be possible to establish an appropriate relationship between the market and non-market productive activity and leisure for the purpose of costing leisure-pleasure time. In order to do this, information is needed about the value of leisure time based on the impact its loss has on market and non-market productivity. This might use the economic concept of *slack* in the household: it is reasonable to suppose that where there is time which is genuinely 'free' it should be costed as such. An ideal costing is further complicated by the fact that within each type of activity each additional unit of time given up will, from the carer's perspective, be more costly (rising marginal cost). While it is unlikely that this could be accurately reflected in any costing in the foreseeable future, a differential costing of types of activity forgone could provide some proxy for this effect.

There is an extensive economic literature concerned with the valuation and allocation of time between different activities, particularly with reference to the use of different means of transport. The focus of most empirical work, however, is the impact of choices made on the productivity of the market sector. In these studies, all non-market activity is classified as leisure. Sharp (1981) reviews the literature and describes a model of time allocation which draws on the concepts of productivity of both waged and unwaged time in terms of direct and indirect utility. Moreover, Wright (1991) examines economic theory from the perspective of putting a monetary value on the contribution of the informal sector.

There are no clear-cut ways of addressing the problem. Extensive theoretically-based research is needed before any sophisticated estimation can be attempted. In this chapter a very pragmatic approach is taken. This is based on the fact that while it is often difficult to identify precisely how time would have been spent in the absence of disability, people are usually clear about whether waged or unwaged time has been given up.

4.3 Unwaged time

Costing unwaged time is an area of considerable debate and a central issue when considering the contribution of the informal sector. Frequently carers of elderly people are elderly themselves (Arber and Ginn, 1990) and the main bulk of the opportunity cost is in the form of unwaged time. Box 5 shows the cost equation for a carer including unwaged time.

Box 5

The cost equation for a carer who has incurred both financial costs and spent some time caring for an elderly person would be:

$$C_c = px + k - m + uT_h$$

Where: uT_h = the lost indirect utility from time

In suggesting an approach to costing time spent on informal care, Wright (1991) draws on the concepts of direct and indirect utility, but in proposing a possible methodological approach to estimating the cost to the carer suggested a weighting based on what the carer provided. Thus coping with incontinence would receive a higher weighting than helping to get dressed. This approach tries to combine the direct and indirect utility effects of caring. The ambition in this chapter is more limited – it seeks to assess simply what has been given up in order to care. Feelings about the caring role and what is involved are seen as more appropriately reflected in such scores as Malaise (Rutter et al., 1970) or General Health Questionnaire (Goldberg, 1972).

In the approach described here, therefore, estimating the opportunity cost of unwaged time requires an estimate of the indirect utility that has been forgone from productive non-market activity: putting a financial value on the gourd of goat's milk or net of fish. The bulk of productive activity that is common to households and for which there is an assessment of indirect utility is housework. The value that society puts on the indirect utility of these activities is the market wage rate: the hourly rate for domestic help.

It is not suggested that this is ideal: clearly in many cases only leisure time will have been forgone which may feed indirectly, if at all, into the productivity of the household. Motivations about the caring activity will vary between individuals, but in costing it is necessary to assume that the underlying motive is a sense of duty or obligation. Whether the carer enjoys the process of providing care is not the issue; it is something that has to be done because of the disability and therefore will incur a cost in the sense of lost opportunities. The decision to provide informal care is not the same as that of volunteer activity where it is reasonable to assume an underlying motive which is related to the appropriate way to spend time that is not committed elsewhere (see Chapters 2 and 9).

4.4 Waged time

Informal care commitments can result in considerable reductions in earnings. A change in working patterns and the subsequent loss of income is one of the principle ways in which savings from initiatives to reduce institutionally-based care result in increased costs in the informal sector (Muurinen, 1986).

Before assessing the opportunity cost of time which would have been spent in waged work, it is important to be clear about the impact of care responsibilities on participation in waged work. Sometimes a few hours have been taken off from work on an irregular basis; in other circumstances the regular hours of work will be adjusted downwards or a carer may give up waged work entirely. All the waged time that has been given up because of care should be costed even if it is not spent on caring.

We have already established that the indirect utility of waged time is the wage rate. If we are concerned with the cost to the carer it is the wages, less tax and national insurance, that constitute the opportunity cost. There is only a cost to the carer, however, if they have lost pay or job opportunities because of caring. If job opportunities have been lost, this is taken as a career effect which is discussed below. In the former, the current wages less tax and national insurance payments are the cost. If a carer changes to part-time work, the expected rate of pay per hour is less than for full-time work so the expected wage rate must be distinguished from the actual wage rate. If the time off work has not resulted in lost pay, the employer has borne the cost rather than the carer.

When a carer has given up waged work entirely because of care commitments the cost is the full-time expected income. In such a situation carers may be eligible for invalid care allowance and other benefits. These need to be deducted from any estimate of lost wage income (see Box 6).

Box 6

The cost equation for the carer allowing for situations where the carer has given up waged work would be:

$$C_c = px + k - m + uT_h + Ew_1.ET_w - w_1.T_w - A$$

Where: Ew_1 = the expected wage rate net of tax and NI

w_1 = the actual wage rate net of tax and NI

ET_w = the expected time spent in waged work

T_w = the actual time spent in waged work

A = benefits, such as invalid care allowance

When the cost to society is estimated, however, the cost is the value of the lost production. This is estimated by the wage rate plus the cost of employing the carer as it is this cost to the employer that will equate to the lost productivity. Allowance is therefore made for national insurance and pension contributions as these form part of the marginal cost of employment (see Chapter 3). All time that would have been spent in waged work is costed this way whether there are lost wages or not. Allowances and benefits should not be included, however, as they do not represent lost production but transfer payments from one sector of society to another (see Box 7).

Box 7

The cost equation to society allowing for situations where the carer has given up waged work would be:

$$C_s = px + k + uT_h + Ew_2.ET_w - w_2.T_w$$

Where: C_s = the opportunity cost to society

Ew_2 = the expected wage rate plus employers contributions

w_2 = the actual wage rate plus employers contributions

In estimating the cost to society it is possible that there will be no lost production where the carer's former job is filled by a person who would otherwise be unemployed. In such situations there is lost non-market production between the carer and formerly unemployed person rather than lost production. One approach to this is to assume that with a rate of unemployment of some 7 to 9 per cent, on average 7 to 9 per cent of the carer's hours would be replaced where the carer effectively left the labour force to undertake the caring tasks.

When costing time, therefore, it is important to establish how it would have been spent. If it has resulted in lost income then the net effect of this is the opportunity cost to the carer. The lost production that results is the cost to society. Time that would not have been spent in waged work, whether the carer is waged or not, is costed in terms of lost home production, society's valuation of which is the domestic wage rate.

The constraints of employment practice on individuals' ability to spend their time exactly as they would wish have already been identified. This also applies to the process of giving up waged time to care. Carers may be forced to give up full-time work and may be unable or unwilling to find another job which takes up the time not spent caring. Thus they have time available for non-market productive activity which they would not have had otherwise. This time available should be counted as a benefit to the carer and to society so the cost of waged time will be reduced by the value of household production or domestic wage rate for those hours not spent caring.

5 Future cost

Another cost of caring can be an impact on the future income of the carer. The disabilities of the elderly person may make it impossible for the carer to meet a requirement to make a heavier time commitment or to move to another part of the country resulting in missed training or job opportunities. Sometimes a carer may change to a less demanding job or one where the hours are more flexible. Such decisions will affect future career prospects, and redundancy and pension rights.

The indirect utility that is lost under these conditions is future income for the carer or productivity for society. The cost would therefore be the difference in expected future earnings or unearned income resulting from caring responsibilities discounted back to the present time to give a weekly expected loss (see Box 8).

Box 8

The cost equation, including future costs, now becomes:

$$C_c = px + k - m + uT_h + Ew_1.ET_w - w_1.T_w - A + \Delta EY$$
$$C_s = px + k + uT_h + Ew_2.ET_w - w_2.T_w + \Delta EG$$

Where: ΔEY = change in expected future income
ΔEG = change in expected future productivity

In estimating the cost to society, the lost production (estimated as the wage rate plus the costs of employment) covers the contributions to pensions and other rights that would have been paid by the carer. The cost to the carer, however, should include discounted future income from pensions in addition to lost future wages.

In empirical work on the cost of child bearing and rearing, Joshi (1987) estimates the career costs when a mother has returned to full-time work after a break for childbearing and part-time work, and the lost career opportunities during that period. Her pay was found to be 14 per cent less than her contemporary who worked over that period (Joshi, 1987). In examining the effect she notes the number of women in part-time employment over the age of 54 exceeds those in full-time work. There is a consequent drop in expected wage rate independent of the cohort effect. This could be due in part to the effect of caring responsibilities among this age group which, in practice, makes it difficult to estimate lost expected future income as a result of caring responsibilities for elderly people.

6 Space and privacy

In most cases where a carer and elderly disabled person share a household, they have done so long before the onset of any disability. The spouse, or a son or daughter who has never left home, is often the principal carer. In such a situation there are no accommodation costs because no change has resulted from disability.

However, in some cases the difficulties of looking after elderly people in their own homes, be it because of distance or frequency of demands made upon carers, mean that there is a net gain in welfare if they live in joint households. This can be organised in a number of different ways and the opportunity cost will depend on the way chosen.

If the elderly person moves into a room in the carer's home, the room could have yielded the carer indirect utility in the form of rent and this is the appropriate method of costing. The capital value of the house does not enter into the costs because the carer would have been living there in the absence of the elderly person's disability (see Box 9).

Box 9
Assuming no effect on capital value when the elderly person moves into the carer's home the cost to the carer, including accommodation costs, would be:

$$C_c = px + k - m + uT_h + Ew_1.ET_w - w_1.T_w - A + \Delta EY + rH_c$$

Where: rH_c = benefit that would have been gained from the room taken up in the carer's household.

In some cases arrangements are more complicated than this, involving transfers of ownership or future expectations in terms of renting or owning property. Where the costs will lie in the case of building a granny flat, for example, would depend on who made the initial investment and the expected distribution of the estate.

In some cases the carer will have moved and in others both the carer and the elderly person will have moved to a different property. When the elderly person is the sole owner or the tenant of the property, the carer could be represented as having given up a great deal more than a room's value in terms of space and privacy. However, it is likely that in such cases there would be expectations in terms of the future ownership or tenancy and this was the reason that the arrangement had been made. In any costing exercise it is necessary to establish just what these future expectations or specific agreements are before estimating the true opportunity cost.

It is possible that there may be a net benefit to society if the altered accommodation arrangements result in a more efficient allocation of housing stock. This would be the case if, for example, the elderly person moved out of a large house releasing it for the use of a family. It is unlikely that a change in accommodation arrangements would result in a more inefficient use of resources. The effect on society would be the difference between the value released from the elderly person's home and the opportunity cost of occupying space in the carer's home (see Box 10).

Box 10

Assuming no effect on capital value when the elderly person moves into the carer's home the cost to society, including accommodation costs, would be:
$$C_s = px + k + uT_h + Ew_2.ET_w - w_2.T_w + EFP + (rH_c - rH_e)$$
Where: rH_e = benefit gained from the elderly person's household.

---

7 Conclusion

In policy discussions much is made of the decline in an important source of care: informal unpaid help. The resources of the informal sector are not restricted to time alone and it is important in costing the contribution to be aware of substitutability of resources. The potential release of assets tied up in housing for use in caring for elderly people has been identified as an important issue in the future provision of care (Age Concern, 1990). Moreover, carers may decide to participate in the workforce in order to pay for the type of care that their dependants need. In both cases, society benefits from the realisation of resources that otherwise might have been underutilised. The comprehensive costing of the contribution of informal carers should inform policy decisions about the demand for care services as these depend fundamentally on the supply of informal care.

Any attempt to provide a detailed opportunity costing requires that the assumptions and estimates made are open to question. This is especially so in this relatively new area where conventions have yet to be agreed. In setting out in some detail this methodology, it is hoped that the assumptions are clear and readers are enabled to assess where and in what directions an estimated cost is likely to vary substantially from the true underlying cost.

In the process of estimation, two leaps of faith are frequently required: between pure theory and the feasible, and between the feasible and the available. The importance of this policy area is such that these problems should not deter attempts to cost informal care; they serve to emphasise the need for more informed research to improve the balance and the quality of information for policy-makers.

Notes

* My thanks are due to Raphael Wittenberg, who provided valuable comments on an earlier paper on which this chapter is based, and to contributors to the workshops, in particular to Karen Traske who 'volunteered' to read through the draft chapter and made helpful suggestions. Vivien Koutsogeorgopoulou was most helpful in discussing algebraic terminology.

1 A cost equation simply sums the different elements of cost. Boxes 1 to 8 throughout this chapter show how each type of cost contributes to the total cost of informal care.

References

Age Concern (1990) The economic equation, *Coming of Age*, Action Pack 2, Age Concern, London.

Arber, S. and Ginn, J. (1990) The meaning of informal care: gender and the contribution of elderly people, *Ageing and Society*, 10, 429-54.

Baldwin, S. (1985) *The Costs of Caring*, Routledge and Kegan Paul, London.

Charnley, H. (1989) Carer outcomes and the social production of welfare, Discussion Paper 595, Personal Social Services Research Unit, University of Kent at Canterbury.

Cm 849 (1989) *Caring for People: Community Care in the Next Decade and Beyond*, HMSO, London.

Davies, B.P., Bebbington, A., Baines, B., Charnley, H., Ferlie, E., Hughes, M. and Twigg, J. (1990) *Resources, Needs and Outcomes in Community Based Care* Gower, Aldershot.

Deaton, A.S. and Muellbauer, J. (1980) A simple test for heteroscedasticity and random coefficient variation, *Econometrica*, 47, 1287-1294.

Finch, J. and Groves, D. (1983) *A Labour of Love: Women, Work and Caring*, Routledge and Kegan Paul, London.

Glendinning, C. (1992) *The Costs of Informal Care: Looking Inside the Household*, HMSO, London.

Goldberg, D. (1972) *The Detection of Psychiatric Illness by Questionnaire*, Oxford University Press, Oxford.

Griffiths, R. (1988) *Community Care: Agenda for Action*, HMSO, London.

Jones, A. and O'Donnell, O. (1992) Household equivalence scales and the costs of disability, Department of Econometrics, University of Manchester.

Joshi, H. (1987) The cash opportunity costs of childbearing: an approach to estimation using British data, Discussion Paper 208, Centre for Economic Policy Research, London.

Levin, E., Sinclair, I. and Gorbach, P. (1989) *Families, Services and Confusion in Old Age*, Avebury, Aldershot.

Muurinen, J.-M. (1986) The economics of informal care: labor market effects in the national hospice study, *Medical Care*, 24, 11, 1007-16.

Netten, A. (1991a) Coming of age: the cost of social care support, Discussion Paper 742, Personal Social Services Research Unit, University of Kent at Canterbury.

Netten, A. (1991b) An economic approach to the study of social care of elderly people: a perspective on informal care, Discussion Paper 781, Personal Social Services Research Unit, University of Kent at Canterbury.

Netten, A. and Davies, B.P. (1990) The social production of welfare and consumption of social services, *Journal of Public Policy*, 10, 3, 331-347.

Parker, G. (1991) Informal care of the older people in Great Britain: evidence from the 1985 General Household Survey, Social Policy Research Unit, University of York.

Phillipson, C. and Walker, A. (1986) *Ageing and Social Policy*, Gower, Aldershot.

Qureshi, H. and Walker, A. (1989) *The Caring Relationship: Elderly People and their Families*, Macmillan, Basingstoke.

Rutter, M., Tizard, J. and Whitmore, K. (1970) *Education, Health and Behaviour*, Longman, London.

Sharp, C. (1981) *The Economics of Time*, Martin Robertson, Oxford.

Twigg, J., Atkin, K. and Perring, C. (1990) *Carers and Services: A Review of Research*, HMSO, London.

Ungerson, C. (1987) *Policy is Personal: Sex, Gender and Informal Care*, London, Tavistock.

Wright, K.G. (1991) Social care versus care by the community: economics of the informal sector, in J. Pacolet and C. Wilderom (eds) *The Economics of Care of the Elderly*, Avebury, Aldershot.

Part II:
The Uses of Cost Information

5 Principles of Applied Cost Research*

Martin Knapp

To the beleaguered social care practitioner, bombarded with needs but no longer showered with resources, the era of efficiency is like a bad dream. The pursuit of efficiency appears as a thinly-veiled euphemism for 'cut', and an attack on fundamental caring principles. Exposed to explanations that efficiency is not all bad – that it is concerned with getting more services and having greater impact from the same pot of money, or doing as well as before but using fewer resources – the downtrodden social worker might see only the word 'cost'. Cost and care simply do not look like comfortable bedfellows. Policies directed at the management of one seem to threaten practices dominated by concerns with the other. Unfortunately, the cost information that needs to go into almost any conceptualisation of efficiency has often been hastily requested, poorly constructed and naively employed. Cost, not surprisingly, has a bad press.

That negative image of cost can be altered by looking at how cost and efficiency enquiries should ideally be conducted and employed – one of the purposes of this book – and by drawing lessons from economics, the discipline which has devoted most attention to the topic. From the study of scarcity, economics has both accumulated theoretical experience and developed comparative empirical advantage in the design and execution of cost research. Some of those theoretical perspectives have already been brought into the discussion of social care, and some have been used to develop conceptual frameworks within which to locate empirical investigations of efficiency (Knapp, 1984; Netten and Davies, 1990).

Thankfully, the arrival of the economist is not seen in the same light by everyone – liberating knight in shining armour to some, vanguard of a hated army of occupation to some others. Neither fantasy guarantees a resolution of resource allocation problems. Economists are as fallible as anyone else, and there is the additional problem that their involvement is commonly too little, too late or too remote. What is needed is the premeditated and purposive integration of costs with other dimensions in the policy or practice debates, and this means the examination of hypotheses which are not 'cost questions' nor, say, 'outcome questions', but are the types of question faced by the policy-maker who has to balance resources against achievements, efficiency against equity, irate social work managers against persistent accountants.

1 Basic principles

The aim of this chapter is to examine the basic principles of applied costs research. The principles are captured by four simple rules which concern comprehensiveness, the treatment of variations, like-with-like comparisons, and linking costs with outcomes:

* Costs should be comprehensively measured.
* The cost variations that are inevitably revealed in any empirical exercise – variations between clients, facilities, areas of the country, and so on – offer a wealth of information which should be explored and exploited.

* Variations encourage comparisons – this service is cheaper than that one, this group of clients is more costly to accommodate than that group – and only like-with-like comparisons have full validity.

* Finally, cost information should be integrated with information on client outcomes. (It is just as wrong to examine costs in the absence of outcome information as it is to study outcomes without paying heed to costs.)

Each of these four rules or basic principles of applied costs research is easier to recite than to observe in practice. They provide the framework for the remainder of this chapter and for the PSSRU's costs research generally. In the next section comprehensive costs are discussed. Sections 4 and 5 examine cost variations and like-with-like comparisons, with illustrations drawn respectively from residential care of elderly people and foster family care for children. Section 6 considers the integration of costs and outcomes data.

2 Comprehensive costs

Most clients receive more than one service, probably from more than one agency. The greater and the more diverse a client's needs, the broader the range of services likely to be utilised. Any evaluation which addresses the resource dimension should therefore aim to cost every service within a care 'package'. Even if the aim of an evaluation is simply to compare the costs of running, say, local authority and voluntary sector hostels for people with learning disabilities, it would be dangerous to define costs narrowly to exclude other services received by residents, for combinations of services tend not to be thrown together willy-nilly. The staff of a local authority hostel may 'network' in different ways from the staff of a non-profit hostel: perhaps having better links with the health service but less access to day care provision, more opportunity to help clients obtain social security entitlement but less independence to advocate change. The purposive combination of services to meet needs is one of the underlying principles of case management, and in Britain at least this mode of working – preferably with budgeting decisions devolved down to case managers – will soon become the norm (Cm 849, 1989). In an age of relative austerity it is hard to imagine effective case management proceeding in a cost vacuum.

Making sensible comparisons and ensuring that new service developments are adequately funded are also compelling reasons for comprehensiveness. For example, most long-stay hospitals in England are scheduled to run down to closure over the next decade. Savings from the rundown of hospitals are expected to fund the running costs of the community services which should replace them. Cost comparisons between hospital and community services are therefore essential in order to plan or monitor these financial transfers. Calculating costs comprehensively ensures that such comparisons are valid.

The comprehensive costing of social care services raises a number of conceptual and practical issues. It is also controversial. It has been pointed out, for example, that it is iniquitous to include daily living expenses, housing rents and routine visits to the family practitioner in the costs of community care since, so the argument runs, every one of us has these basic needs and incurs equivalent costs. But only if utilisation of these services is identical for the options being studied is it legitimate to ignore the associated costs.

It is unnecessary to illustrate the comprehensive costing of social care services here as there are plenty of examples elsewhere (see Chapters 3, 11 and 12 in particular). In moving to a broad view it is not expected or necessary that each agency involved in providing care will use comprehensive costs in their decisions, but they need some appreciation of them in order to understand the incentives and disincentives at work within the care system.

3 Exploring and exploiting variations

Interclient and interfacility variations in cost are generally marked. They should not be ignored. Good social work practice is individually tailored, and practitioners talk about the 'average client' only in order to make some temporary general remarks. Service packages reflect individual needs, and because needs vary, so too should costs. The correspondence between needs and services is not perfect but is sufficient for us to have reservations about those policy recommendations based solely on averages. Unless the organisation of care is so routinised or regimented as to utterly disregard individual circumstances, the costs of care will reflect client differences.

Service responses are also shaped by, *inter alia,* the preferences and perspectives of other professionals working with these clients, the bureaucratic tendencies of organisations, their scales of operation, and the characteristics of local economies and their implications for the price of labour.

3.1 The 'behavioural' cost function

A large and impressive body of applied economics research has explored the extent of, and reasons for, cost variations. The most favoured route is to estimate a statistical cost function, a multivariate technique designed to simultaneously tease out the many influences on cost. The cost function has impressive theoretical credentials – it follows directly from the economic theory of production, and is based on assumptions which have been exhaustively debated in a wide variety of market and non-market contexts – and in application has proved manageable and informative (Knapp, 1984, Chap. 9). If it is reasonable to make the analogy between, on the one hand, the production model of inputs and outputs that is the bread and butter of microeconomics and, on the other, the processes of delivering social work services, then the cost function has currency. It is, however, a data-hungry tool, and in the hands of the inexperienced, uninitiated or unscrupulous it is as dangerous and misleading as any other empirical procedure.

The cost function is most commonly estimated for a cross-section of 'production units' known or assumed to have similar objectives and to employ reasonably similar production techniques. In the study of manufacturing goods, the study of costs would ideally be based on data from a sample of factories (or work teams within factories) producing a similar if not identical product. In human service applications 'production' is certainly not routinised or standardised, and the terminology of business is unfamiliar, but the production metaphor has considerable validity (Davies and Knapp, 1988a). Using economic theories and analogies, the 'production of welfare' approach can organise, locate and connect with many relevant parts of the social work, philosophy, public administration, psychology and sociology literatures on social care. It can do so in ways which are most likely to maximise the applicability of economic tools of analysis (of which the cost function is one), but least likely to jettison either principles of social care or the empirical insights that come from other disciplines. Under the terms of this production of welfare approach the cost function has a behavioural interpretation.

In practice, a cost function is a multiple regression equation, with a dependent variable of either total or average cost, and the explanatory or independent variables suggested by a pragmatic blend of theory and experience. These determinants of cost are selected in an actual empirical study on these same criteria plus statistical significance.

3.2 Cost variations between residential care homes

The cost function can be illustrated by looking at residential care homes for elderly people. For simplicity consider only those homes in the public sector. Even when aggregated up to the local authority level, average revenue cost per resident week varies by a factor of more than two (Chartered Institute of Public Finance and Accountancy, 1991), and within these areas the variations are even greater. Yet local authority homes all concentrate mainly on delivering long-term care for what one would expect to be similar populations of frail elderly people, hiring staff covered by nationally-agreed terms of employment and salary scales, governed by common regulations, enmeshed within similar care systems, and collectively guided by many decades of research-based social work training. The cost variations might therefore reflect slight differences in these factors as well as the efficiency with which facilities deliver residential care services of a given quality and impact upon the well-being of residents.

In an early study, a cost function was estimated using data for a nationally-representative sample of local authority homes in England and Wales. Although the data are now quite old, this study helpfully illustrates many of the uses of cost functions, and the reasons for exploring cost variations (see Darton and Knapp, 1984, for a full account). Average revenue cost per place normally in use was taken as the dependent variable. (Capital costs and any costs falling outside homes' budgets were omitted.) The variables examined as possible (statistical) explanations for the cost differences covered: characteristics of residents (especially dependency or activities of daily living), staff and homes; non-residential services; and the localities and labour markets within which homes were located. The investigation was underpinned by theoretical arguments (Davies and Knapp, 1981), and informed by previous empirical research. After a deal of statistical analysis, the 'best' cost function most closely met the conventional criteria of parsimony, statistical significance and interpretability in the light of theoretical arguments (see Table 1). It is unnecessary to fully detail the function here, but some of its policy conclusions illustrate both the power of the technique and the need to explore cost variations.

The cost function 'explained' 76 per cent of the observed variation in average cost; that is, the differences between homes were largely accounted for by the factors listed above. This emphasises the need to examine costs in their proper context – indeed, some high-cost homes and local authorities proved to be costing less than would have been expected once resident dependency and home, labour market and other factors had been taken into account. The residual or unexplained 24 per cent of the variation in cost might then be interpreted as picking up differences in efficiency, although there is need for caution. The cost function also tests for the existence of economies and diseconomies of scale. In this case average cost per resident

Table 1

An estimated average operating cost function for old people's
homes, 1981-2

The estimated cost function indicates that average expenditure on manpower and
running expenses per bed normally in use per resident week is equal to:

-552.83*		
+1.74**	x	labour cost index
-3.26**	x	number of beds normally in use in group-living homes
-1.60**	x	number of beds normally in use in non-group homes
+0.02*	x	number of beds normally in use in group-living homes, squared
+0.01**	x	number of beds normally in use in non-group homes, squared
+10.73*	x	percentage occupancy level (at 31.10.81)
-0.06*	x	percentage occupancy level (at 31.10.81), squared
+6.00*		if staff of home have duties in sheltered housing
+4.36*		if all laundry done within home
+7.74*	x	number of permanent admissions in 12 months prior to 31.10.81 per number of beds normally in use
+3.19*	x	number of short-stay discharges in 12 months prior to 31.10.81 per number of beds normally in use
+4.93*		if mixed-sex non-group-living home
+34.82**		if single-sex group-living home
+63.29**		if mixed-sex group-living home
-12.49**	x	proportion of residents in limited dependency category
+51.71**	x	proportion of residents in appreciable or heavy dependency categories
-0.81**	x	number of beds normally in use weighted by proportion of residents in appreciable or heavy dependency categories

Significance levels: * $0.01 \leq p < 0.05$, ** $p < 0.01$
F-value for equation: $F = 37.58$, $p < 0.0001$
$R^2 = 0.76$, adjusted $R^2 = 0.74$
$n = 218$

was found to be lowest at a scale of between 55 and 70 beds (depending on
whether or not the home was designed around group-living units).

Not surprisingly, resident dependency and cost are positively related. The
advantage of the cost function is that it quantifies the cost-dependency
association and can therefore feed into debates about the balance of care
between, say, hospital, residential and domiciliary settings (Davies and
Knapp, 1988b). Some residential homes also offer day facilities for non-
residents, or act as the hub of a meals service, and via an empirical enquiry
of this kind we can separate the joint costs of these different services.

The estimated cost function reported in Table 1 also allowed interauthority
differences to be set in a better-informed context (castigating authorities for
high costs is meaningless without standardising for factors beyond their

control), and was used as the basis for studying differences between the public and private sectors (Judge and Knapp, 1985; Judge et al., 1986).

The cost function approach offers other insights, and is equally relevant in other social care contexts. Two general points must be made. First, social care and therefore its cost is inherently variable. Second, the variations tell us a great deal about practice and policy. We should not shy away from them.

4 Like-with-like comparisons

Cost variations invite comparisons. Why is one residential home more costly than another? Why does one group of residents impose a greater care burden than another group? Why is residential care more expensive in some parts of the country than others? In answering these important questions, the problem is to avoid drawing inferences from misplaced or misjudged comparisons. Usually, only like-with-like comparisons offer admissable evidence.

Consider the comparative costs of foster family care and residential homes for children (Knapp and Fenyo, 1989). Foster family care has long been preferred to residential care for the majority of children who cannot be accommodated with their natural parent(s), and for whom adoption is not an option. This preference has been couched overwhelmingly in terms of child welfare outcomes, and does not apply to every child in care (Parker, 1988; Parker et al., 1991). If we put these 'welfare' arguments to one side for the moment – they are not to be ignored, of course – we can examine the frequently-made claim that foster family care is cheaper than residential accommodation, a claim that is frequently used to bolster the 'welfare' arguments.

The two placement types do not accommodate identical populations of children. Those in residential care are typically more 'difficult' than children boarded out – they are more likely to have physical handicaps and learning disabilities, delinquent tendencies or backgrounds, and emotional or behavioural problems such as aggression, hyperactivity or propensity to self-mutilation (Millham et al., 1986; Packman, 1986). The relevance of these differences between the two child care populations stems from the cost correlates of 'difficulty'. Evidence of cost-difficulty associations comes from cost function explorations of the kind described earlier (Young and Finch, 1977; Knapp and Smith, 1985; Knapp and Fenyo, 1989). For foster family care, for example, we have found that the weekly boarding-out payment and the costs of social worker time were found to be associated with: child characteristics (such as age, gender, legal status, health status, emotional and behavioural characteristics, educational needs, previous placement and time in care); placement experiences (duration to date, location, composition and previous fostering experience of the family, objectives and plans, housing size and tenure); characteristics of the natural family (parents alive, visiting frequency, their own long-term care experience, siblings) and some features of the supervising social worker.

The differences between the two child care populations, and the links between child characteristics and costs, have important implications for the current policy emphasis in Britain on shifting the balance of care away from residential accommodation. In projecting the savings to be reaped from shifting the balance towards foster family care, one must be sure only to compare like with like. It is, for example, all too easy to exaggerate the cost differences between placement options. Simple cost averages for residential and foster family care are compared without paying heed to the child characteristic differences that lie behind them. If a child whose need-generating characteristics are typical of the residential population moves from such a setting to a family placement, the costs of the latter will be somewhat higher than today's foster care average. If *today's* average costs are employed to justify savings, and to justify a changing balance of care, there is a danger of grossly underpitched funding for family placements.

There are two corollaries. The most common way to alter the balance of care is to place with families children whose needs are more difficult or demanding to meet than the average for the foster care group but less difficult than the average child in residential care. The effect will be to raise the average difficulty and average cost in both foster and residential care. This is seemingly a perverse consequence of a policy which has cost savings as one of its aims, but in fact the total costs of the child care system will fall. This helps to explain the (constant-price) cost inflation in both services in England in the last few years. The proportion of children boarded out has risen from 33 per cent in 1976-77 to 57 per cent by 1990, and over the same period the 'inflation-adjusted' costs of both placement types have risen by rather more than 30 per cent. Further changes in the balance of care will mean higher direct and indirect costs for foster care. But residential care will then also be accommodating a more difficult clientele, raising its average cost, and making it more conspicuous to politicians and policy-makers in budget-conscious agencies. (It is also worth noting that falling numbers and changing characteristics of children in local authority care have also made it harder for local authorities to find foster placements for children; see Knapp et al., 1990.)

The second corollary concerns placement breakdowns. There is evidence to suggest that a high breakdown propensity is associated with foster child and foster family characteristics (Berridge and Cleaver, 1987; Fenyo et al., 1989), and that local authorities placing a relatively low proportion of children in their care with families have higher rates of successful placement endings (fewer breakdowns) in both the foster family and residential home populations (Rowe, 1989). This exactly parallels the cost implications. Placement break-down is by no means the only or best indicator of outcome (Parker et al., 1991), but higher breakdown rates could be expected from the under-resourcing of services, since boarding-out payments to families would then be lower, and there would be less support for families from social workers.

In common with a number of today's debates about social care, the encouragement of foster family care as an alternative to residential care is based primarily on assumptions (and some evidence) about comparative effectiveness gauged in terms of client welfare, and reinforced by assumptions (but usually *no* evidence) about comparative costs. But valid comparisons are made all too infrequently, with the result that major resource implications of care decisions are overlooked, wide variations around averages remain unexplained (and unexploited), and the system effects of changes in the balance of provision are missed.

The research evidence that has been gathered to date for the two principal forms of out-of-home child care may not be perfect, but it has cumulative force. It does not imply that recommendations to expand the proportion of children in care in family placements rather than residential settings are inappropriate, but it implies that the commonly-employed cost argument for this expansion seriously underestimates the future costs of foster family care and dangerously exaggerates the savings that will flow from changes in the balance of care.

5 Merging costs and outcomes

It is inadvisable to separate discussions of costs and outcomes. Ideally, the two types of information will be merged in any policy review, research endeavour or practice decision. The pragmatic second best is to recognise that one source of information is missing when drawing conclusions from the other. Costs and outcomes are two parts of the same production system – the inputs and outputs, means and ends, causes and effects.

Costs and outcomes can be examined together using one or more of the various evaluative techniques developed by economists. *Cost-effectiveness analysis* examines the costs of achieving a specified level of outcomes, for example change in client welfare. The efficiency rule could be to compare the costs of obtaining certain levels of outcome, and to conclude that the option with lowest cost per given level of outcome is the more efficient. This is obviously not always an easy rule to apply in practice, particularly with multidimensional outcome measures which do not move in concert. In the case of the PSSRU's evaluation of the rundown of Friern and Claybury hospitals, and the earlier evaluation of the Care in the Community demonstration programme (Renshaw et al., 1988), community care costs were lower than in-patient hospital residence for people with long-term mental health problems (excluding dementia). In both cases, the outcome results suggested that community care was no worse than in-patient residence and, along one or two dimensions, significantly better, so that the comparative cost-effectiveness of community over hospital care was clear (Knapp et al., 1992; and see Chapter 11). If some outcome dimensions register improvements and others indicate deterioration, or if the cost and outcome comparisons point to different preferred solutions, it is not the task of the researcher to advocate a particular policy or treatment option. It is the task of the researcher to point to the various consequences and to leave decisions to the politician, clinical manager, or care giver.

A *cost-benefit analysis* differs from a cost-effectiveness analysis in that it seeks to attach monetary values to the outcomes. This is an eminently sensible objective in some contexts, but not likely to be feasible or particularly sensible in social care evaluations. While cost-effectiveness analyses aim to show how a given level of outcome can be achieved at minimum cost (or maximum outcome at given cost), cost-benefit analyses seek cost-benefit ratios or differences. A third type of economic analysis has been labelled *cost-utility analysis*, and is essentially a cost-effectiveness analysis conducted with a uni-dimensional outcome measure. In health care studies, this measure is usually the quality-adjusted life year (QALY). With a cost-utility analysis it is possible to calculate the cost per QALY for different procedures or even different health problems, comparing kidney transplants with treatment of cystic fibrosis with cetfazidime, for example (Gudex, 1990). No progress has been made towards a uni-dimensional outcome measure for constituent social care services, and the primary concern about any such measure would be the loss of information consequent upon the subsuming of the many different facets usually taken to comprise outcomes of social care into a single scale.

With our present knowledge about outcomes, and given enough inform-ation, the most illuminating way to explore the links between outcomes and costs is to examine the associations with the help of appropriate (multivariate) statistical methods. *Cost function analysis* is an obvious methodological candi-date, and we illustrate its use in Chapter 11 when looking at the costs and outcomes of community care for former long-stay psychiatric hospital residents. The cost function can handle a large number of outcomes, help to overcome the difficulties that can follow from a less-than-perfect research design forced upon a study, and can simultaneously test a host of hypotheses.

6 Conclusion

Cost analyses should never 'make decisions', but they can 'make decisions better informed' (Weisbrod, 1979). Cost information is an indispensable part of most efficiency and equity studies, and policy or practice changes which ignore costs, or which embody cost information without obeying or recognising the four basic rules discussed here, will often be of dubious validity, and will sometimes offer advice which is dangerously inaccurate or misleading.

This is inexcusable, for, as shown by the illustrative studies reported in this chapter and elsewhere in this book, cost analyses need not be horrendous, ideologically compromising or scientifically complex. There are enough examples of bad costs research in the social care literature to demonstrate that it is not as simple as some people may think, but there are also enough examples of good research to encourage further attempts.

Note

* This is a substantially revised version of a paper, 'Cost', published in *Administration in Social Work*, volume 15, 1991, pp.45-63.

References

Berridge, D. and Cleaver, H. (1987) *Foster Home Breakdown*, Basil Blackwell, Oxford.

Chartered Institute of Public Finance and Accountancy (1991) *Personal Social Services Statistics: Actuals*, CIPFA, London.

Cm 849 (1989) *Caring for People: Community Care in the Next Decade and Beyond*, HMSO, London.

Darton, R.A. and Knapp, M.R.J. (1984) The cost of residential care for the elderly: the effects of dependency, design and social environment, *Ageing and Society*, 4, 157-183.

Davies, B.P. and Knapp, M.R.J. (1981) *Old People's Homes and the Production of Welfare*, Routledge and Kegan Paul, London.

Davies, B.P. and Knapp, M.R.J. (eds)(1988a). The Production of Welfare Approach: Evidence and Argument from the PSSRU. *British Journal of Social Work*, 18 (supplement).

Davies, B.P. and Knapp, M.R.J. (1988b) Costs and residential social care, in I. Sinclair (ed.) *Residential Care: The Research Reviewed*, volume 2 of the Wagner Report, HMSO, London.

Fenyo, A.J., Knapp, M.R.J. and Baines, B. (1989) Foster care breakdown: a study of a special teenage fostering scheme, in J. Hudson and B. Galaway (eds) *State Intervention on Behalf of Children in Youth*, Kluwer, Dordrecht.

Gudex, C. (1990) The QALY: how can it be used, in S. Baldwin, C. Godfrey and C. Propper (eds) *Quality of Life: Perspectives and Policies*, Routledge, London.

Judge, K.F. and Knapp, M.R.J. (1985) Efficiency in the production of welfare: the public and private sectors compared, in R. Klein and M. O'Higgins (eds) *The Future of Welfare*, Basil Blackwell, Oxford.

Judge, K.F., Knapp, M.R.J. and Smith, J. (1986) The comparative costs of public and private residential homes for the elderly, in K. Judge and I. Sinclair (eds) *Residential Care for Elderly People*, HMSO, London.

Knapp, M.R.J. (1984) *The Economics of Social Care*, Macmillan, London.

Knapp, M.R.J., Baines, B. and Gerard, B. (1990) Performance measurement in child care: when a falling boarding-out rate should attract congratulation and not castigation, *Policy and Politics*, 18, 39-42.

Knapp, M.R.J., Cambridge, P., Thomason, C., Beecham, J., Allen, C. and Darton, R.A. (1992) *Care in the Community: Challenge and Demonstration*, Ashgate, Aldershot.

Knapp, M.R.J. and Fenyo, A.J. (1989) Economic perspectives on foster care, in P. Carter, T. Jeffs and M. Smith (eds) *Social Work and Social Welfare Yearbook 1989*, Open University Press, Milton Keynes.

Knapp, M.R.J. and Smith, J. (1985) The costs of residential child care: explaining variations in the public sector, *Policy and Politics*, 13, 127-54.

Millham, S., Bullock, R., Hosie, K. and Haak, M. (1986) *Lost in Care*, Gower, Aldershot.

Netten, A. and Davies, B.P. (1990) The social production of welfare and consumption of social services, *Journal of Public Policy*, 10, 331-47.

Packman, J. (1986) *Who Needs Care?* Basil Blackwell, Oxford.

Parker, R.A. (1988) Residential care for children, in I. Sinclair (ed.) *Residential Care: The Research Reviewed*, volume 2 of the Wagner Report, HMSO, London.

Parker, R.A., Ward, H., Jackson, S., Aldgate, J., Wedge, P. (eds)(1991) *Assessing Outcomes in Child Care*, Report of an Independent Working Party established by the Department of Health, HMSO, London.

Renshaw, J., Hampson, R., Thomason, C., Darton, R., Judge, K. and Knapp, M.R.J. (1988) *Care in the Community: The First Steps*, Gower, Aldershot.

Rowe, J. (1989) Paper presented at NATO conference, Maratea.

Weisbrod, B.A. (1979) A guide to benefit cost analysis, as seen through a controlled experiment in treating the mentally ill, unpublished paper, Institute for Research on Poverty, University of Wisconsin, Madison.

Young, D.R. and Finch, S.J. (1977) *Foster Care and Nonprofit Agencies*, D.C. Heath, Lexington, Mass.

6 Proceed with Caution?
The Use of Official Sources
of Cost Information
in Social Services Departments

Aidan Kelly and Andrew Bebbington

Some years ago, Webb and Wistow (1983) found that the increase in personal social services expenditure during the late 1970s was virtually accounted for by increased unit costs. During the 1980s, after allowing for inflation, increase in the average recurrent unit cost of all main services continued (Bebbington and Kelly, 1992). One implication of such findings is that unit costs are of major significance in determining the variation in local authority expenditure on the personal social services. Equity and efficiency are unlikely to be promoted in circumstances where costs are not monitored and controlled, or where unit costs are escalating yet little is known about cost trends.

It would seem to be a primary management task, therefore, to monitor a flow of information about activity, manpower and cost, yet social services information systems are still relatively underdeveloped. This has been the case since the early 1970s and a dearth of uniform and reliable management information was still evident in the mid-1980s (Miller, 1986, pp.9-10). As a result, our knowledge of the costs of social services is based on specific academic studies of the cost implications of design features and client dependency (Knapp and Smith, 1985); the comparative costs of alternative modes of care (Davies and Knapp, 1988; Wright and Haycox, 1985); and variations in local cost-raising conditions (Baker et al., 1990; Bebbington and Kelly, 1991, 1992). Essential as these studies are, they use methodologies that are unlikely to be useful in the social services management context in the short term. It is far more likely that, where services cost information is used, it will be based on readily-available data sources such as annual statistics supplied by the Department of the Environment (DoE), Department of Health (DH) and Chartered Institute of Public Finance Accountancy (CIPFA). This paper describes one approach to analysing these data in the light of known problems and provides an explicit rationale about what they can contribute to our understanding of unit costs and trends in unit costs.

1 Constructing unit cost estimates from official government sources

The process of constructing unit costs from official data sources is one of secondary analysis, and the reader is directed to more general discussions of this method of social research (Hakim, 1982; Dale et al., 1988). Secondary analysis involves the use of (often official) data for purposes for which they were not primarily designed. The existing data sets contain explicit or implicit conceptualisations of the real world objects that data categories seek to describe. The conceptualisations reflect the aims and assumptions of those who constructed the categories and developed the guidance on the completion of the returns. For secondary analysis, these categories and concepts are not taken for granted but reworked and assessed in the pursuit of specific theoretical and analytical objectives. This chapter offers an illustration of what can be done with readily-available official data on expenditure and service activities. As it proposes a method for estimating unit costs that is, perhaps, inherently problematic and far from the ideal proffered elsewhere in this book (see, for example, Chapter 3), it should carry an organisational health warning: 'Proceed With Caution!' Cautions about the data and their use in policy-making notwithstanding, it is recommended to the reader on the highly pragmatic grounds that it allows a start to be made on what will become an increasingly important task for social services departments: the costing of their services.

The process of service costing by secondary analysis can be illustrated by recasting the service costing diagram described in Chapter 3 (see p.29). As in that diagram, the first stage is to arrive at a clear description of the service activities which are being costed, but there the similarity ends. Figure 1 shows that the second and third stages are to identify available sources of resource input and service activity data, and then engage in a process of 'double-fitting': the matching of service activity and expenditure categories in order to get definitions of each that are reasonably consistent. Stage four is the calculation of unit costs. As in any process, the results can lead to a questioning of the adequacy of the procedures and the process beginning again. The next two sections describe the official sources of expenditure and service activity data for the main social services.

1.1 The identification of resource inputs

Every local authority is required to supply the Department of the Environment with details of its expenditure on personal social services. The official return is known as the *DoE rate fund services revenue account* or *R03A-E*. Expenditure on social services is organised in rows, and Table 1 shows the main service rows for 1988-89. DoE data have the advantage of completeness and reliability, but the definitions are not compatible with DH definitions of social services

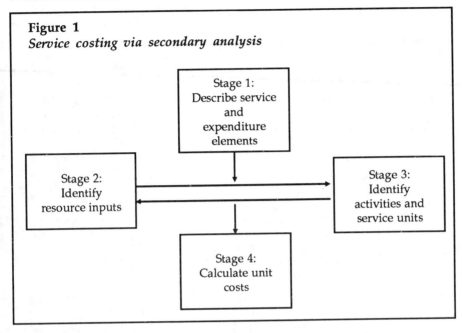

Figure 1
Service costing via secondary analysis

activity. The data were not designed to be in an ideal form for unit cost calculations, but they can be used as such if care is exercised in the selection of the appropriate variables.

DoE revenue accounts permit a further breakdown of costs, most usefully for capital facilities, into both running costs and manpower costs. They also permit an estimate of cost recovery rates from fee income, and the cost of contracted-out services. They do not, however, provide information on the recharging of overhead costs to client group activities. In this respect, the CIPFA Personal Social Services (PSS) data are more comprehensive, but are usually thought to be less reliable.

1.2 Activities and service units

Unit costs are measured by the division of gross cost as defined above by the annual volume of activity. Estimates of the volume of activity supported by expenditure may be based on the published activity data collected by the DH from social services departments (see Table 1). The volume denominator for each service is a measure of the principal intermediate output of that service. For residential homes for elderly people, maintained and controlled community homes for children, boarding out, day nurseries, and homes for people with learning difficulties, this is the number of client-years of service provided, in each case estimated by the numbers cared for (or on the register)

Table 1

Personal social services resource inputs and activities

Client	Activity	Data sources	
		Volume	Expenditure
Children	Total number of children in community homes at 31 March each year	A/F/12 Table 6	Community homes RO3A row 1
	Total number of children boarded out in foster homes	Table 6	Boarded out RO3A row 7
	Children on register of facilities provided by LA and children paid for by LA in other facilities, as 31 March each year	A/F/6 Table A	Day nurseries RO3A row 8
Elderly	Supported residents aged 65+, all forms of accommodation, at 31 March each year	RA/1 Table A	Residential care RO3B row 1
	Places in local authority day centres (all client groups) at 31 March each year	A/F/8 Table B	Day centres RO3B row 3
	Meals at home, each year	A/F/18 Table A	Meals RO3B row 5
Learning difficulties	Residents of LA homes/hostels and places available in other organisations at 31 March each year	A/F/11B Tables 1, 2, 4	Residential care RO3C row 1
	Places in LA day centres (all client groups) at 31 March each year	A/F/8 Table A	Day centres RO3C row 3
Mental health	Total supported residents in homes and hostels at 31 March each year	A/F/11B Table A	Residential care RO3C row 7
Fieldwork	No. of full-time equivalents in post at 30 September each year	A/F/1 Table 1	RO3E row 1
Administration	No. of full-time equivalents in post at 30 September each year	A/F/1 Table 1	RO3E rows 9, 10, 11

at the beginning and end of the year. For day centres for the elderly and adult training centres, there are no DH statistics of numbers of people cared for, so numbers of places in centres have been substituted. For the home help/home care service there are no DH statistics on levels of activity, but the number of client-hours of service delivered during the year is available from the CIPFA PSS Actuals. For meals-on-wheels, the denominator is the number of meals supplied at home.

Local authority personal social services expenditure listed in the Revenue Outturn RO3A-E includes support services: management and administration; research and development; training; and field social work. Spending on these items comprised 26 per cent of gross recurrent expenditure in 1988/9. Between 1978 and 1988 the number of managers, administration and social work staff remained a constant 22 per cent of all staff nationally, but within that group managers have been one of the most rapidly expanding subgroups of social services employees, increasing from 3,160 in 1978 to 5,849 in 1989. The number of other staff supported by each member of management staff fell from 60 to 39.

The implication behind the term 'support services' is that they do not create output in their own right but support other activities. Therefore output from these services is implicit in the volume of other activity taking place. Such an interpretation is quite reasonable for management and administration, but only partially so for social work. Social work does support other services but also makes a direct contribution in ways independent of the other services. Indeed, it is a direct substitute for some services in that the aim of much social work is to prevent the need for other direct services. However, there is no convenient means, even crude, of measuring the output of social work's independent contribution in a manner which would reflect variations through time or between authorities.

There are three ways of regarding the output of support services:
• the cost of support services per pound of direct expenditure;
• the cost of support services per 'direct' care provider;
• the cost of support services per cost-weighted unit of output.

This last method of constructing a cost-weighted index of all recorded activities that are likely to contribute to the social work caseload is reported in Bebbington et al. (1979). They found that the number of children in care was by far the most significant single predictor of social work levels. However, this method will exaggerate the average unit costs of authorities whose social workers are effective at keeping down the number of children in care by preventive work.

It is suggested that for most purposes unit costs estimates should be based on DH and DoE statistics rather than taken direct from the better-known figures provided by CIPFA PSS Actuals. It should be noted that for some services there are very substantial differences between unit costs calculated this way and those provided by CIPFA. Caution should be exercised in the use of both data sets as will become clear in the discussion about the fourth and final stage: calculating unit costs.

1.3 Calculating unit cost estimates

The normal method of calculating unit costs using these data is to apply the formulae shown at the top of Box 1 to calculate the gross cost to the authority of providing the service for clients, and to divide this by the number of service

---

Box 1

Costs definitions for calculation of unit costs from DoE R03 returns[1]

Method (A): Supported users

Recurrent gross cost on own supported people	= Manpower cost (1) + Running cost (2) – Income from other agencies – Contributions to voluntary organisations (16)[2]
Recurrent net cost on own supported people	= Gross cost – Sales to persons (17) – Fees from use of local and health authority services (18) – Fees from persons using voluntary and private services(19)

Method (B): All users

Recurrent gross cost on users of own services	= Manpower cost (1) + Running cost (2) – Other income (12) – Services provided by independent sector (14) – Services provided by other authorities (15) – Contributions to voluntary organisations (16)[2]
Recurrent net cost on users of own services *where:*	= Gross cost – Sales (9) – Fees (10)
Income from other agencies	= Sales (9) + Fees (10) + Other income (12) – Sales to persons (17) – Fees from use of local and health authority services (18) – Fees from use of the independent sector (19)

1 Figures in brackets relate to column numbers of the R03 return.
2 This assumes that contributions to voluntary organisations are primarily to enable then to provide a separate service.

---

outputs. Where the reported total expenditure includes spending on own services for own clients, spending on own services provided to clients of other agencies, and spending on contracted-out services for own clients, some care is needed to ensure the appropriate denominator is chosen.

For example, if, as is the case for elderly services, only the numbers of own supported residents in the care of the authority are available, then Revenue Outturn expenditure data used in unit cost calculations must refer only to expenditure on these clients. This recurrent gross cost of an authority's own residents is the sum of the manpower cost plus the expenses of running the service minus income from other agencies (for support of residents) and the contributions to voluntary organisations.

The DH returns for day centres and special needs centres, on the other hand, refer to places available for all the users of an authority's services. When this is the case, the unit cost is the sum of the manpower cost and the running costs minus the following:

- other income;
- services provided by the independent sector;
- services provided by other local authorities;
- contributions to voluntary organisations (assuming provision of a separate service); and
- income from sales, fees, sales to persons, fees from persons using local authority/health authority services or the independent sector, and other income.

2 The validity and reliability of official sources of unit costs estimates

The rather limited use of cost data by management and monitoring agencies is probably due to the persistence of widely-acknowledged problems of validity and reliability associated with these data. Validity criteria refer to the quality of concept indicator links: what are the 'real' costs and what are the 'real' activities being covered? Reliability concerns the consistency over time and across departments in the use of categories of cost information: would two accountants arrive at the same expenditure totals for each service in a local authority? Are different guidelines or norms used in different authorities? Do definitions change over time?

A major problem of validity arises in the conceptualisation of the services that are being costed. The methodology of unit cost estimates outlined above assumes that categories such as residential child care, for instance, are appropriate ways of classifying the activity of social services departments which cover a range of services having different aims and objectives, and where there are policy-led variations in the degrees to which different departments emphasise different approaches. Here the CIPFA data have an undoubted advantage over DH/DoE data. Whatever the questions about the reliability of CIPFA data, their more refined classification of child care activities scores higher on validity criteria.

Costs are expressed per unit of output, but this term raises questions of validity: what really is output? In an ideal world, costs would be expressed per unit of outcome, but this seems a distant prospect. At a more mundane level, cost per resident (for example, the number of children in homes 'as at' 31 March) or per place is a relatively poor substitute for cost per resident week or user day, as Table 2 shows. Until 1987, CIPFA routinely provided unit costs on the basis of such figures. Table 2 compares estimates using both denominators and illustrates the degree to which the 'as at' estimate of activity conceals wide variations in the intensity of use. For elderly residential care, the 'as at' occupied place provides between 47 to 62 resident weeks. Day care 'places' are used for part-day attendances explaining why mental health day care attendances vary between 22 and 1482 'days' per year! Clearly variations in 'as at' unit costs might be accounted for by variations in the intensity of use.

Table 2
User activity per 'as at resident' or per place 1986

	Mean	Standard deviation	Minimum	Maximum
Children				
– resident weeks	30.98	18.11	2.23	182.00
– nursery days	418.17	336.66	47.00	1591.03
Elderly people				
– resident weeks	53.64	2.63	47.75	62.11
Learning difficulties				
– child resident weeks	93.82	91.24	15.00	403.75
– adult resident weeks	48.92	15.85	12.82	167.59
– day care sessions	98.42	28.57	31.50	216.50
Mental health problems				
– resident weeks	48.48	13.81	5.06	104.80
– day care sessions	152.63	173.89	22.17	1482.00

Source: CIPFA Actuals (1986).

If turnover, occupancy and vacancy rates vary, there can be large differences between the services delivered when using nominal measures of output such as the 'as at' figure. March 31 may be a reasonably typical day, but may not reflect the total number of service outputs when services are expanding or contracting rapidly. The average of the two-year-end reports is a better estimate but again this may be a poor approximation for authorities making rapid changes (more than 25 per cent per year) and for authorities making low levels of provision (for example, under 30 places) and for authorities with a high throughput of clients.

Problems of reliability – the consistency of the measures across location, period and local authority officer – are considerable. Variations in unit costs may reflect differences in reporting or accounting procedures associated with different management arrangements, or some other statistical artifact. For example, the data on home help hours reported by CIPFA contain a useful distinction between hours paid and hours delivered. Hours delivered is the favoured measure of output but differs from hours paid only in the practices used to estimate hours delivered. In some authorities hours delivered is approximated by hours paid less 25 per cent to allow for travel; in another authority, hours delivered is equal to hours paid, as travel is included in the clients' receipt time. The official categories also change over time: in 1978/9, assisted homes were included with maintained and controlled homes for children, whereas later data collections categorise them separately.

Some activity data can be tricky to collect centrally: for example, the number of home help contact hours or number of attendances in day care. Even residential care can be difficult; for example, in children's homes the number actually present is sometimes only a fraction of those registered as resident. Often approximations are used and again methods vary. Sometimes this relies on taking 'snapshots' at particular times or the unit cost calculations use year-end figures to estimate volume. This will be inappropriate, however, during times of change, in particular where the change is subsequently reversed, for example where a home is closed down and its replacement does not come on-line for some time.

Social services departments are part of the local authority, and as such receive a share of common inputs from central administration: for example, personnel and transport. The allocation of overhead costs to particular services ('recharging') is a relatively recent practice dating from the revised Standard Form of accounts introduced in 1987/88. It has become usual practice for such shared inputs to be recharged among departments for accounting purposes, although this is not universal practice. Also, the separate services for client groups or functional divisions or areas receive inputs from the central services of the social services department, and indeed one service may provide help to another. Variations between social services departments in recharging practices may reflect the degree of decentralisation: where administration is decentralised it is more likely to be allocated to a client group or functional division. In addition, the job descriptions of care staff might include administration in one authority but not in another. A similar problem arises with references to services provided by other agencies. The National Health Service, the voluntary sector and informal carers may provide services free or at highly subsidised prices. Where services are run jointly there is little consistency in the level of subsidy or the reporting of costs. For example, a local authority may count as part of its provision services which it allocates but which are mainly paid for by another agency. A general note of caution must be entered about the comparability of apparently similar definitions of direct and indirect services since quite arbitrary conventions may be used by those deciding what services and expenditure to include.

Expenditure and output data are usually the responsibility of different sections of social services departments – finance and research, for example – and sometimes the financial return is completed by central local authority staff. Many authorities do not combine data from these different sources but rely on CIPFA data for their unit cost estimates. In addition, those responsible for routine data recording may have little or no use for the data and thus have little incentive to ensure its accuracy and consistency. It requires a concerted effort from senior management to overcome these problems.

Given these problems of validity and reliability it is not surprising that the initial and perhaps only consequence of exercises in interauthority costs comparisons is an extensive correspondence between authorities about the 'real' meaning of the revealed differences (Miller, 1986, p.15). Given a valid definition of what constitutes a unit cost for a service, it could prove to be inoperable as a research tool if doubts remain about the accuracy and consistency of coding practices in social services departments. In the end, however, judgements about the worth of the exercise are themselves based on the costs of not undertaking it, and on the risk of making erroneous policy conclusions. In our judgement it is worth proceeding, but with full knowledge of the problems.

For social services managers seeking an overview of their costs profile, an index showing the unit costs for each service relative to the average costs for 'similar' or otherwise comparable authorities will prove useful, as is illustrated in Figure 2. This shows the position of one London authority's costs relative to the Inner London average and highlights where the authority appears to be providing high-quality services or providing services inefficiently.

The unit cost profile shows a social services department with below-average costs relative to its comparison group, but with high support costs for both administration and fieldwork. Residential care (which accounts for a high proportion of social services department expenditure) for children and for people with learning difficulties is either of low quality or highly efficient – the very question that the use of cost information in social services departments is likely to beg.

3 Costs and services planning after the purchaser-provider split

The social services department purchasers will seek the benefits of marketisation by developing alternative sources of supply. The contracts they enter into should be, therefore, the 'best buys' in community-based services on cost-outcomes considerations. The arrival of the purchaser-provider split has forced authorities to routinely consider the costs of services they provide. The purchaser-provider split in the social services is not simply about the introduction of market principles of allocation; indeed, progress may be rather slow in this respect (Wistow et al., 1992). Rather, the division of responsibilities can be seen as a way of combining technocratic and market principles of allocation in a post-bureaucratic system of welfare production (Hoggett, 1990; Kelly, 1991).

Social services departments as purchasing authorities are required to be *technocratic* in order to combat the problem of consumer irrationality: the principle objection to the operation of autonomous consumer choice in welfare. They are required to purchase services for welfare 'consumers' who do not necessarily demand them; for example, health promotion, preventative services and services that control socially unacceptable behaviours. The purchaser function will continue to operate some form of 'top-down' needs-based planning, but once sufficient care management data are on-stream it will codify and collate the needs assessment of case managers. The purchasing should then provide a rational counter-balance to the tendency for resources to flow in accord with provider interests and the distribution of power within the provider group as a whole. Sole reliance on bottom-up costs, needs and outcomes data is likely to lead to planning that reinforces the current bias of the service delivery system: the bias towards certain professional preferences

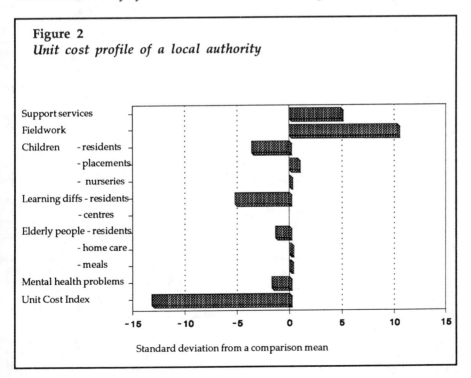

Figure 2
Unit cost profile of a local authority

Standard deviation from a comparison mean

for service delivery and towards existing expressed demands. Only a system that uses data independent of the service provision process can effectively counter the weaknesses of the current system.

Current research, such as that reported in other chapters of this book, is very much focused on costing packages of care, assessing needs and evaluating outcomes as an aid to the development of care/case management. These studies require the collection and analysis of highly disaggregated data. Invaluable as these are, they are not, at the moment, comprehensive enough to provide an adequate database for resource allocation in social services departments. The development of client information systems recording demographic, service use and outcomes of care may in the future provide for the systematic input of 'bottom-up' data into higher-level planning and policy-making (see Figure 3).

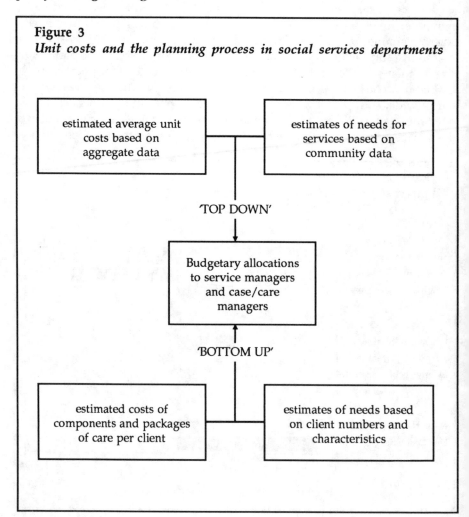

Figure 3
Unit costs and the planning process in social services departments

This chapter has discussed an interim, top-down methodology. However, the development of bottom-up management information systems in the social services will, paradoxically, improve and not replace top-down aggregate methodologies. For reasons outlined above it is important to use information that is independent of the service delivery system itself to overcome its biases, but the newer bottom-up systems will provide a sound basis for inferring from demographic information the likely service needs and outcomes. The early years of implementing *Caring for People* (Cm 849, 1989) should, as a result, see equal emphasis placed on top-down and bottom-up methodologies.

4 Conclusion

Perhaps the biggest obstacle to the development of either methodology and the use of cost data in the social services is the widespread cynicism which many professionals and some managers view proposals to use cost information in the planning process. Similar suspicion is directed at quantitative studies such as those produced by the Audit Commission (1985, 1987) and the Key Indicators System (Gostick, 1989). Improvements in the quality of data will help, although there will always be some for whom the nature of human services requires a substantial reliance on qualitative evidence and professional judgements. The separation of purchaser-provider roles will help to counter the dominance of such perspectives. Social services department purchasers, as surrogates for the community and service users as a whole, must be concerned with costs per client and with the most cost-effective options among alternative packages of care. This is the only way in which they can maximise the delivery of care within available resources. Providers in all sectors will be sensitised to cost implications of their day-to-day practices, and will have every incentive to investigate sources of high unit costs, if only to justify them to purchasers and clients on quality grounds.

In sum, the reforms could lead to an improved understanding of the relationship between various packages of costed inputs and outcomes for the client. A clearer focus on the relationship between resources, needs and outcomes will be welcomed by those concerned with efficiency and equity in the delivery of publicly-funded social services.

References

Audit Commission (1985) *Managing Social Services for the Elderly More Effectively*, HMSO, London.

Audit Commission (1987) The management of London's authorities: preventing the breakdown of services, Occasional Paper 2, Audit Commission, London.

Baker, J., Dilworth, J. and Kenny, D. (1990) *Care and Care Homes in the 1990s: An Analysis of Trends and Costs*, London Research Centre, London.

Bebbington, A.C. and Kelly, A. (1991) The London Costs Project: stage one report, Discussion Paper 757, Personal Social Services Research Unit, University of Kent at Canterbury.

Bebbington, A.C. and Kelly, A. (1992) Unit costs, policy drift and territorial justice in the personal social services, Discussion Paper 799, Personal Social Services Research Unit, University of Kent at Canterbury.

Bebbington, A.C., Davies, B.P. and Coles, O. (1979) Social workers and client numbers (a research note), *British Journal of Social Work*, 9, 1, 93-100.

Chartered Institute of Public Finance Accountancy (1986) *Personal Social Services Actuals*, CIPFA. London.

Cm 849 (1989) *Caring for People*, HMSO, London.

Dale, A., Arber, S. and Procter, M. (1988) *Doing Secondary Analysis*, Unwin Hyman, London.

Davies, B.P. and Knapp, M.R.J. (1988) Costs and residential social care, Appendix to *Report to the Residential Care Review Committee* (Chair: Lady Wagner), HMSO, London.

Gostick, C. (1989) A good start is not enough, *Social Services Insight*, 7 March, 15-16.

Hakim, C. (1982) *Secondary Analysis in Social Research: A Guide to Data Sources and Methods with Examples*, Unwin Hyman, London.

Hoggett, P. (1990) Modernisation, political strategy and the welfare state: an organisational perspective, *Studies in Decentralisation and Quasi-Markets*, No. 2, School for Advanced Urban Studies, University of Bristol.

Kelly, A. (1992) The new managerialism in the social services, *Social Work and Social Welfare Yearbook, 1992*, 179-93.

Knapp, M.R.J. and Smith, J. (1985) The costs of residential child care: explaining variations in the public sector, *Policy and Politics*, 13, 2, 127-54.

Miller, N. (1986) Management information and performance measurement in the personal social services, *Social Services Research*, Issue 4/5, 7-55.

Webb, A. and Wistow, G. (1983) Public expenditure and policy implementation: the case of community care, *Public Administration*, 61, 21-41.

Wistow, G., Knapp, M.R.J., Hardy, B. and Allen, C. (1992) From providing to enabling: local authorities and the mixed economy of social care, *Public Administration*, 70, 25-45.

Wright, K.G. and Haycox, A. (1985) Costs of alternative forms of NHS care for mentally handicapped persons, Discussion Paper 7, Centre for Health Economics, University of York.

7 Costs, Prices and Charges*

Ann Netten

Putting a price on services is becoming an increasingly important issue with the separation of purchaser and provider functions in government-funded health and social care. Frequently, therefore, the purpose of estimating costs will be to affix a price or a charge to a service. Costing services is clearly an important stage in this process but, in setting prices and charges, organisations which are acting as providing agencies need to be clear about their objectives. Pricing services is not simply a mechanistic process but one that involves policy values and choices.

This chapter is limited to addressing the pricing of services in the statutory sector, with particular emphasis on local authority social services departments. First the use of the terms prices and charges in this context is defined. The various objectives of pricing and charging for services are discussed and the importance of the pricing environment described, before identifying strategies that can be employed to meet the objectives. The chapter concludes by identifying some important challenges and implications when estimating costs, and setting prices and charges.

1 Price or charge?

There is no theoretical difference between a price or charge: they are both the amount for which a good or service is sold or offered. The term 'charge' tends to be used in statutory social and health agencies when referring to the amount that is paid by the final consumer for services such as meals-on-wheels or home help. There is usually an implicit understanding that the cost represents, or ought to represent, the upper limit of these charges, adhering to the principle that public services should not make a profit. The objectives and strategies used to price services for the final consumer are often different to those for pricing services within or between agencies. Throughout this chapter, therefore, the distinction between charges and prices is the nature of the purchaser: clients and patients are final consumers who pay charges, while agencies – or budget-holding individuals within agencies – pay prices.

2 Pricing and charging objectives

In setting prices and charges social services departments will have a number of objectives, many of which will not be fully articulated. It is essential that there is a clear understanding of the aims of pricing and charging policies and how these complement or conflict with each other and with wider organisational objectives. In the absence of such an understanding, strategies may be employed that create perverse incentives or are inoperable because the explicit aims conflict with implicit organisational objectives. For example, if those involved in directly delivering and charging for services believe that services should be free at the point of delivery, they may undermine a charging policy intended to establish whether clients find services value for money. Parker (1980) illustrates this point by describing the changes in prescribing practice that followed the introduction of prescription charges. When the charges were made per prescription form, doctors wrote more prescriptions per form. When this was changed to a charge per item, doctors increased the amount of each item they prescribed.

In identifying the different potential pricing and charging objectives it is useful to put them in the current policy context. Parker (1976) suggests a number of different purposes for consumer charges which can, for the most part, also be applied to prices as defined here. These have been generalised and supplemented to produce five types of objective:

- to act as symbols;
- to prevent waste or abuse;
- to reduce total cost;
- to shift priorities; and
- to influence the social care market.

Knapp points out that two general justifications for using prices are 'the pursuit of efficiency and the promotion of consumer choice' (1984, p.101) both of which are primary aims of the *National Health Service and Community Care Act 1990*. Prices and charges, therefore, can be seen as tools which local authorities can use as part of a strategy in implementing policies to increase value for money and to increase consumer choice. It is in the context of these overall policy aims, and the underlying goal of enhancing independence, that the individual pricing and charging objectives need to be examined.

2.1 Prices and charges as symbols

The mere fact of establishing prices for services represents a profound change in the organisational culture of social services departments. This shift in attitudes is as great as the shift that took place in the 1940s with the development of the post-war welfare state and the move from regarding social services as charity for the 'deserving' poor to perceiving them as a right for every citizen 'in need'. Prices are both symbolic of changes that have taken place and are likely to affect organisational attitudes particularly among people using prices, whether as budget-holders or service-providers (Kelly, 1990). It is probable, for example, that budget-holders will feel they have the right to be more demanding of quality when allocating services they have 'bought'.

While pricing statutorily-provided services is relatively new, charging for these services has a long history. Knapp notes that charges have long had a symbolic value 'to clients, the electorate, the Cabinet or even to foreign opinion' (1984, p.104). In particular, charging for residential care for elderly people was part of the process of separating the provision from the Poor Law workhouses they were replacing, symbolising the change in the relationship between the carer and the cared for (Judge and Matthews, 1980a). However, in recent years there has been a shift in attitudes to this symbolic role of charges. The issue is now less that they perform an important role in preventing services being perceived as charity and more that people are responsible for self-provision and ought to contribute towards their own care (Davies, 1990).

In terms of current policy concerns, charges also have a symbolic role to play in consumer empowerment. Consumers who are paying for a service will feel more able to complain, or to exercise *voice* (Hirschman, 1970). This is of particular importance when the capacity to reject a service (or *exit*) is limited. This sense of empowerment may be related to levels of charges, however. Judge and Matthews (1980b) report how an increase in charges for meals-on-wheels resulted in an increase in consumer criticism of the quality of meal served. Once charges start to approach a level where consumers feel that they are not getting value for money they are more likely to complain or reject the service. The increase in meals-on-wheels charges also resulted in a large number of people dropping out of the service although they were replaced by others from the waiting list.

2.2 Reducing waste and abuse

It could be argued that those who dropped out from the meals service were in a sense wasting or abusing the service as they were only prepared to receive it at the lower price and those on the waiting list, who were prepared to pay more, valued the service more highly. This is unlikely for, as Judge and Matthews (1980a,b) and Knapp (1984) point out, the main gatekeeping role is performed by professionals. Thus while it is unlikely that a free service will lead to abuse or waste by consumers, it is clear that the relationship between charges and service use could be used to monitor whether consumers find the service value for money. Judge and Matthews (1980a) point out that parental contributions to child care services are the principal social services where prevention of misuse is the main objective of charging.

For social services in the current context, the more appropriate mechanism by which waste can be reduced is by pricing services to care managers. The primary rationale behind introducing the separation of the purchaser and provider functions is to make use of the price mechanism. It is this which is credited with increasing efficiency by making individual decision-makers and agencies more aware of the resource implications of decisions. Thus it is through making professional gatekeepers aware of prices rather than through client charges that the objective of reducing waste and increasing value for money is most likely to be achieved.

2.3 Reducing total cost

Parker (1976) distinguishes two ways in which cost is reduced: by raising new or additional revenue and by reducing demand and lowering the level of supply. Clearly in the context discussed here setting prices on local authority services will not raise new revenue. It may, however, reduce demand for specific services. In addition, awareness of the resource implications should make gatekeepers consider alternative ways of meeting needs and thus potentially reduce the total cost of 'producing' a given level of welfare. Thus a set level of resources could meet more needs.

Charges, on the other hand, can result in additional revenue. There are considerable fiscal pressures on local authorities who are limited both by the level of revenue they can raise through local taxation and by central funding based on the Standard Spending Assessment. These pressures are such that revenue raised from charging for services may become a more important ingredient over time in ensuring an adequate and consistent level of provision. Judge and Matthews suggest that the principal objective of home help and meals-on-wheels charges was to raise revenue. Hi torically, however, a very small proportion of service cost is met by charges (Judge and Matthews 1980a; Kelly, 1990) and there are limits on how much revenue can be raised from people who often have minimal incomes.

The scope for using charges to reduce cost by lowering demand is also limited: the *National Health Service and Community Care Act 1990* states that identification of need must not be related to ability to pay (para. 3.3.1). While a discriminatory charging policy could prevent excessive demand, it is more likely that the assessment process would be seen as the appropriate and equitable tool for gatekeeping. The reduction of demand through charging is in any case an unlikely aim, but where authorities are aiming to improve targeting they may wish to consider using charges and prices as a means of shifting priorities.

2.4 Shifting priorities

One of the original purposes of the *National Health Service and Community Care Act 1990* was to remove the perverse incentive by which people moved into residential care rather than received support in their own homes (Audit Commission, 1986). Thus substitutability of services may be a pricing issue: 'care in the community' may mean that local authorities would wish to include among their pricing objectives the discouragement of the use of residential care and encourage the shift to domiciliary-based care. It will be important in organising the process of budget-holding and pricing services not to build in perverse incentives. For example, it is unlikely that care managers will be expected to hold budgets for those in residential care. If appropriate safeguards are not built in, it is conceivable that exactly the same perverse incentive to place people in residential care that existed between agencies will be reproduced within social services departments.

There is a limit to which charging can be used to shift priorities either in terms of need or modes of care while ensuring that identification of need is not limited by ability to pay. Judge and Matthews (1980b) identify the reduced priority for day nursery provision which followed the end of the second world war. The number of free day nursery places expanded rapidly during the war because of the need to release womanpower. At the end of the war, government funding was reduced and local authorities pressed for legislation to enable them to charge. Attendance at day nurseries fell by over 20 per cent in the year following the *National Health Service Act 1952*, which allowed local authorities to charge for day nursery places. Knapp (1984) points out, however, that there are few modern instances in the field of social care where charges have been used to shift priorities.

2.5 Influencing the market

Another function of a pricing policy may be to influence the market structure: to encourage the 'development of a flourishing independent sector' (Cm 849, 1989, p.5) in order to encourage diversity of provision and thus consumer choice. The division between purchaser and provider need not necessarily result in increased competition; some local authorities may only be interested in encouraging competition if short-term costs can be cut by encouraging other providers to supply the same services at a lower cost. Other local authorities may see the encouragement of the independent sector, with only a residual market share held by local authority services, as a fundamental aim. Before deciding on a pricing policy, local authorities need to be clear what their intentions are with respect to the independent sector.

The relationship between charges set by local authorities and the independent sector is less clear. When consumers can purchase services provided by social services departments directly, the charges made by local authorities will affect the market. But where charges are well below the price of alternatives and rationing is on the basis of professional judgement, this impact will be negligible. With the introduction of new financing arrangements as a result of the *National Health Service and Community Care Act 1990*, local authorities will be responsible for the social care element of publicly-funded residential care. As a result of this, local authority residential care charges may well have a more direct impact than charges for other services and authorities will need to consider how they would wish to influence the market in this area more than any other.

These pricing and charging objectives are not mutually exclusive but a coherent set of objectives needs to be developed if pricing policies are to reinforce and provide a useful mechanism for the furtherance of community care policies as a whole. But it is in the context of the market structure of each service that local authorities will need to develop appropriate pricing and charging strategies to meet these objectives.

3 The pricing environment

Whether the local authority regards influencing the independent sector to be a priority or not (Allen et al., 1991), the price at which it sets its own services will have a major impact on the development (or otherwise) of the market structure. In analysing what market structure forms the pricing environment, local authorities will have to decide what exactly it is that each service provides in order to determine what is being priced. The clearest existing market is in residential and nursing home care of elderly people. There has been an expansion in the 1980s of independent sector provision, with many of the homes run by owner-managers. The characteristics of homes differ and proprietors can vary their charges to reflect this. This type of market, in which each provider is producing a slightly different service and charges accordingly, is a form of monopolistic competition.

In other cases the situation is less clear. For example, a voluntary organisation providing meals-on-wheels for an entire local authority can be seen as representing a monopoly (a single provider) facing a monopsony (a single buyer). Such markets arise where there are barriers to other providers and purchasers entering the market. In this example the level of trust built up between a local authority and local volunteer organisation may be such that competitors are not considered. Such *brand loyalty* can be seen (perhaps more importantly) as a way of reducing *transaction costs* (Hansmann, 1980). Moreover, if other services such as luncheon clubs, day centres and so on are regarded as alternative providers of meals, then an entirely different market structure emerges. Local authorities will need to decide what types of service are regarded as alternatives, and on what basis, before they can analyse their local market structures.

One way to deal this problem and to determine what is priced would be to draw on the concept of *basic commodities* of social care (Netten and Davies, 1990) and on the theory of *characteristics* of goods (Lancaster, 1966). Rather than considering services in terms of their titles (day care, home help, meals-on-wheels, for example) they can be analysed in terms of the commodities they provide, such as social contact, housework, nutrition and so on. Any other service or source of these commodities (social clubs, private domestic help, luncheon clubs) are *substitute* services. These provide the same commodity but may differ in terms of characteristics, such as being provided in people's own homes, variety, choice of menu and so on. Day care and transport services are *complements* in that the increased demand for day care will tend to lead to an increased demand for transport services.

Using the concept of commodities to analyse the market accords with the philosophy of the White Paper *Caring for People* (Cm 849, 1989) which emphasises the importance of needs-based assessment and flexibility in meeting these needs. The approach represents needs in terms of problems in producing commodities which it is the function of social care services to provide or assist people in producing. By defining markets in terms of commodities, the substitutability of different services in meeting these needs is clarified, with characteristics defining important properties about the way in which the needs are met.

The process of using the concepts of commodities and characteristics to clarify exactly what local authority services are providing and thus what budget-holders are purchasing will help to inform potential entrants to the market. They will be clearer both about what it is that budget-holders are purchasing and the potential for innovative approaches to supplying the commodities in question. By improving the information to potential entrants to the market, the local authority is making the market more *contestable*. A contestable market is one which is accessible to potential entrants so there are no barriers to entry or exit (Baumol et al., 1982). There may only be one provider but the conditions are such that independent providers have the opportunity to compete if they choose to do so. Clearly in social care there need to be some barriers to entry: there has to be an element of trust that other providers will not abuse their position in caring for the more vulnerable members of society. Within limits, however, contestability is a desirable attribute in the mixed economy, encouraging innovative approaches to the supply of social care and helping ensure that services provide value for money.

In most of the markets in which it is operating a local authority will at least initially be the major provider and thus the price leader. It may be the only provider and be less concerned with encouraging the independent sector than ensuring that each of the markets in which it is operating is at least partly contestable. The prevention of unnecessary barriers to entry to markets is clearly central to achieving policy aims through pricing strategies and to a lesser extent through charging strategies.

It is important therefore in deciding on a pricing policy that local authorities are clear about the nature of the market in which they are operating and which they are affecting by their actions. They need to understand what services act as substitutes and complements for one another, what barriers exist to entry and to what extent these barriers are necessary. Moreover, they must be aware that prices should reflect their longer-term needs as providers, including sustaining their position in the market.

4 Pricing and charging strategies

Before discussing specific pricing and charging strategies, it is important to be clear about the different types of cost used in setting prices. *Fixed costs* are those unaffected by the level of output during the period that the price or charge is in effect. These include management salaries, depreciation on equipment, capital costs and so on. *Variable costs* are proportional to, and affected by, the number of units bought or sold: direct labour or transport, for example. Clearly, what costs are considered fixed and what variable will depend on the time period under consideration and on what is being priced and for what purpose. The term *marginal cost* refers to the cost of providing an additional unit of output and in the long run includes both fixed and variable costs (see Chapter 2 for a more detailed discussion).

4.1 Prices

In discussing specific pricing strategies it is helpful to consider the pricing objectives identified above. In the pure market there is no need for the price to reflect the cost: firms can set whatever price they can get for a service. When prices are *acting as symbols*, however, budget-holders attempting to purchase the best value for money for their clients will consider that prices for statutorily-provided services 'ought' to be based on or less than the cost of providing the service. Moreover, the two pricing objectives of *reducing waste and abuse* and *reducing total cost*, which clearly link into the policy objective of achieving value for money, require that prices reflect the costs of services. In the light of these objectives, it is appropriate, therefore, to start by discussing cost-based pricing strategies.

Once the different resource elements of the service to be priced have been identified, estimating variable costs such as wages is relatively straight-forward. Most problems arise in estimating the fixed cost overheads associated with service delivery and how to allow for these. Three cost-oriented pricing strategies identified by Alpert (1971) focus on this problem.

Mark-up pricing adds a fixed percentage to variable costs of all services provided in order to cover the fixed cost overheads associated with the delivery of the service. This type of approach is most often used in the retail trade.

Cost-plus pricing allocates total overheads associated with service provision on a proportional basis depending on the share of those overheads which are assumed to be attributable to the service being priced. This approach is most frequently used by wholesalers and is closer to the opportunity cost approach to costing services described in Chapter 3.

In the absence of adding any risk premium, both these methods assume that the amount of service to be produced is known in advance and that all of it will be sold. Clearly this can be assumed if the level of output is fixed in advance as happened previously in the provision of home care, for example. The whole impetus of current reforms, however, is to place the onus for rationing resources on budget-holding purchasers rather than providers. Fixed purchasing budgets need to be accompanied by flexibility in provision if the reforms are to have the desired impact in terms of value for money. Those responsible for pricing services will need to anticipate demand but be aware of the cost implications of variations from planned levels of service provision.

Break-even analysis emphasises the sales volume required in order that a firm breaks even or achieves a target rate of return. Once the time period over which the price is expected to operate, what is being priced and for what purpose are determined, the total revenue at a given price can be plotted against total cost (see Figure 1) and the break-even point determined. On this basis a number of break-even points can be compared and the price associated with expected levels of output can be forecast.

Using break-even analysis it is possible to look at the implications of actual demand above or below planned levels. If, in practice, more services are demanded and produced than anticipated, the provider will generate excess revenue or profit. If, however, the price is too high or quality of service too low and demand is lower than anticipated, then total cost will exceed total revenue and there will be a loss during the period the price is in effect.

Each of these strategies sets the price at the average cost at a given level of output which, as was discussed in Chapter 2, is a reasonable approximation

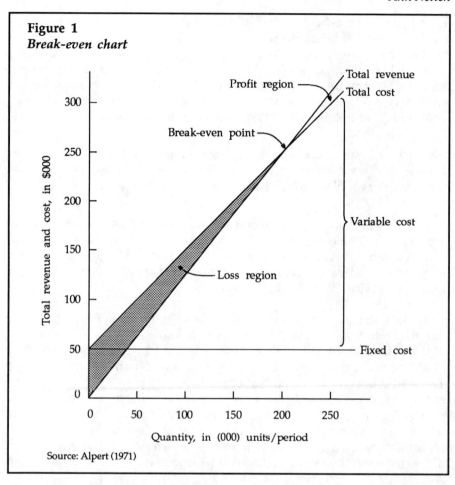

Figure 1
Break-even chart

Source: Alpert (1971)

to long-run marginal cost. Setting prices equal to marginal cost was seen as
the starting point in public enterprises in the 1960s when the objective was
to ensure the best use of resources (Cmnd 3437, 1967) but this does not always
result in a pattern of consumption that uses resources most efficiently (Davies,
1978). *Optimal* pricing of a range of services increases the prices of those
services for which demand changes very little as prices alter (that is, demand
is *inelastic* with respect to price) and sets prices close to the marginal cost for
those services for which demand is very responsive to (or *elastic* with respect
to) price (Baumol and Bradford, 1970). *Second-best* pricing takes into account
the relative costs and prices of services that are complements and substitutes
for each other in a way that keeps the relative quantities of services sold
equal to the proportions that would result from setting prices equal to
marginal cost (Webb, 1976).

In the public sector the demand for peak and off-peak services such as electricity and public transport are often given as examples of situations where optimal or second-best pricing are appropriate strategies (for example, Webb, 1976). Davies (1978) discusses the use of such an approach in setting a charging policy for school meals. In both these cases the price is charged to the final consumers who directly express demand by purchasing the service. In the field of social care where most services are allocated on prescriptive grounds, pricing examples are less easy to identify. The next section discusses the relationship between charges and demand for services.

Apart from the complexity of setting optimal or second-best prices, the primary problem with adopting such pricing strategies is lack of information. As markets continue to develop and with devolved budgeting among purchasers of services, it may be possible to estimate appropriate price elasticities. Without such information it will be difficult to devise an effective pricing strategy which aims at encouraging specific modes of care for any other reason other than pure cost criteria.

One of the objectives identified earlier was *influencing markets* and it was noted that frequently the local authority will be the only or dominant provider. In these situations the level at which it sets prices will dominate the going rates or *normal prices* (Downie, 1958). While independent providers may be able to sustain lower prices, they will be unable to maintain prices much above those of local authority services without providing a demonstrably different service. Thus the temptation to charge a very low price for in-house services with the aim of demonstrating value for money may actively work against the creation of a 'flourishing independent sector' and effectively provide a barrier to entry, reducing the contestability of the market.

Some of the services local authorities produce are likely to be more attractive to independent producers than others. It has been argued, for example, that the private sector will be less likely to provide high-quality residential care for elderly people with dementia as the costs are so much higher than providing residential care for elderly people who do not have mental health problems (Cox, 1990). If the same price is charged for all people in residential care then new entrants to the market will tend to focus on the groups that are cheaper to care for, leaving the local authority to provide care for only the most costly groups. Similarly, if mark-up pricing is used as a strategy and there is a high level of variation in the degree to which different services attract overheads, then new entrants will be attracted to those services which incur lower overheads.

Whatever pricing strategy is adopted there is an underlying problem in estimating demand. The level of variable and marginal costs depends on the level of output. Local authority social services departments have tended to assume that services are needed rather than demanded, and that refusal of a service represents the expression of a problem with the potential consumer rather than a problem with the service itself. With the introduction of the reforms and a policy to increase consumer choice, patterns of demand could provide indicators of how well services are meeting the needs they are designed to fulfil. Consumers themselves, however, will be valuing services in the context of the charge rather than the price.

4.2 Charges

Severe limitations were noted on the use of charges to reduce waste, reduce demand, shift priorities and influence markets. The principal objectives in charging were identified as raising revenue and acting as symbols. These objectives need to be set in the context that charging strategies should be demonstrably equitable, affordable and cost-effective. By *equitable* it is usually understood that people are charged similar amounts, thus a flat rate for the receipt of home help could be represented as equitable. However, such a strategy does not reflect the variations in the level of service provided, since some people receive a great deal more than others for the same charge. A strategy that is demonstrably equitable, in that all consumers are charged the same for each unit of service received, is then likely to encounter the problem that those in the greatest need are the least able to afford the total of the charges for services they receive.

Affordability is central to charging. Knapp (1984) defines charges as the cost less a subsidy and this subsidy is to ensure that all those who need a service can afford to pay the charge. Among other reasons the state subsidises services, or indeed funds any service, is because the welfare of other members of the community is in some way diminished if those who need services do not receive a minimum standard (Le Grand, 1975). This is demonstrated by ministerial comments resulting in such headlines as 'Homeless former patients an affront to society' (*The Independent*, 20 January 1992). Moreover, it is in local authorities' interests that people are not made poor, indeed that their income is maximised, since poverty increases the chance that people will need state-funded services. It was pointed out earlier that the *National Health Service and Community Care Act 1990* specifies that assessment of need should not be influenced by ability to pay. Clearly, charging more than can be afforded prevents take-up of services and is against the spirit of the Act.

One way to ensure that services are affordable is to keep the charge very low or not to charge at all. But this runs counter to the objective of reducing costs by raising revenue. The most frequently-used methods of charging while ensuring people can afford services is by means-testing and/or linking charges to the receipt of specific benefits. In the past much debate centred on the stigma attached to means-testing and its role in the prevention of take-up of benefits (Judge and Matthews, 1980a). This does not appear to affect the take-up of local authority residential care, the charges for which have been based on long-standing rules for means-testing. At the time of writing the whole mechanism for meeting the costs of publicly-funded residents is under review. Concerns about the way new arrangements for means-testing will be implemented focus on the practical implications for elderly people and their carers rather than issues of stigma. What, for example, will be the rights and responsibilities of family members in paying for their elderly relatives' care (Age Concern, 1991)?

As residential care provides for all or most living expenses, the process of establishing a charge is in fact less complex than establishing an affordable and appropriate charge for community-based services. One way to approach the problem of setting appropriate charges for these services is to link charges to benefit entitlements. This can lead to problems, however. A common policy is to charge those on income support very little or nothing at all while others have to pay the standard (subsidised) charge. This can lead to anomalies as those on income support are eligible for other benefits so their resulting income can be higher than that of other people who are not eligible for income support. Another way is to ensure that charges for different services do not build up to an excessive total is by putting an upper limit on the amount an individual can be charged for the service package. Residual income should be sufficient to pay for normal living expenses. A strategy of this sort is being introduced in one local authority using the *Family Expenditure Survey* as a basis for estimation, and relying on the appeals procedure to identify exceptional circumstances. The introduction of care management is an important element in facilitating the communication and coordination required to implement this strategy successfully.

To be *cost-effective* when raising revenue is a primary objective; a charging strategy must yield more revenue than it costs to administer. As Birch (1986) points out in his analysis of prescription charges, however, the process of revenue-raising will usually conflict with other objectives of the organisation providing the service. In the targeting of social care, people with the highest level of need are most likely to be those who are on the lowest income and most likely to be deterred by a charge.

One way to reduce administrative and collection costs is to charge a flat-banded rate. But this type of charge is not an effective way of ensuring value for money because while consumers are unaware of the relative costs of different services they are unable to exercise informed choice about the services on offer. Moreover, charging consumers the same for services that incur very different costs is not equitable. For example, should an elderly person attending a day centre that provides a range of services including chiropody pay the same as an elderly person who is provided with a cup of tea and a chat? This is particularly likely to become an issue if invoicing consumers so they are aware of the different costs incurred becomes a widespread policy.

The best judges of the value of services in meeting their needs are (usually) the consumers of those services. In assessing value for money, however, consumers are dependent on the charging structure together with opportunities for voice and exit. There is an enormous variation in the way that consumers are charged for services but little information about how they respond to different levels of charges. Judge and Matthews (1980a) investigated the relationship between changes in charges and patterns of consumption. They hypothesised that demand for publicly-provided personal social services was likely to be less elastic (less responsive to price changes) than for the same service produced in a private market. This is because subsidies would result in publicly-provided services being favourably priced compared to the privately-produced substitutes and because charge levels were linked to recipients' ability to pay. In analysing the evidence, they suggested that rationing of services by social services departments meant that consumers did not receive as much of a service as they would like at any given charge, so small changes in charge level had a limited effect on demand for services.

In discussing the symbolic function of charges it was noted that the level of charges was important if people were to respond to falls in quality by exiting or complaining. If charges are to be used as a means to establish whether consumers themselves feel that they are getting value for money, it is clearly important to get the level of charges right. Figure 2 depicts the relationship between the level of service demanded and the price to the care manager and charge to the consumer. The price charged to the care manager as budget-holder (P) results in an allocation of service (S) at which the ideal

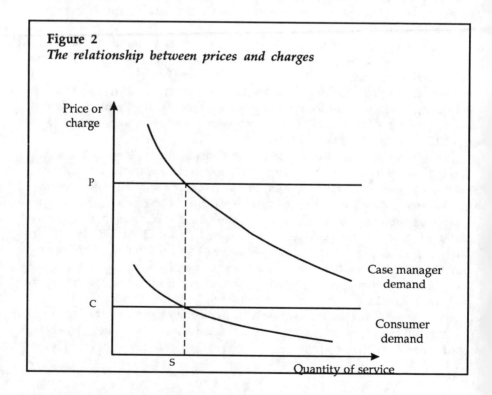

Figure 2
The relationship between prices and charges

charge to the consumer is C. At this point the consumer will respond to falls in service quality. As quality falls they would demand less for any given level of charge (the *demand curve* would shift downwards) so they would complain about or drop out of the level of service allocated by the care manager.

The major problem in setting charges at this appropriate level is lack of information. With time it will be possible to monitor the different levels of service allocated by care managers at different price levels. But the consumers' demand curve is inherently unobservable because of the way in which services are allocated. As pointed out above, however, charges are frequently set well below the level consumers would be prepared to pay so they do not respond to changes, be they minor increases in charging levels or changes in the quality of the service. This is not a reason to despair, however. There is potential through research to establish 'ball park' figures which can aid the initial setting of charging levels. Proper monitoring could also provide useful information. Once charges are set, assessment and review procedures provide an opportunity to establish how much of a service consumers would like to have, given their circumstances. Monitoring the relationship between charge levels and expressed demand for services would allow constant feedback about appropriate charging levels and the way that consumers perceive services as providing value for money.

Exploiting the potential of charging as a policy tool while ensuring affordability and choice presents a formidable administrative challenge, but it is one that has to be faced if charging is to form part of a coherent strategy in achieving value for money in the provision of social care. Moreover, deciding on appropriate pricing and charging strategies to meet the objectives is made more difficult by the two-tier nature of the system. Just as wholesalers and retailers both influence the market through their pricing decisions, both prices to budget-holders and charges to final consumers will affect demand for services.

5 Conclusion

A number of different objectives have been identified in pricing and charging for services, and the importance of being clear about these and how they fit in with other policy objectives has been emphasised. National policies will, of course, have very different interpretations locally. Local authorities will need to make explicit these interpretations and within these the role and objectives of pricing and charging. In particular, prices and charges provide valuable mechanisms in providing value for money, a fundamental aim of the reforms.

Those making decisions about prices in statutory agencies also need to be aware of the indirect effects of their decisions. Whether they like it or not they are operating in markets, if only internal markets. As local authorities are the major provider in most of these markets, their pricing strategies will have a profound effect and they need to assess the current market structures and the likely impact of their strategies. An awareness of the pitfalls in setting prices is essential but it is clear that for pricing strategies to reinforce the aims of the reforms, prices should be based on the opportunity cost of services. In deciding how to estimate the cost, it is necessary to go through the four stages identified in Chapter 2 while keeping in mind the pricing objectives.

A major obstacle in the process both of estimating costs and setting prices and charges is lack of information. Problems of inadequate information in estimating costs have been dealt with elsewhere in this volume. In deciding on prices and charges local authorities will have to learn largely from experience. To do this, comprehensive monitoring and evaluation of the information collected are essential. Monitoring systems need to allow analysis of the links between prices and charges and patterns of demand. It is only by monitoring such changes and maintaining the link between costs, prices and charges that social services departments can keep in touch with the resource implications of changing patterns of preferences for the way in which needs are met.

Note

*   I am particularly indebted to the advice and support of my colleagues in the production of this chapter. Jeni Beecham, David Challis, Bleddyn Davies, Shane Kavanagh, Aidan Kelly, Jeremy Kendall, Martin Knapp and Robyn Lawson were very helpful in my early attempts to grapple with this subject. My thank are also due to Ken Judge who provided very helpful comments on a later draft.

References

Age Concern (1991) Care costs two: a discussion paper, *Briefings*, Age Concern England/National Council on Ageing, London.

Allen, C.F., Hardy, B., Knapp, M.R.J. and Wistow, G. (1991) Managing the mixed economy of care: an interim report, Nuffield Institute/PSSRU.

Alpert, M. (1971) *Pricing Decisions*, Scott, Foresman and Company, Glenview, Illinois and London.

Audit Commission (1986) *Making a Reality of Community Care*, HMSO, London.

Baumol, W.J. and Bradford, D.F. (1970) Optimal departures from marginal cost pricing, *American Economic Review*, 60, 265-83.

Baumol, W.J., J.C. Panzar, J.C. and Willig, R.D. (1982) *Contestable Markets and the Theory of Industry Structure*, Harcourt Brace Jovanovich, New York.

Birch, S. (1986) Increasing patient charges in the National Health Service: a method of privatising primary care, *Journal of Social Policy*, 15, 2, 163-84.

Cm 849 (1989) *Caring for People: Community Care in the Next Decade and Beyond*, HMSO, London.

Cmnd 3437 (1967) *Nationalised Industries: A Review of Financial and Economic Objectives*, HMSO, London.

Cox, P. (1990) Care for elderly mentally ill people: a special market niche presentation of elderly care prospects for the 1990s, given at a conference organised by Laing & Buisson and Healthcare Information Services, March, London.

Davies, B.P. (1978) *Universality, Selectivity and Effectiveness in Social Policy*, Heinemann, London.

Davies, B.P. (1990) Social services in the city: context change, service response and service outcomes, *The Statistician*, 39, 229-45.

Downie, J. (1958) *The Competitive Process*, Duckworth, London.

Hansmann, H. (1980) The role of nonprofit enterprise, *Yale Law Journal*, 89, 835-901.

Hirschman, A. (1970) *Exit, Voice and Loyalty*, Harvard University Press, Cambridge, Mass.

Judge, K.F. and Matthews, J. (1980a) *Charging for Social Care*, Allen and Unwin, London.

Judge, K.F. and Matthews, J. (1980b) Pricing personal social services, in K. Judge (ed.) *Pricing the Social Services*, Macmillan, London.

Kelly, A. (1990) Enterprise culture and the welfare state, in R. Burrows (ed.) *Deciphering Enterprise Culture*, Routledge, London.

Knapp, M.R.J. (1984) *The Economics of Social Care*, Macmillan, London.

Lancaster, K.J. (1966) A new approach to consumer theory, *Journal of Political Economy*, 74, 135-45.

Le Grand, J. (1975) Public price discrimination and aid to low income groups, *Economica*, new series, 42, 32-42.

Netten, A. and Davies, B.P. (1990) The social production of welfare and consumption of social services, *Journal of Public Policy*, 10, 331-47.

Parker, R.A. (1976) Charging for social services, *Journal of Social Policy*, 5, 359-73.

Parker, R.A. (1980) Policies, presumptions and prospects, in K. Judge (ed.) *Pricing the Social Services*, Macmillan, London.

Webb, M.G. (1976) *Pricing Policies for Public Enterprises*, Macmillan, London.

8 New Policies and Old Logics: Costs Information and Modal Choice

Bleddyn Davies

The current dominant concern in the field of cost information is with social services departments' financial control systems. The consequences of their inadequacy have too often been shocking. The effect usually quoted is how they have discouraged social services departments from pushing discretion about resources and policy decisions far enough down the organisation (Audit Commission, 1992a). It is considered too impolite to mention examples in which services to increasingly needy people have been arbitrarily withdrawn or spread so thinly as to have little effect and that no new clients are taken on, however needy they are, after reins have been pulled in as a response to overspending. Many social services departments and others are working hard, however, on the development of systems which will integrate information about resources and needs.

This essay discusses an issue with which the real world will be more preoccupied when it has all the paraphanalia of the new community care in place: the implications of rewording an old question in the context of new policy assumptions. The question is what costs (and outcomes) research has to tell the real-world manager about how to conceptualise the achievement of the most equitable and efficient matching of 'mode of care' to the circumstances of persons. (By 'mode of care' is meant the broad alternative[1] care forms: for instance, community-based or residential-based.)

The answer will illustrate two general truths. One is that broad questions in social science are often much the same over a generation. Not so the detailed answers. That is because it is at the level of working out the arguments that we embody the new values, assumptions, causal knowledge, and 'quasi-technological' knowledge about the relations between ends and means.

This has certainly happened in community and long-term care. At the most general level, many of the the basic questions had been worked out by the late 1970s. But the answers given now are different in their precision, depth and breadth, even if they are elaborations of the same basic insight. The elaboration changes their emphasis. But also it changes their degrees of detail and 'groundedness'; that quality of being based on a realistic appreciation about how things do and can be made to work. And so they differ in practical usefulness to the policy world.

Modal choice is one of those issues which are a research director's dream, because it may be said of it: *'plus ça change, plus c'est la même chose'*. Such issues are a research director's dream because one can be confident that long-term intellectual investments in providing answers will pay handsomely.

The second general truth is that there is one respect in which Keynes' dictum – paraphrased, that practical men thinking that they have thought things out for themselves are often merely restating the ideas of some long-dead scribbler – was a wild distortion, almost a gross academic conceit. The case of modal choice illustrates that it is changes in the practical world which give direction and relevance to the academic scribblers more than *vice versa*.

Section 1 outlines the initial logical insight from which subsequent argument is built. The rest of the essay develops the argument about changes in policy argument and their implications. Section 2 summarises the changes in the policy and examines the implications for the use of costs information in a care-managed world with micro-budgets. The significance of the issues raised are discussion in section 3.

1 The traditional logic

The traditional logic is embodied in Figure 1. To simplify, it assumes that 'dependency' is the main predictor of costs. The concept implicitly subsumes factors other than functional dependency itself. Indeed, dependency is so defined as to make its measurement partly dependent on costs (see below). The diagram implicitly assumes outcomes yielding equivalence in all modes of care of quality of life for dependants and an acceptable quality of life for informal carers.[2]

The principal explicit assumptions are that costs to the agency rise with increases in 'dependency'. It further assumes that costs rise with disability faster for low overhead modes of care (for example, community-based care without special arrangements for shelter). The conclusion is that the most efficient use of agency resources would require that persons with a dependency level up to A would receive community-based care; that those of levels between A and B should receive the lower-level mode of residential care; and those of greater disability than B should receive nursing home care. It also suggests that the availability of extensive informal support so reduces costs to the agency given the level of 'dependency' that it is efficient for those with much informal support to be cared for in the community to a higher 'dependency' level: level B.

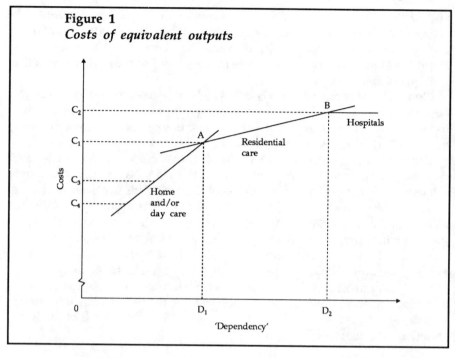

Figure 1
Costs of equivalent outputs

2 Implications of changes in policy ends and means

How policy assumptions are changing is discussed elsewhere. To summarise:
- More ambitious goals require the recognition of variety and complexity in need and responses to them. In some respects that will increase organisational control but will also increase budgetary devolution.
- Both the supply and financing of care are becoming more pluralistic and, as a result, it will be more difficult to achieve policy goals using the traditional command-control techniques of the kind relied on within simple hierarchical organisations. Instead, organisational control will rely more on incentives with information for setting them and for allocating the rewards.
- Local variations in the relative prices of alternative means will matter more when making the most equitable and efficient use of resources.

The changes require an adaptation of the original model of modal choice. The new logic must be around a world with a much larger number of modes and so choices; a world in which the critical decisions about modal choices are dispersed among care managers and for whom the crucial costs and other information refer to small areas.

There are user circumstances in which there are great potential gains to be made in welfare and/or savings in costs to public funds. To facilitate such gains requires the careful performance of care management by persons able to be flexible and resourceful in mixing inputs, and to be flexible in responding to the needs of users and informal carers. The first of these tasks must include finding the best roles for informal carers, tapping quasi-informal sources of care like the paid and expense-compensated 'helpers' in the PSSRU projects (Qureshi et al., 1989), as well as formal agency inputs. Care managers must be responsive to users and potential carers, partly because it is that which helps to achieve the reduction in the costs of outcomes.

Costs information is a basic requirement for these tasks. If care managers are to have great discretion in mixing inputs and setting target outcomes, they need information and policy guidelines of kinds which incorporate costs. Moreover, cost information can help to show what care management arrangements are most appropriate for users in what circumstances.

2.1 The need to integrate the choice of priorities in needs-based planning and care management arrangements

The new policy, and to a greater degree the Griffiths Report, aims to integrate needs-based planning at one level with entrepreneurial fine-grained care management at another. The Griffiths model was an integrated system of needs-based budgets from the national level to the care management team. This model was one of interdependence: interdependence between priority decisions at various levels and groups. At each level, the responsibility, authority and accountability for resources and outcomes were to be concentrated. At each level there was to be a clear framework within which managers could be resourceful in achieving the goals set for them. No logic which did not reconcile these levels would be adequate. No logic would do if it failed to make central the trade-offs between the opportunity costs of outcomes.

Consider the nature of the problem in a simplified model which links both the general level of needs-based planning and the narrower world of the care management team for one kind of client. The assumptions of the model are stated in Box 1. These basic relationships are expressed in diagrammatic form in Figure 2.

Figure 2 portrays the logic of the world of the needs-based planner. One can start the logic from either of two ends: the total budget, which is equal to the area under the curve in the South-West quadrant (called the DEPINDEX integral), or the numbers in client subgroups in the North-East quadrant.

Starting in the North-East quadrant, the needs-based planner estimates numbers of potential users in each of the various groups, each group being defined to be similar with respect to the nature of the the mix and cost of

Box 1

Cost relationships and case management parameters:
setting parameters to achieve greater equity and efficiency

What follows is part of a model for setting parameters in a case management system with devolved budgeting. Its focus is the logic of setting guidelines about the maximum expenditure per case receiving care while living at home. This box defines model concepts and specifies model assumptions.

Model concepts defined

AVBUDGET	Average weekly budget for home care excluding case management costs: ie TOTHCCOST *less* CMCOST.[a] AVBUDG = OTHHCCOST.
AVBUDG curve	The curve describing the relationship between AVBUDG, BUDGCAP, and TARGFLOOR.
BUDGCAP	The guideline weekly cost of home care which case managers should not exceed (or expect to exceed) over more than a short time without managerial review of the case. The text argues that BUDGCAP = CMCOST and an element which varies with AVBUDG in a way which reflects the distribution of the cost-determining characteristics of the persons between TARGFLOOR and BUDGCAP and the position of the HORIZTE curve.
CMCASELOAD	Number of cases per case manager.
CMCOST	Average weekly costs of case management.
DEPINDEX	Index of characteristics affecting costs of achieving equivalent outcomes in home care (given CMCASELOAD) associated with targeting criteria.
DEPINDEX curve	The curve describing the numbers of persons in the potential target population at every level of DEPINDEX.
DEPINDEX Integral	The area under the DEPINDEX curve between TARGFLOOR and BUDGCAP. The DEPINDEX integral measures the total cost of home care (with equivalent outcomes) assuming 100 per cent target efficiency.
	Average duration of stay cared for living at home.
HORIZTE curve	The curve describing the postulated or selected degree of horizontal target efficiency given the DEPINDEX score and which given DEPINDEX determines the AVBUDG required.
LIFEDUR	Average expectation of life: LIFEDUR = HOMEDUR + RESDUR.
OTHHCCOST	Average weekly cost of home care services other than case management.
OTHHCCOST curve	Curve describing the dependence of OTHHCCOST on AVBUDG given the level of CMCASELOAD.
RESCOST	Weekly care cost in residential facilities.[a]
RESCOST curve	Curve describing the dependence of RESCOST on RESDUR.
RESDUR	Average duration of stay in residential mode of care: RESDUR = LIFEDUR - HOMEDUR.
TARGFLOOR	The minimum level of DEPINDEX, the index of dependency-generating characteristics, for which care to be publicly funded.
TOTHCCOST	Total weekly cost of home care: TOTHCCOST = CMCOST + RESCOST

a Dependency of 'care' costs only; that is, excluding 'housing benefit' costs for non-dependent persons.

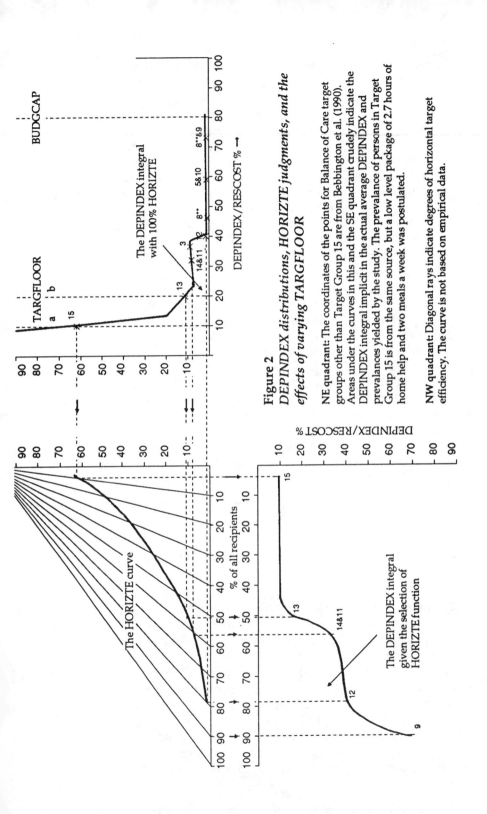

Figure 2
DEPINDEX distributions, HORIZTE judgments, and the effects of varying TARGFLOOR

NE quadrant: The coordinates of the points for Balance of Care target groups other than Target Group 15 are from Bebbington et al. (1990). Areas under the curves in this and the SE quadrant crudely indicate the DEPINDEX integral implicit in the actual average DEPINDEX and prevalances yielded by the study. The prevalance of persons in Target Group 15 is from the same source, but a low level package of 2.7 hours of home help and two meals a week was postulated.

NW quadrant: Diagonal rays indicate degrees of horizontal target efficiency. The curve is not based on empirical data.

the packages of publicly-financed care provided. This top right-hand quadrant is based on some fifteen groups derived from a PSSRU needs-based planning study by Bebbington et al. (1990) for services for elderly persons. The groups each have an estimated average cost of intervention expressed as a proportion of the opportunity cost of residential care.

In the North-West quadrant, the planners seek the proportion of potential users in each group at which the group member receiving care with the lowest ratio of benefits to costs is the same for all groups. (For simplicity, the diagram postulates a curvilinear relationship between the proportions chosen and the proportion of all recipients in the target subgroup. The reasons are stated in Davies et al., 1990.) Putting the criterion as a proportion of persons in a subgroup who should receive priority recognises that the outcomes for persons in each group can be very different, and so can be the value of these outcomes.

In the South-West quadrant, the implications are worked out for the total spending on each group. That, together with the number of clients given priority from that subgroup, yields the average cost of services per client expressed as a ratio of the marginal cost of residential care. This can be translated into a basic cost guideline for the case management team. Figure 3 shows what the average service costs of clients in one care-managed experiment was, and how that related to the size of the budget cap for any client beyond which care managers could not spend without management sanction based on the review of the particular case.

So much for reconciling the level of needs-based planning and the lower level of the care manager facing individual clients. Between them, needs-based planning and the average service budget for care management teams are seen to be interrelated. Unless they are reconciled in a two-way process, inequity and inefficiency must result.

2.2 *Setting the guidelines to use resources most efficiently in modal choice*

The managers of care managers must both set the arrangements and parameters which balance 'technical knowledge' about the quantitative relationships between ends and means in the alternative modes, and provide information to aid care managers' judgments. Working within the policy framework (elements of which are about costs), care managers facing the choices about modes must use guidelines about costs and benefits in alternative modes to make predictions about likely outcomes for particular cases. Costs information is vital at all stages of this process.

In the model depicted in Figure 4, we assume two kinds of care: community-based home care and residential. Two further assumptions are necessary. First, that there is a predictable relationship between the 'price' of residential

Figure 3
A DEPINDEX distribution for a case-managed community care caseload

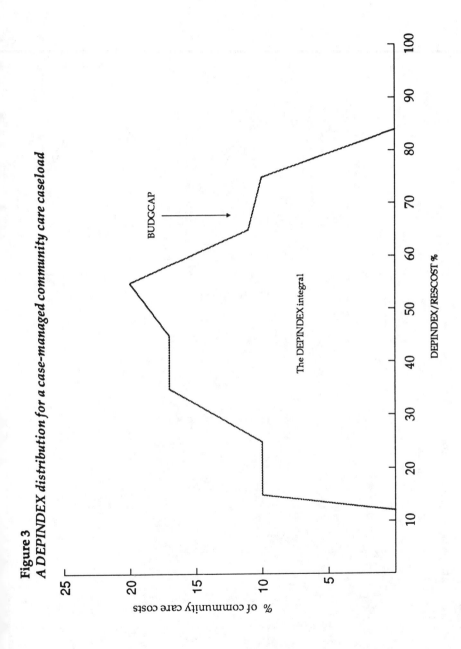

Figure 4
Cost relationships and case management parameters

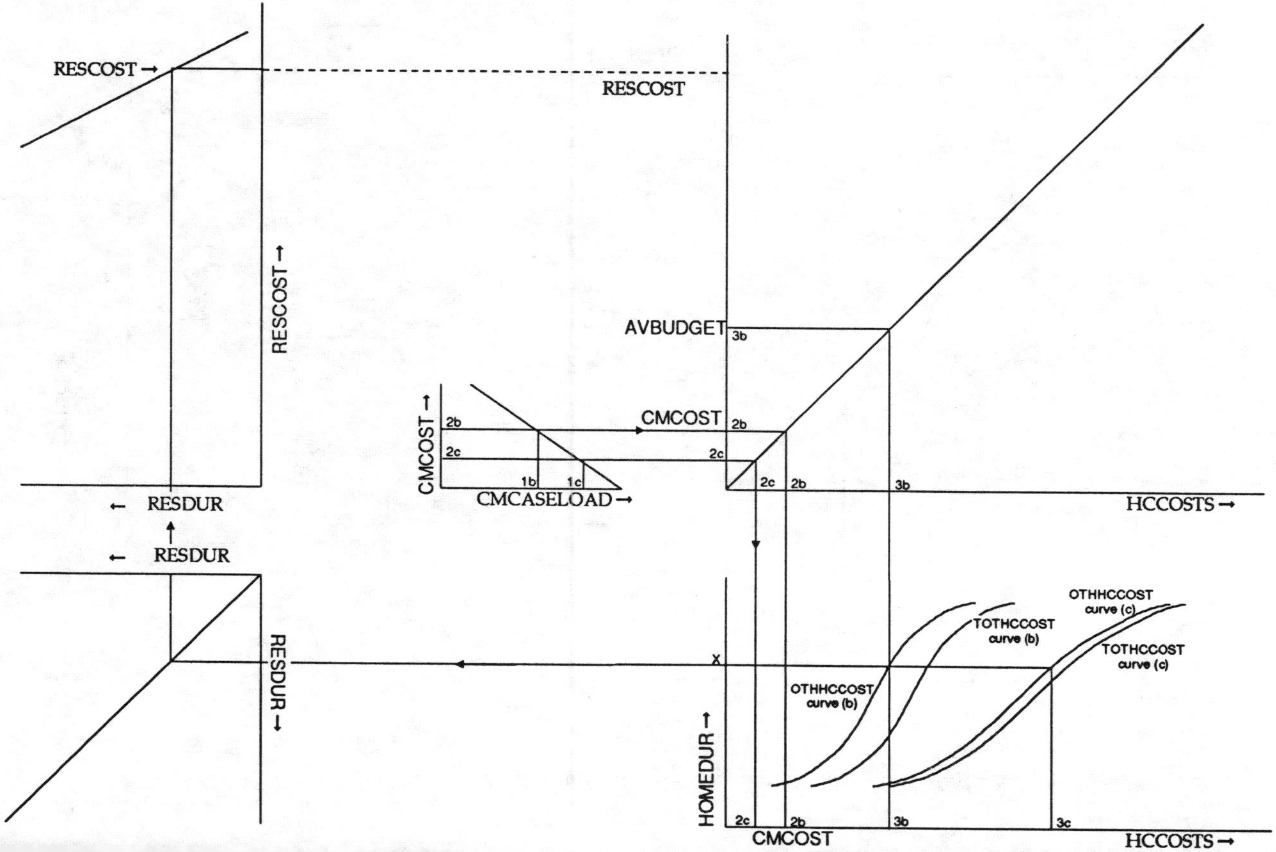

care and the demand for resident days. The lower the demand for resident days, the higher is likely to be the dependency of residents, and so the higher the unit costs in residential homes, given that quality of care is the same. But the lower the demand for resident days, the lower the price asked for care by the most expensive provider whose services must be consumed in order to obtain the requisite numbers.[3] These two effects pull in different ways. The relationship is described in the North-West quadrant of the diagram.

Second, it is necessary to assume that there is a predictable relationship between the time and skill of the care manager, the average number of days in the home which a given amount of community-based services will purchase, and the number of additional days in the client's own home which an additional pound's worth of home care service will achieve. For many groups, the effectiveness of community-based services is improved by the amount of care management activity. However, at high levels of such activity in relation to the circumstances of persons on the caseload, additional inputs of care management are likely to make little improvement in outcomes, which include the client remaining at home rather than entering a residential or nursing home. Indeed, there is some evidence from both the PSSRU community care experiments and the US suggesting that high levels of care management inputs actually increase the probability of admission to institutions for long-term care for some clients.

In the South-East quadrant of Figure 4, OTHHCOST refers to the cost of community services and TOTHCCOST to the cost of these together with the costs of case management. Thus the gap between each pair of curves represents the cost of care management. The position of the curves along the horizontal axis is determined by the size of the caseload. That is to say, there is a pair of curves for each level of case management caseload. The curves (b) illustrate a situation where case management costs are high but the cost of service packages are low for each level of duration of stay in the client's own home (3b for HOMEDUR = X). Curves (c) demonstrate the opposite case: care management costs are low but service package costs are high (3c for HOMEDUR = X). The South-West and North-East quandrants simply link the associated diagrams leaving values unchanged.

The logic starts with setting the level of case management in relation to the population. Setting a higher level of care management per case (by reducing the caseload from 1c to 1b in the centre of the diagram) causes care management costs of 2b. The outcomes of needs-based planning set cost guidelines for the average home care budget for the expected clientele. That sets the level of the average budget, and so the point on curves (b). That in turn determines the length of time people can be maintained in their own homes. Given the assumptions of the model, that in turn determines the number of residential days required, and so the average price of residential care.

The average price of residential care must be equal to the budget cap if resources are to be efficiently used. So the best budget cap reflects the starting values of the caseload of case managers given the nature of their cases, and the average budgets per case manager. Therefore the best budget cap, the best level of the average budget, and the case managers' loads are interdependent; and all of them are interdependent with the priority decisions made in the needs-based planning process.

2.3 Costs-based guidelines and other care management arrangements and parameters[4]

The average home care budget and the budget cap beyond which care managers should not spend are only two of the costs-related parameters and information required in care-managed community care. These analyses are the beginnings of a 'contingency theory' of care management arrangements. The parameters are based on international experience: a body of theory which suggests the consequences of different combinations of arrangements. (Argument about what the body of knowledge implies for care management arrangements for persons in different need-related circumstances in UK home care services for elderly people is presented in Davies et al., 1990, pp.321-7). The 'contingency theory' is based on, though it always needs more evidence about, the consequences of setting cost guidelines at different levels.

Box 2 contains a list of examples of arrangements and parameters which differentiate care management systems. The costs-based signals implicit in the list are connected with what is called 'span': the range of services and resources covered by the budget, each with a 'price' known to the case manager and set, where appropriate, to encourage the best use of resources. The economic principle for fixing the span is clear: the span should as far as possible cover the most important inputs which can be combined together to provide community-based care. If important inputs are excluded, there is an incentive for the case manager to use time to attempt to procure their use. (Case managers would have an incentive to do so up to the point at which

---

Box 2

Variations in arrangements for case management

- Targeting
- Cases/case manager
- Size of budget/budget capital
- Organisational focus
- Budget span
- Skill mix within team
- Locus for management of case management

the expected cost to their budgets, including case management time, equals the reduction of the burden on the budget they control.) There is evidence from other countries that this incentive can considerably distort allocations.

The arrangements and parameters can vary within teams. The Social Services Inspectorate (1991) and the Audit Commission (1992a) have shown interest in varying the budget limits for spending according to the circumstances of clients.

2.4 Investing in people: decision criteria and lifetime costs

A great deal of the new community argument is about seizing opportunities for investment: the input of more resources in the shorter run in order to prevent changes or secure amelioration which will make fewer resources necessary in the longer run. The notion of 'investment' is well established in geriatrics and some conspicuous successes have been due to it (Ratna, 1982; Hendriksen et al., 1984; Rubinstein et al., 1984, 1985; Vetter et al., 1984).

Indeed, much of the point of the changed philosophies and arrangements of the new policies for community and long-term care is to be able to make the most of these investment opportunities: the practical support of carers and the doctrine that only by being responsive to the wants, wishes and values of dependants and their supporters can the greatest success be achieved. These arrangements include the development of a new occupational group, care managers, and the separation of responsibilities for performing care management from supply, and more.

However a traditional criticism of field activity in social services departments has been vagueness about ends and means (Goldberg and Connelly, 1982). One aspect of this is tunnel vision and with it, short-sightedness.

For instance, users have not been helped to obtain medical and other interventions which would reduce or remove some of the causes of need for social care inputs. For a reform putting so much emphasis on pinning responsibility and authority on the social services departments, what is interesting is how much of the DH and other guidance about community care arrangements is designed to coordinate inputs from other agencies: that is, how to create or get recognised incentives to work together in a framework in which the most obvious incentives are to work independently. Field personnel have focused insufficiently on predicting future need patterns to make the most of the opportunity to provide services now which could save money later. This is made difficult because of the problems in collating views of other professionals, who have often been acutely conscious of professional identities and the protection of their turves, and the unpredictability of many of the events of decisive importance.

The formal evidence is more in the nature of examples than of precise estimates of the extent and scale of these classes of inefficiency: the use of drugs in ways which exacerbate dependency; the influence of conditions which could be ameliorable with treatment on the decision to admit to institutions for long-term care; the lack of understanding among social care staff of diseases and their consequences; the absence of contact between health-related and social care personnel at the field level; the paucity of the information flowing from health to social care staff; the failure of the latter to obtain prognostic information and judgements relevant to medium-term care planning; and the opportunities for independent social services department action to support and maintain situations with bigger immediate inputs but lower long-term costs in relation to the benefits.

But the problem is more general: even within the range of independent interventions of the social services departments, field personnel have not set out to take 'investment opportunities'. Field managers of the flows of service – such as social workers and home help organisers – have had neither the breadth of authority and responsibility nor the time (and in many cases the skills) to do the groundwork necessary to put in place what will be the most cost-effective plan for the long run.

We cannot claim to be able to quantify the losses. But their resource consequences must be enormous.

The following section discusses a few of the key concepts for evaluating the costs and benefits of investment decisions and relates them to needs for costs information.

2.5 The theoretical decision criterion: when is an investment worthwhile?

The theoretical decision criterion for an investment decision is that the positive difference between the values of the stream of benefits and costs through time should be maximised. It requires:

- The appropriate time over which benefits and costs should be compared: the only time period which is other than purely arbitrary is the remainder of the lifetime.
- The appropriate application of opportunity costing to the estimates of costs.
- Actual empirical information about costs and benefits in each time period.

The comparison of the differences between benefits and costs in different time periods should not be based on simply adding them over the lifetime. Benefits and costs in different time periods should not be treated equally. The differences, the 'net benefits', in a later period should not be treated as equivalent to earlier differences because resources saved early can (in principle) be used for 'investment' to increase the total resources available later. So the net benefits in later years should be reduced in value to make them equivalent to earlier benefits.

The device used to reduce benefits to equivalence, a 'present value', is the application of 'a rate of time discount'. This is a rate per annum. How to select the rate has been the subject of much discussion. What rate is appropriate varies between circumstances.[5] In practice, some Alexander the Great in H.M. Treasury cuts through the Gordian knots of economic theory by nominating a rate for public investments (see Chapter 3).

Ideally then, a formula such as that shown in Box 3 is used and correctly identifies the lifetime costs and benefits that should be taken into account. But social services departments' databases do not provide the information to describe these and so put the decision criterion into effect.

Box 3
One formula for estimating present value is:

$$PV = B_0 - C_0 + \frac{B_1 - C_1}{(1+r)^1} + \frac{B_2 - C_2}{(1+r)^2} + \frac{B_3 - C_3}{(1+r)^3} + \dots + \frac{B_i - C_i}{(1+r)^i}$$

where PV is the present value of the net benefits; B and C are Benefits and Costs respectively for the sucessive years indicated by 1, 2, 3, 4 and i – by 'i' is meant any and each subsequent year; and r is the rate of time discount.

2.6 Qualifications and complications of the decision rule: uncertainty

In social care, needs-related circumstances are often complex and difficult to identify. So are the circumstances which influence the outcomes of interventions. Indeed, some of the latter are essentially unpredictable which would seem to imply that the pervasiveness of uncertainty makes the enterprise of social care different in kind, not merely in degree, from other areas in which we struggle to make the best use of limited resources. It becomes an alibi. Vagueness, indecision, the lack of testing of skills, a sloppy neglect of the measurement of who gets what and with how much benefit to whom comes to be explained as part of the special characteristics of an area dominated by uncertainty. The apologists say such things as: 'We risk inequity and a more fundamental ineffectiveness and inefficiency were we to produce confusing descriptions of the indescribable and biased measurements of the immeasurable.' To this, the reply is surely: 'True, but research evidence shows that there is already confusion, inequity, inefficiency, ineffectiveness and bias and that, used in the right context, information can reduce them.'

The principal technical issues are twofold. First, is the uncertainty so great that no useful statistical generalisations are worthwhile? Second, how should we balance relatively certain judgements about likely costs and benefits with highly uncertain ones? In balancing the 'certain' with the 'uncertain', the first task should be to define the areas in which the best predictors are measurable

and the outcomes broadly predictable, then undertake the research in order
to make the predictions for those areas.

The real difficulty is in balancing the priorities between persons for whom
outcomes are predictable to quite different degrees. Cost-benefit analysts
suggest mapping the probability of different levels of costs or outcomes for
various combinations of circumstances. That is, obtain a set of probabilities
for each outcome for each combination of user circumstances. Then obtain
information about the valuations of each outcome. In that way, for instance,
one could register the kinds of outcome which in few or no circumstances
could be tolerated with a probability higher than a certain level, and either
value them accordingly or automatically exclude the alternative. More
commonly, the issue is to examine whether the average outcome was the
result of more than average benefit for a lot of people with a few having
very large disbenefits, or vice versa. Then the valuation of the outcome would
be the sum of the products of values and probabilities implicit in the selection
of an alternative. These are not the kinds of exercises which agencies would
perform. But the results of research aimed to map them could be of great
benefit as background information for case decision-making and planning.

2.7 Estimates in social care

The basic decision criterion is anything but new. The period when the theoretical argument developed most rapidly ended by the mid-1960s. From the
time when Barbara Castle was Minister of Transport, it was increasingly used
in some British departments. There were early attempts to apply the general
ideas to British social care in the late 1960s.[6] But the progress since then has
been modest. Most such estimates have been of costs, so they have presented
a one-sided story. Moreover, gaps in the data have either forced those making
the estimates to make them incomplete, or to improvise.

Examples from PSSRU work illustrate this.

- Chesterman et al. (1988) estimated *discounted costs over four years* to various
  agencies and society as a whole for the first of the PSSRU community care
  experiments, the Thanet (commonly called 'Kent') Community Care Project,
  comparing the costs with locational outcomes at the end of the period. The
  point was to establish whether an experiment, highly successful over one
  year, would appear equally highly successful over a much longer period.
  That was necessary, because the pattern of costs and benefits has been
  shown to be different in the long and short runs for some experiments.
  The only benefits measurement available over the whole period was
  survival and place of residence. So the emphasis was for costs only, and
  not costs over the lifetime.
- Davies and Baines (1991) estimated discounted *lifetime opportunity costs of
  standard community-based social services* to the social services departments

for a cohort of persons first receiving community-based social care in twelve areas of England and Wales during the mid-1980s. Also, less reliable estimates were made of costs to the social services departments of residential care. The estimates were less reliable because there appear to be no British data for a representative group of recipients of community-based care predicting lengths of stay in residential care from needs-related circumstances prior to admission. The focus was the prediction of variations between individuals, not broad groups. The aim was to show how such analyses could provide clues and the background information against which could be set the dialogue between case managers and their managers about cases on whom it would be most worth investing heavily in current treatment. The components of lifetime costs were also predicted: the period of utilisation and the amounts utilised. Though based on a substantial number of cases (see Davies et al., 1990), information was available over only three years. The missing information for subsequent years was estimated by applying models which assumed that the rates of attrition established by the end of the period continued thereafter. The results showed great variation between individuals and substantial predictability from information available at the first assessment and by the time of the second review.

• Davies and Baines (1992) also made estimates of *costs of standard community-based services over five years*, using the same database but for a different purpose: to explore the implications of varying targeting on the pattern of commitments of costs and the disability characteristics of caseloads. Here the emphasis was on broad groups categorised by disability. The analysis was based on the actual changes in state and input responses to them during the first six months, and a similar pattern of variation between groups was found but smaller changes in each subsequent six-month period.

3 Begged questions: some needed developments in logic and evidence

3.1 The argument must now postulate a larger number of modes

We have now created both a financing mechanism for shelter-with-care which separates the former from the latter, and an incentive to social services departments to think imaginatively about what shelter-with-care arrangements would best suit people. The consequence will be a massive increase in variety. So from now on, as Kane et al. write about new forms of shelter-with-care in the USA:

the policy issue becomes one of whether long-term care will be envisaged as a continuum with a niche for each client or whether it will be viewed as a repertoire of services that allows considerable choice based on lifestyle preferences and prices (Kane et al., 1991, p.1119).

One way to look at it is that growing variety in home care will be matched by growing variety in shelter-with-care. A more accurate perspective is that the old distinction between care for persons living at home and in facilities will break down. The Danes and Dutch argue – sometimes too dogmatically, one senses – the merits of their experiments in bringing services from outside congregate living facilities. That will grow in importance here.

Seeing the issue thus will greatly enhance the needs for cost information and complicate the task of obtaining and analysing information to provide it – all the more so because a system which not merely accidentally, but consciously, seeks to release Variety, Choice, and Change from Pandora's box will need to put more resources and effort into the collection and analysis of information.

3.2 *Make the most of the new user information systems and systematically establish ways of supplementing them*

A theme of this chapter has been the amazing lacunae in our knowledge. One example: think again about the context of the work on lifetime costs. The context is the new emphasis on potential for investment. One of the key features is the assessment of the reduction at acceptable cost of the unwanted and technically unnecessary utilisation of residential modes of care. It has been possible to estimate some prediction equations for lifetime costs of home care (Davies and Baines, 1991). However, there are simply no real data for the prediction from preadmission assessment information of the length of stay of persons in residential facilities. As was pointed out in Davies and Baines (1991), this is at a time when authorities are about to shoulder the responsibilities for a high proportion of persons so accommodated, and when it is at least possible that authorities might so dramatically change the pattern of admission as to make the cross-section average length of stay data now available extremely misleading. It is a fact of life that such spending will account for a high proportion of the total, so that gross errors in expected durations of stay could simply make massive cuts inevitable for others in need. There are authorities which simply have accepted no new cases for months on end. The price of ignorance can be colossal in terms of human suffering.

The costs estimated are often costs to the social services department of the community-based care. It is true that most of those costs now fall on the social services department. However, there are certainly other cost effects: to the National Health Service, to the social security services, to relatives and others. It is important to show the degree to which basing decisions on costs to the social services department would cause inefficiency by wider criteria and, to the degree that it does, provide additional information about the likely costs to other groups. Already some health and social services have joined forces to create information systems for some client groups; for example East Dyfed's Community Operational Support System (Audit Commission, 1992b).

The only discounted estimates discussed here are for costs. The economists' basic decision rule compares the present value of costs with those of benefits. To apply it requires comparable effort in both the estimation of benefits through time and in the valuation of the benefits. Experience in the measurement of outcomes of the last fifteen years suggests that estimating benefits through time is more a matter of expense in the collection of data than of the inherent difficulties of conceptualisation and measurement. Attaching values to outcomes is more difficult on both counts. Such valuations are likely to vary with user circumstances, and users themselves can be expected to have different valuations. The estimation of quality-adjusted life years (QALYS) seems to raise more difficulties for community and long-term care than for some acute treatments. The goals of the estimation suggested by Goldberg et al. (1980) were more modest and might raise fewer difficulties, but both estimating and valuing benefits are necessary.

There is hope, however. For the first time, there is a powerful thrust to the development of computerised information systems containing the basic building blocks of the production of welfare analyses on which this essay has drawn. Not only are individual agencies working on them. There are attempts to pool information across traditionally unbridgeable gulfs; between family health services, community health services and the social services departments, for instance. So far, there has been more effort than success. But if the momentum continues, we shall soon be able to have much of that localised information needed to support the application of the new logics in at least some areas.

Notes

1 Modes of care are alternatives at a point in time in the sense that two modes cannot be simultaneously consumed, though a care plan might combine them through time. For instance, the care plan might be to maintain someone in community-based care for some time, with the expectation that at a later stage shelter-with-care will be necessary.

2 The argument was first stated in the UK and the US at much the same time (in the UK: Wager, 1972; Wright, 1974; Mooney, 1978; and in the US see Homemakers Upjohn, 1975; Pollak, 1973).

3 Producers differ in the costs which they face and in their efficiency. So in a competitive market there will be a range of prices on offer for care of much the same quality given the characteristics of the potential resident.

4   By arrangements is meant broad structural choices, often set in by higher management for long periods. Examples are disciplinary mix of care management teams and their organisational locus, how much freedom the care managers have in deploying their budgets and the range of kinds of inputs on which the budget can be spent (and the aims the spending are intended to achieve).

    While 'arrangements' are characteristics, and so qualitative, 'parameters' are variable quantities: the budget limit beyond which each case has to be considered by higher management, the average budget per case, the average number of cases on the load of a care manager given the nature of the case mix.

5   Indeed, it might be appropriate to discount elements of costs and benefits differently; for example, if clients have higher valuations of present over future consumption than society in general (or, by implication, central and local government), the user-responsive social services department should arguably apply a higher rate of time preference to benefits to them.

6   Institute of Municipal Treasurers and Accountants (1969), PA Management Consultants Inc. (1969), Wager (1972) and Ratcliffe (1974) gave a general critique of the state of the literature.

References

Audit Commission (1992a) *Community Care: Managing the Cascade of Change*, HMSO, London.

Audit Commission (1992b) *The Community Revolution: Personal Social Services and Community Care*, NHS Report No. 8, HMSO, London.

Bebbington, A.C., Charnley, H. and Fitzpatrick, A. (1990) Balance and allocation of services to the elderly in Oxfordshire, Discussion Paper 700, Personal Social Services Research Unit, University of Kent at Canterbury.

Chesterman, J., Challis, D.J. and Davies, B.P. (1988) Long-term care at home for the elderly: a four-year follow-up, *British Journal of Social Work*, 18 (Supplement), 43-53.

Davies, B.P. and Baines, B. (1991) On lifetime costs and targeting: effects of current case management policy on future resources commitments with entropic assumptions about productivities, Discussion Paper 738, Personal Social Services Research Unit, University of Kent at Canterbury.

Davies, B.P. and Baines, B. (1992) Targeting and the silting-up of resources in community-based social services: the consequences of alternative policies, Discussion Paper 770, Personal Social Services Research Unit, University of Kent at Canterbury.

Davies, B.P., Bebbington, A.C. and Charnley, H. and colleagues (1990) *Resources, Needs and Outcomes in Community-Based Care*, Avebury, Aldershot.

Goldberg, E.M. and Connelly, N. (1982) *The Effectiveness of Social Care of the Elderly: An Overview of Recent and Current Evaluative Research*, Heinemann, London.

Goldberg, E.M., Barnes, J., Davies, B., Fruin, D., Harewood, P., Plank, D. and Timms, N. (1980) *Directions for Research in Social Work and Social Services*, report of a DHSS working party chaired by Miss E.M. Goldberg, Department of Health and Social Security, London.

Hendriksen, C., Lund, E. and Strongard, E. (1984) Consequences of assessment and intervention among elderly people: A three-year randomised control trial, *British Medical Journal*, 289, 1522-4.

Homemakers Upjohn (1975) *Cost Analysis: Home Health Care as an Alternative to Institutional Care*, Homemakers Upjohn, Kalamazoo, Michigan.

Institute of Municipal Treasurers and Accountants (1969) *Cost-Benefit Analysis in Local Government*, IMTA, London.

Kane, R.A., Kane, R.L., Illston, L.H., Nyman, J.A. and Finch, M.D. (1991) Adult foster care for the elderly in Oregon: A mainstream alternative to nursing homes, *American Journal of Public Health*, 81, 1113-20.

Mooney, G. (1978) Planning for balance of care of the elderly, *Scottish Journal of Political Economy*, 25, 2, 149-64.

PA Management Consultants Inc. (1969) *Cost-Benefit Analysis for Social Services for the City of Leicester*, PA Management Consultants, Leicester.

Pollak, W. (1973) *Costs of Alternative Care Settings for the Elderly*, Urban Institute, Washington D.C.

Qureshi, H., Challis, D.J. and Davies, B.P. (1989) *Helpers in Case-Managed Community Care*, Gower, Aldershot.

Ratcliffe, D. (1974) Cost-benefit analysis and the personal social services, *Policy and Politics*, 2, 237-48.

Ratna, L. (1982) Crisis intervention in psychogeriatrics: A two-year follow-up study, *British Journal of Psychiatry*, 141, 296-301.

Rubinstein, L.Z., Josephson, K.R., Wieland, G.D., English, P.A., Sayre, J.A. and Kane, R.L. (1984) The effects of geriatric assessment and managed intervention, *New England Journal of Medicine*, 311, 1664-70.

Rubinstein, L.Z., Kane, R.L., Josephson, K.R. and Wieland, G.D. (1985) The effects of geriatric assessment and managed intervention, *New England Journal of Medicine*, 312, 1066.

Social Services Inspectorate (1991) *Case Management and Assessment: Managers Guide*, HMSO, London.

Vetter, N.J., Jones, D. and Victor, C. (1984) Effect of health visitors working with elderly patients in general practice: a randomised controlled trial, *British Medical Journal*, 288, 369-71.

Wager, R. (1972) *Care of the Elderly*, Institute of Municipal Treasurers and Accountants, London.

Wright, K.G. (1974) Alternative measures of output of social programmes: the elderly, in A.J. Culyer (ed.) *Economic Policies and Social Goals*, Martin Robertson, Oxford.

Part III:
The Application of Costs

9 Calculating Unit Costs of a Centre for People with AIDS/HIV*

Andrew Bebbington

Recent policy developments have served to focus the attention of managers of small social centres on their unit costs. The 1980s saw a trend to decentralise financial management, with the managers of such facilities becoming increasingly responsible for managing their own budgets. This brought an increasing familiarity with costing inputs – staff, supplies, maintenance – as part of the auditing process. In the 1990s managers need to justify their cost-effectiveness, and to demonstrate their competitiveness in an increasingly open market. There has to be a progression from determining the costs of inputs, to determining the costs of outputs.

This chapter describes how output unit costs were calculated for a grant-funded non-profit-making day centre for people with AIDS and HIV infection situated in South London, which relies heavily on the use of volunteers and contract workers supported by a small core of permanent staff, and has an annual turnover of about £250,000. It illustrates a practical approach to solving some of the knottier problems associated with calculating unit costs which have been raised earlier in this volume; there are several distinct outputs created by the centre; the costing involved estimating long-run unit costs which combine both capital and recurrent expenditure; some costs are 'hidden'; and costs may appear different from different standpoints. Although every case is unique, this costing is in many ways typical of what managers of small cost centres in both the statutory and voluntary sector need to do in preparation for implementation of the 1990 *National Health Service and Community Care Act*.

The costing had the following purposes:
- to calculate the unit costs for each element of the service provided, to enable the managers of the centre to identify potential for improved

efficiency, and which would be of assistance in predicting the cost consequences of changing service levels;

- to calculate unit cost per client, on a basis that would meet the sponsors' 'need to ensure quality, consumer choice, and value-for-money' (Department of Health, 1990), which would help them in assessing the comprehensive costs of care, and would facilitate cost comparisons with alternative forms of care; and
- to provide information which would be of assistance in devising an equitable charging policy should the need arise.

These purposes are all associated with planning and evaluation, and require an assessment of the long-term opportunity costs of particular courses of action. The general approach is known as *ratio analysis* which 'should yield evaluative data on agency or program development that are useful to outside funding sources and the community, and also useful for internal management and planning purposes' (Lohmann, 1980, p.249). The essential building-block for ratio analysis is what it costs to produce a unit of each required output.

The outputs of social care ultimately concern benefit to clients' welfare and more general benefits to society as a whole; but usually, as in the present case, it is the intermediate outputs – the activities and services provided – which are costed (see also Chapter 2).

This exercise illustrates in particular the problems of determining unit costs when inputs and outputs are interrelated in a complex manner; and when there is no direct means of establishing the short-run marginal costs for each output.

The costing process followed four stages:

- defining units of output and measuring their volume (section 1);
- relating outputs to inputs (section 2);
- determining expenditure on inputs (section 3); and
- calculating unit cost of services, and hence cost per client (section 4).

Each of these sections describes how the issues raised elsewhere in this volume, particularly in Chapter 5, were dealt with. Section 5 of this chapter describes the consequences of this costing exercise, and its effect on subsequent policy.

1 Defining and measuring outputs

1.1 Defining outputs

With a multipurpose centre, several outputs are involved. Evaluations of social care invariably require some preliminary work to establish and agree with managers the exact definitions of the outputs, which for this centre included:

- social activities, including drop in, meals, library, laundry facilities;

- therapeutic services provided by sessional staff including massage, acupuncture and shiatsu;
- advisory services mostly provided by other agencies, both voluntary and statutory, but based within the centre, such as nursing consultation, social work, and legal, money and housing advice;
- services provided by volunteers on an outreach basis, including home support and transport;
- activities associated with promoting, developing and coordinating activities by other agencies;
- health education and training; and
- facilities for use by other AIDS/HIV organisations.

This list is inclusive, in that it contains all activities which take place under the centre's auspices, including some which do not fall within its own budget.

1.2 Output units

For unit costing, a unit must be defined for each output. Services, that is activities in the first four groups above, can have the unit defined in more than one way; for example;

- the number of 'usages': separate contacts between each client and the service provider(s);
- the number of sessions: periods of activity by a service provider;
- the number of appointments made (which will typically be less than the number of usages); and
- the unit length of 'usage': hours of time given exclusively to the client by the provider(s).

An ideal unit has two desirable properties. First, the unit is such that it is realistic to assume that the cost will be reasonably constant across units in the short term (see section 2.2 below). As a service usage might range from a five-minute fleeting contact in a group, to intensive one-to-one work taking all day, we might perhaps guess that it is the last of these four definitions which is likely to be most suitable. Second, the units must be easily measurable, for which reason one of the first three is often preferred to the last. Different units may be preferable for different purposes. For example, in establishing a charging policy, appointments booked may be more relevant than actual usage.

Box 1 summarises the volume of each service activity during the year 1 October 1989 to 30 September 1990, showing the units which were used. The last three of the outputs in section 1.1 are not services. As these are a comparatively small part of the total activities (in cost terms at least), only total rather than unit costs were calculated in this exercise. However, it was most important to disentangle the cost of these when determining the cost of services.

Box 1
Principal activities, year ending September 1990

Social and resource centre

Drop in   This was open for 247 days during the year. There were an estimated 6,700 attendances by clients, with an estimated total duration of usage of 16,000 hours.

Women's   14 with an average attendance of 8.
meetings

Meals   An estimated 4,750 meals were served to users and volunteers (excluding staff and other visitors).

Counselling and advice

Service	Operational	*Sessions*		*Consultations*		Av. length
		Year total	Av. per month	Year total	Av. per month	consult. (mins)
Counselling and drug advice	Mar. onwards	40	5.7	61	8.7	45
Diet	Throughout	35	2.9	27	2.3	40
Housing	Aug. onwards	9	4.5	22	11.0	60
Immunity (legal)	Throughout	41	3.4	75	6.3	30
Money	Oct. to May	24	3.0	39	4.9	45
Nursing	Throughout	58	4.8	118	9.8	60
Social work	Throughout	104	8.7	244	20.3	30
Threshold (housing)	Oct. to Nov.	5	2.5	4	2.0	60

Health promotion

Service	Operational	*Sessions*		*Treatments*		Av. length
		Year total	Av. per month	Year total	Av. per month	treatment (mins)
Acupuncture	Throughout	86	7.2	850	70.7	-
Homeopathy	July to Aug.	3	1.5	7	3.5	50
Massage	Throughout	87	7.2	247	20.6	60
Reflexology	Sept. onwards	2	2.0	3	3.0	-
Shiatsu	Nov. onwards	21	1.9	39	3.5	90

External services

Home   Operational from January onwards. Recorded 76 visits (average 22
support   per month), with an average visit length of 2hrs 40 mins.

Transport   Operational throughout. Recorded 743 journeys for users (average 62 per month).

2 Relating inputs to outputs

The costs of outputs are determined from the cost of inputs, since it is the latter which are normally available in accounts. In the present case these comprise the building, equipment, the internal staff, contracted staff, consumables and volunteers. This section describes how the volume of input required to produce each unit of output was determined.

When multiple outputs are involved, part of the task in costing is to determine the specific inputs for each output. Many inputs will be shared between outputs and must be subdivided. However, invariably there are some inputs which are essentially indivisible, and in practice it is too difficult to attempt to disaggregate others, and this presents a conceptual problem.

2.1 Divisible inputs

First we summarise the methods used to separate divisible inputs.

- *Staff time.* Internal staff inputs were divided among the outputs according to the proportions found in a study of staff time use. External staff work regularly at the centre but are not on the payroll. These staff can be divided into three groups: staff seconded to the centre by other agencies; sessional staff providing services but funded by other agencies; and sessional staff contracted by the centre itself. Most external staff contribute to one particular output.
- *Building.* Premises, maintenance and furniture inputs were divided among inputs according to the time and size of the rooms they used.
- *Equipment and consumables.* Specific item costs are attributed to the appropriate service where possible, though in practice this heading covers office equipment and publicity, which cannot be divided.
- *Volunteers.* Volunteer inputs, including volunteer coordinator and other staff support are redistributed between services according to the number of hours of volunteer input each service was estimated to have received. Three services were run by volunteers: drop in, home support and transport (see Box 1).

2.2 Indivisible inputs

The inputs which are regarded as unallocatable include labour, mainly staff time spent on general administration; and capital, including reception and administration, and offices and equipment.

At this point we need to introduce the distinction between average costs and marginal costing. In reality, many of the inputs which have been divided among outputs are not actually divisible. For example, all activities share the building. We may attribute to an activity the pro-rata share of the building space it uses, but there is no sense in which that part of the building cost could be removed if the activity did not take place. The approach applied is an average costing, and the rules we have applied for dividing inputs in section 2.1 must be understood as essentially arbitrary.

It is of course possible to argue that it is pointless to divide inputs if one is concerned with marginal costs; all that then matters is the *extra* input required for an additional amount of any particular output. Marginal costs are in principle most relevant to future planning decisions about adding facilities or improving productive efficiency, though for some purposes average costs may be more useful: for setting an equitable charging strategy, or as a convenient means of summarising the comparative costs of facilities.

Ideally, we would like to know the production function that defines the relationship between inputs and outputs. The problem is that we are observing the level of inputs and outputs only at one particular point in time. The production function can only be determined empirically if we observe the organisation running under a wide variety of input combinations. This is never possible for a single site costing although it may be estimable when one can observe a number of very similar organisations operating at different levels of output.

Conclusions that need to be drawn about marginal costs for the purpose of planning and evaluation, for example about the cost implications of making modest changes to the outputs, must in effect involve assumptions about the shape of the production function. These should be kept as simple and realistic as possible. As was pointed out in Chapter 2, often the best that can be done is to assume that the long-run marginal costs will be similar to the current average costs (including appropriately treated capital costs), within the limits of common sense and general understanding about the way the facility operates. This is the reason why it is desirable to choose units for measuring outputs that are likely to have reasonably constant costs over a range of circumstances and to employ 'sensible' disaggregation rules. It is also why the exercise was undertaken when the centre was operating at a stable level so that the estimation of average costs was not disturbed by changing marginal costs.

The usual convention for distributing indivisible inputs among outputs for average costing purposes is to do so pro rata with allocatable expenditure.

3 Costing inputs

The next step is to determine expenditure on inputs during the year. For planning and evaluation purposes we are primarily concerned with the opportunity cost, what is lost in the long run by using resources for this centre rather than on the best alternative. While opportunity cost is not in principle measured in monetary terms, in practice this is always the most convenient common factor. For current account expenditure, money is the natural measure of cost over a period. But there is other expenditure to consider that does not appear on the current account: 'hidden' costs. These are of two types: expenditure which falls to other organisations' accounts; and costs which are time-lagged, that is outputs which are produced some time removed from when the expenditure was made.

3.1 Other accounts

Some hidden costs are those attributable accounts other than the centre's. There are, as in all such costings of individual facilities, four sets of accounts to consider.
- The centre's own budget.
- The cost to other agencies of items not in the budget. There are three main ways that the centre may receive unbudgeted support from external agencies. First, there may be a hidden subsidy in the rent, which is discussed further in section 3.2. Second, the sponsors are in effect providing some administrative support, though in practice we believe this was minimal. Third, staff are provided by other agencies, particularly for counselling and advice. The cost of each of these must include not only the staff member's pay but also the related costs: travel, administration and so on in their own organisations. These were estimated from an hourly cost analysis of staff time in one of the sponsoring health districts.
- The cost to volunteers of their input. It is important to distinguish the cost to the organisation of supporting volunteers from the opportunity cost to the volunteers themselves (see Box 2). The former is discussed in section 3.2, but the cost to volunteers is not considered further here.
- The overall cost impact on society of the centre. The full social cost (such as effect on employment) is usually only relevant in the context of planning social programmes, and is not considered further here.

3.2 Capital and start-up costs

Other 'hidden' costs relate to inputs which create output over a different period from the accounting period. This applies particularly to capital, start-up and training costs where the benefits of initial expenditure may be felt over several years, and where the opportunity cost can vary considerably between alternative courses of action. The general approach is to discount fixed costs over their expected life. For each of the main fixed assets, the following methods were used.

Box 2

The cost and benefit of volunteering

Broad introductions to the principles of costing volunteer input are given by Weisbrod (1988) and, less formally, by Knapp (1990). There are two accounts to consider: the cost to the agency and the opportunity cost to the volunteers themselves, though occasionally the costs to society may also be relevant. It is customary for the benefits of volunteering to the agency to be valued in cash terms and we summarise some of the issues involved.

Costs and benefits to the agency

The cost to the agency includes the recruitment, training, support, perks and maybe ex-gratia payments that are made to volunteers. These are the support costs.

The benefits to the agency and its clients are conventionally measured by the substitution cost: the marginal cost in the market place to the agency to obtain an equivalent level of output to that created by the volunteer activity. It is often described in terms of the rates for paying staff to undertake activities which will achieve the same outputs.

Though it is generally assumed that the benefits to the agency from volunteers will far outweigh the support costs, this may not be so. Certain economic laws apply as much to voluntary agencies as they do to private companies. There will be a diminishing rate of return to additional volunteer activity. Also, as the demand for volunteers increases, there will be an increasing marginal support cost to the agency since presumably the recruitment drive must be stepped up and/or greater effort must be given to encourage volunteers to stay. Indeed, in a voluntaristic 'free market', a voluntary agency could be regarded as acting efficiently if it continued to recruit volunteers until it felt that a balance had been reached between the support cost and the benefits volunteers were bringing (Knapp, 1990). In this case the benefits to the agency of volunteers could be valued by the support costs. (The benefits to recipients of the agency's activity may be intentionally less than the support costs, if one of the agency's objectives is itself to encourage volunteering. More volunteers may be used than are strictly needed for an activity, or the volunteers chosen are not necessarily those who could undertake the work most efficiently.)

If the benefits to the organisation are to be measured by the substitution cost, it is rarely adequate to assume that there will be a one-to-one trade-off between volunteers and paid staff. There has to be some understanding of the 'production

---

- The cost of fixed items including building refurbishment, equipment including a car, and furniture which were purchased new were annuitised as follows. The annual opportunity cost was calculated from the present value of an annuity (with the same value as the initial value of the resource) over the expected life of that resource is calculated as

$$A = \frac{C_i}{P_i} \times \left\{ \sum_{n=1}^{Y} (1+R)^n \right\}^{-1}$$

relationship' for both. Often this can be difficult. Volunteers and paid staff may both create the same outputs but at different rates, or in different manners. For example, a paid help may be more reliable but a volunteer more flexible in meeting similar needs. Some assessment of their relative efficiency, or 'quality', is necessary in order to determine equivalence. The situation is further complicated if, as is common, volunteers are providing more than one output, say both practical help and emotional support. Volunteers, unlike paid staff, have considerable freedom to provide the combination of benefits that they themselves think appropriate. The recipient, or the agency for which the costing is being made, may well value things differently – they may rate certain outputs highly, and regard others as less important. In many cases, if the volunteer was not available, they might consider paying only for a part of what the volunteer does. So substitution costings also have to take account of relative marginal values of outputs of different kinds.

Costs and benefits to the volunteer

The cost to the volunteer stems from what the volunteer may be sacrificing. In the present context, the main resource input of volunteering is usually the volunteer's time. A method of valuing the indirect utility for this (that is, the benefit experienced by the volunteer as a result of the activity) is by placing a market value on the activity that the volunteer might have otherwise been undertaking, such as the loss of waged time, in which case the volunteer's employers will also lose the surplus value of that time, or the extra housework which the volunteer might otherwise have done. But in practice it is often leisure time which is sacrificed, so the opportunity cost depends on the volunteer's direct utility for this. (The direct utility of any activity is the satisfaction or value of actually participating in an activity.) As yet there are only speculative ways of attaching a cost value to direct utility.

The volunteer gains external benefit from the improvement in recipient's welfare as a result of his or her activity. There is also direct utility from the positive experience of having contributed, or perhaps some expectation of future reciprocity. The volunteer may also benefit from the human capital investment, and it is worth noting that many staff employed in AIDS/HIV centres were first involved in a related volunteer role.

where C_i is the capital spent in year i, P_i is the price index for that year relative to the current year, R is a constant discount rate and Y is the expected years of use of the item. Currently the Treasury advise (Circ. 32/89, 1989) a minimum public sector discount factor of 6 per cent (the factor R). The retail price index was used for the annual price index (P). Auditors' assumptions for the depreciation period tend to be rather pessimistic for the present purpose and we assumed a fifteen-year life for the refurbishment, and a five-year life for other items.

- For the building, the centre pays a rent which appears in their current account. The concern was that this might contain an element of hidden subsidy which would need to be added to the appropriate agency account. To determine this is difficult. Indeed, it is not easy to place a value on the building which is owned by an NHS trust. An alternative approach is to employ Treasury recommendations and conventions (see, for example, Cmnd 7131, 1978) for assessing the opportunity cost of capital in terms of an investment based on the replacement cost of the building and the land value (using Davis et al.'s, 1989, estimates). This gives a figure of about £400,000 for the premises in use as a health clinic. A 6 per cent discount factor over a 60-year life span gives a figure sufficiently close to the actual rent to assume that the hidden subsidy in the rent would be small. It has been ignored in subsequent calculations.
- For training volunteers the concern was that volunteers have an intermediate status between input and output, as the training process itself uses inputs that are accounted elsewhere. For this reason we calculated a unit rather than an overall cost for volunteer input. The cost in the year to September 1990 of training, including staff time but not overheads, was estimated at £8400, equal to £131 per volunteer. A separate exercise revealed that the average return per volunteer was 130 hours from training to resignation – so the average unit cost of training volunteers was £1 per hour of volunteer activity. The additional cost of the two volunteer coordinators brought the total support cost per hour of volunteer time to £4.42, excluding administrative overheads.

4 Determining unit costs

4.1 Unit costs of services

The stages are to determine the input costs over the year ending 30 September 1990 using the methods described in section 3 and then apply the relationships between inputs and outputs outlined in section 2 to calculate the cost per output for the year ending 30 September 1990. The expenditure on general administration and other expenditure not otherwise allocated amounted to 50 per cent of the total current expenditure which by convention is distributed pro rata with allocatable spending. The size of this overhead confirms the arbitrary nature of average cost calculations. Table 1 shows the estimated total cost of each output. Following the approach of section 3.1, three separate cost components are developed: the annual current account expenditure; the capital opportunity cost; the cost of paid inputs to other agency accounts (excluding volunteers) which are presented here *en masse*. Finally, administrative overheads were re-allocated.

Table 1
Output costs, year ending 30 September 1990

Item	Current account		Capital costs (annuitised)	Hidden costs (to external agencies)	Total (including recharge)
	Staff	Premises & other			
Drop in	16116	23267	14727	4376	109216
Informal support	4298	0	0	2804	13262
Meals	4813	13905	1459	0	37678
Home support	2963	1959	405	519	10915
Transport	7516	9703	2965	713	39022
Services					
Counselling	1493	444	340	3539	10862
Diet	0	389	298	2037	5085
Housing	2707	100	77	0	5385
Immunity	0	455	349	1902	5053
Money advice	0	266	204	1436	3560
Nursing	0	644	493	5609	12597
Social work	0	1155	884	6223	15428
Threshold	0	56	43	232	616
Acupuncture	0	955	731	5762	13908
Homeopathy	0	243	26	0	502
Massage	0	7056	740	0	14557
Reflexology	0	162	17	0	335
Shiatsu	0	1703	179	0	3514
Community action	25206	2859	2189	2804	61730
Total	65112	65320	26125	37956	
Admin. and sundry	69822	68525	28494	1870	(0)
Grand total	134934	133845	54619	39826	363224

The final column includes a 86.7 per cent mark up for recharged administration costs
for each service.

Table 2 shows these expenditure totals converted to a unit cost for each of the main services, using volume estimates from Box 1. Two forms of unit cost are presented; the cost to the current account only excluding administration recharges and the cost to all current accounts. Unit costs including capital and administration recharges are not shown in Table 2, though they are easily calculated.

Table 2
Output unit costs at September 1990

	Units	Cost to own account £	Cost including others' accounts £
Drop in	per hour	2.50	2.50
Meals	per meal	4.00	4.00
Home support	per week	20.00	20.00
Transport	per trip	21.00	21.00
Services			
Counselling	per consultation	7.00	65.00
Diet	per consultation	7.00	50.00 *
Housing	per consultation	30.00 *	30.00 *
Immunity	per consultation	7.00	32.00
Money advice	per consultation	7.00	43.00
Nursing	per consultation	5.00	52.00
Social work	per consultation	4.00	30.00
Threshold	per consultation	7.00	32.00 *
Acupuncture	per treatment	1.00	8.00
Homeopathy	per treatment	35.00 *	35.00 *
Massage	per treatment	29.00	29.00
Reflexology	per treatment	35.00 *	35.00 *
Shiatsu	per treatment	44.00	44.00

These unit costs are current account only (staff and premises) *excluding* administration and capital costs (except transport includes owned car).
* Insufficient information for accurate estimation (under 40 consults/treatments) and partly based on similar services. Included to enable cost per user to be calculated.

4.2 Costs per client

In order to investigate the pattern of use and costs per client, a sample of 95 clients were tracked to identify all resource use during the year. This sample was representative of all clients at that time.

Cost per client per year through the period was calculated by combining the number of visits (other than as a volunteer), meals, treatments by any of the various therapies, counselling or advice sessions received, and visits by outreach services, with their respective unit costs. Care must be taken to ensure like is being compared with like. A few clients first joined after the beginning of the year, so to compensate the following adjustment was made. For those who were still attending the centre at the end of the year, an estimated amount was added to their cost to give them the equivalent of a full year's cost. The average full-year current cost to the centre excluding administration was £420 with this adjustment; or £519 if the recurrent costs to other agencies were also included. There were wide variations between clients: three cost over £2000.

5 Consequences

It is of interest to report on the conclusions that were drawn from the costing exercise, in relation to the original exercise, and the consequences for development of the centre over the subsequent year.

5.1 Improving efficiency

The first objective had been to use the costing to improve productive efficiency, to identify activities which were expensive in relation to outputs. The costing proved generally reassuring about the sessional and other specific activities, with the small exception of the transport service, where some economies were later sought. The analysis revealed the comparatively high proportion of direct expenditure going to the drop-in facility. But by far the most striking consequence of the costing of activities proved to be the realisation of the very high administration component of total expenditure, nearly one-half of all costs including activities funded by outside agencies. This high ratio was attributed to three hings:
- the inclusive definition of administration which incorporated, for example, reception facilities;
- the cost of operating an essentially facilitative organisation, one in which most of the core staff were in a support rather than a service-providing role; and
- diseconomies of scale associated with managing a relatively small autonomous organisation.

In the year that followed, the developmental role of the centre was shifted in favour of direct service provision. New posts and vacancies were generally re-oriented towards providing specific services for clients. Towards the end of 1991 a major re-organisation was announced to reduce the management staff and hence the administration costs. These changes came about as the board attempted to align the centre into a favourable position ahead of the introduction of the purchaser/provider arrangements proposed by the *National Health Service and Community Care Act 1990* in which cost awareness, if not cost competitiveness, was seen as increasingly important to funders.

5.2 Equity

The costs analysis also contributed directly to a debate about target efficiency. The centre had originally espoused a non-interventionist policy of open access to all affected by HIV. However, the question arose of whether the services were going to those whom could most benefit from them; and this became translated as an issue of equity between the various social groups using the centre. Client registration information showed that although young white gay men were in preponderance among clients joining the centre, minority groups including blacks, women and those who had become HIV+ through intravenous drug abuse were represented according to their known incidence in the population. However, the cost analysis told a rather different story. The breakdown of the annual cost by type of user, shown in Table 3, revealed that people in these minority groups were, on average, using significantly

Table 3

Use of facilities from October 1989 to September 1990 and annual cost per user, by type of client. Based on a sample of 95 people

	Overall cost	
	Average £	Proportion of total %
Gender		
Men	556	89
Women	336	11
Ethnic group		
UK white	607	83
Irish	387	7
Other white	366	6
Black	181	4
HIV transmission group		
Gay sex	661	66
Heterosexual sex	174	2
IVDU	304	8
Other HIV+	257	3
Not HIV+	531	11
Unknown	487	10
Residence		
Lambeth	575	45
Southwark	325	12
Elsewhere	554	43

These are current account costs only, including costs to other agencies but excluding capital and administrative overheads.

fewer resources than others, attending less often and dropping out sooner. It also showed that a significant and perhaps undesirably high amount of resources was going to clients affected by HIV, but not themselves HIV positive, such as partners.

In the year following, targeting as an objective became pervasive at all levels in the organisation. Specialist services targeted at women and ethnic minorities were introduced, and attention was paid to improving the suitability of the service for all minority groups.

5.3 Charging policy

The intention was that the costing exercise would be used to set a service charging structure for purchasing agencies. At the time of writing, a charging policy is made impossible by the inconsistent position of these agencies, some of which are contracting through a bidding system for inputs while others want service level output agreements. Within the centre itself there remains resistance to a charging system, which is felt by some to be inconsistent with the voluntary nature of much of the input.

The individual client analysis showed spending divided by local authority of residence (shown in very summary form in Table 3). It had been expected that clients living locally would use more services than those living further away, but this was not so. The information has helped the centre to put pressure on local authorities whose residents were among the clients, but which were not providing funds.

One thing all purchasing agencies want is the introduction of information systems for monitoring, costing and evaluation. The clerical exercise of monitoring client use has created a heavy additional administrative burden. The costing exercise provided, as a spin-off, a computer database which would somewhat ease this burden by linking client information to recorded use of each service and calculating total cost automatically.

5.4 Pervasive influence of costing

There is an unusual degree of cost awareness among staff within the centre mainly due to its exposed financial position as a small autonomous unit, but to which the costing exercise undoubtedly contributed, through its presence in monitoring activities. In 1991 it was almost the only centre of its type in London not working to a deficit budget. Initially, services tend to be judged by the volume of demand, though management have been careful that this does not result in a preoccupation with maximising activity levels regardless. However, pride is taken in the high volume of activity that has rapidly outgrown the building and keeps staff stretched. Visitors familiar with the more traditional type of day centre are invariably impressed by the bustle during opening hours.

Notes

* I would like to thank staff at the centre for assisting with the collection of information on which this report is based. The work was undertaken with funding from the Department of Health, and is reported fully in A.C. Bebbington, R. Feldman, P. Gatter and P.O. Warren (1992) *The Evaluation of The Landmark*, Personal Social Services Research Unit, University of Kent at Canterbury.

References

Cmnd 7131 (1978) *The Nationalised Industries*, HMSO, London.

Davis, Langdon & Everest (1989) *Architects and Builders Price Book 1990*, E. and F.N. Spon, London.

Department of Health (1990) Caring for People Implementation Documents, Draft Guidance for Purchasing and Contracting, DH Report CCI7, Department of Health, London.

H.M. Treasury (1989) *Discount Rates in the Public Sector*, Circ. 32/89, 5 April, Press Office, London.

Knapp, M.R.J. (1990) *Time is Money: The Costs of Volunteering in Britain Today*, The 1990 Aves Lecture, Volunteer Centre, London.

Lohmann, R.A. (1980) *Breaking Even: Financial Management in Human Service Organisations*, Temple University Press, Philadelphia.

Weisbrod, B.A. (1988) *The Nonprofit Economy*, Harvard University Press.

10 Case Management: Costing the Experiments

*David Challis, John Chesterman
and Karen Traske*

In this chapter we focus on the analysis of costs and its application in service evaluation. Three examples are given. Two are of a case management service located purely within the social services department and the other is of a case management service located in a geriatric multidisciplinary team: a joint health and social services initiative. These were evaluations of the costs and effectiveness of different ways of providing long-term care for frail elderly people. The focus was on the individual users of services, hence the unit of analysis was the individual elderly person.

Six stages have been identified in the cost-effectiveness analysis: specifying the alternatives to be analysed; listing costs and benefits; measuring costs and benefits; comparing costs and benefits; testing those results in the light of uncertainty and sensitivity; and examining the distributional implications of the alternatives (Challis et al., 1984; Knapp, 1984). Our concern in this chapter is to examine three of these factors: listing costs; collection and measurement of costs; and comparison of costs. The main focus here is therefore on the costs elements rather than on outcomes.

1 The costing process

Four key issues concerning the costing process are addressed in this chapter:
- what information to collect;
- how to collect the data;
- how to measure the value or price of a commodity or unit of service; and
- how to use the cost information.

1.1 What information to collect?

The first task is to identify which costs are significant and who bears these costs. The second is that when calculating them, it is necessary to avoid transfer costs and double-counting. At a more pragmatic level, when the obsessional researcher is given full rein, the costs and benefits of the research itself and the danger of diminishing returns must also influence decisions. This requires consideration of the relative importance of particular costs; for example, an error in measuring time spent in residential care will have far greater consequences than an equivalent error in measuring the consumption of meals-on-wheels. A further complication occurs when some data are unobtainable, perhaps due to non-compliance, or to the large numbers of actors involved, or to the confidentiality of the data. In principle, such omission is acceptable where the level of unseen cost is broadly similar for the different groups being compared.

1.2 How to collect the data?

Whereas the answer to such a question may seem self-evident, a number of complications have to be considered. First, a decision must be made about the time period for the evaluation. Second, there is the decision about whether to collect cost data over the whole period or by sampling: on the one hand, it is economic of research time to sample the consumption of resources in a particular week, but on the other hand, if sample sizes are relatively small and the level of care is volatile, then there is a danger that sampling may under- or overestimate costs. Obvious examples of this include periods of admission to institutional care and the varying demands of particular clients upon staff during periods of crisis. Third, a decision has to be made about the units of time for data collection.

A further complication is that the routinely-available sources of information generated by care-providing agencies do not necessarily distribute staff time between different recipients of services, and special methods of data collection may be required. Sometimes such information has to be obtained indirectly or even estimated from other sources.

1.3 How to measure the cost of a unit of service?

There are four major issues: the use of opportunity costs rather than accounting costs; the need for a common price base; time lags between the incidence of cost and benefits; and overhead costs.

In making decisions about costs of services, an underlying principle has been to use estimates of opportunity costs of services (see Chapter 2). In contrast, cost information held by agencies is usually in the form of accounting costs. Moreover, the conventions employed in the collation of these accounts will vary across agencies. Opportunity costing may be particularly useful in treating capital costs in different settings equivalently (Knapp, 1984).

A second issue is that the price information for all the different bearers of costs should be related to the same point in time: in short, a common price base. This may be difficult to achieve in projects which are monitored over several years and when different organisations work to different financial years. Suitable indices can assist in deflating costs to a common base (see Chapter 3).

Third, since there are likely to be time lags between the occurrence of costs and some of their associated benefits, adjustments will be necessary to make comparisons between services. An obvious example is that of a multi-disciplinary assessment which, although immediately costly, may yield benefits over a considerable time. Another example is the setting-up and development costs of a new service, which will be high proportional to the number of users in its early period. For example, there is clear evidence that case management services have very high unit costs in their first year when development work is high and the number of clients is relatively low (Kane et al., 1991). There is therefore a need to consider how these set-up costs can be discounted. A fourth problem is the allocation of overhead costs, particularly in respect of staff time when a considerable proportion of this is not spent in direct client contact.

1.4 How to use the cost information?

Having identified the bearers of costs, the ways in which the quantities of costs borne by these parties may be measured, and the way in which costs may be allocated, the use of that cost information must be considered. The first and most obvious application of this information is in a straightforward comparison of the costs of the different approaches to care. This will be related to specific case studies in the following two sections. A more complex use involves comparing information on costs and benefits of one style of service with another, and this will be considered in the final section.

2 Costing the Gateshead Community Care Scheme

The Gateshead Community Care Scheme was an experimental evaluation of a case management service, located in the social services department, which was designed to prevent unnecessary admission of elderly people to institutional care. Through the devolution of control of resources to individual social workers, acting as case managers, it was designed to permit more flexible responses to needs, and the integration of fragmented services into a more coherent package of care to provide effective care at home. A matched group of elderly people receiving the usual range of services from adjacent areas within Gateshead provided a comparison group for the evaluation. Ninety matched pairs of cases were identified for comparison. Both groups of elderly people and their carers were interviewed upon identification and followed up a year later. The costs of services were monitored over a one-year period for both groups (Challis et al., 1988, 1990a, 1992).

The costs of care for both groups were determined for a number of parties, as shown in Box 1. Let us consider how the four issues were tackled for each of these parties.

Box 1
Parties incurring costs and benefits

The *social services department* – domiciliary services such as home help, meals-on-wheels, social work and case management (including flexible budgets); day care and residential care.

The *National Health Service* – hospital in-and out-patient services; day hospital; community nursing.

The *Department of Social Security* – pensions and benefits paid to elderly people and benefits paid to carers.

Private and voluntary establishments – residential and nursing homes.

The *elderly person* – living and care costs.

The *principal informal carer* – care costs.

Society as a whole – services; elderly person and carer costs; housing.

2.1 The social services department

Data collection. Special record systems were created to collect the amounts of each service used by each elderly person on a weekly basis. In the area receiving the case management service these were completed by the staff of that service and in the comparison area by the researcher. This was because existing records did not readily aggregate the mix of services received by each person. These records were designed to monitor the weekly care costs of elderly people over a twelve-month period (52 observations in all), since vulnerable elderly people were seen as subject to too many changes in levels of care for a sampling approach to provide an adequate picture of their costs of care. Tracking people in this way was particularly important because of the transitions which many people experienced between different settings.

Unit costs. The single most costly service to estimate was that of the local authority old people's homes. Given that the case management service was designed to prevent unnecessary admission of elderly people to residential care, the running cost of residential care was estimated as the revenue cost of a new residential care home rather than the average of all residential homes, which is influenced by older establishments. This was the best estimate of the marginal cost of care, since, with increasing demand caused by an ageing population, marginal costs could be seen to approximate to the average cost of a place in a new home (see Chapter 2). This cost was derived from local authority accounts. The capital cost element was estimated from the building costs of a new home, including the cost of land, discounted over a 60-year period. This was a more realistic conception of opportunity cost than the annuitised capital repayments in the local authority accounts. Together, the revenue and capital costs provided an estimate of gross costs, and net costs were estimated by subtracting the average contribution paid by elderly persons to the authority. The capital and revenue costs of day centres were estimated in a similar way. One interesting problem arose in attaching a cost to the provision of day care within a residential home, since apparently such care was absorbed within the existing staff time and spatial facilities. Thus the marginal cost of this form of care was estimated as the cost of meals and transport to and from the home. Of course, since some staff time was expended on attention to day care visitors, an alternative solution would require precise measurement of the distribution of staff time during the day to different activities.

The unit costs of domiciliary services such as home help and meals-on-wheels were estimated from the gross expenditure on each service divided by the number of units of service provided, with an allowance added for administrative and managerial overheads. This was an attempt to avoid the danger of merely costing the direct service without taking account of the broader infra-structure required in its management and delivery. The costing of meals-on-wheels was more feasible in this authority than in many, since the service was provided and monitored by the social services department rather than a voluntary organisation, such as the WRVS.

The cost of social work time posed interesting problems. On the one hand, the case management service, consisting of a team leader (carrying a caseload) and two level 3 social workers with their own administrative support, was directly responsible to an assistant director. The organisational overheads were therefore relatively low. On the other hand, workers in an area team, although greater in number, carried considerably more overhead costs: senior social workers (non-caseload carrying), principal social workers and an assistant director, as well as administrative support. In order to avoid biasing cost comparisons in favour of the experimental service, the same unit cost was used for each. Measurement of the precise allocation of social work time between cases also posed problems. Even allowing for errors in recording direct contact and visits, a great deal of social work time related to individual cases does not take the form of direct contact. Therefore it was necessary to devise a means of estimating how 'indirect activities', as well as overheads, were distributed. Based on studies of social work time use and previous case management schemes (Carver and Edwards, 1972; City of Manchester, 1981; Challis and Davies, 1986), as well as direct observation of the scheme in practice, it was possible to estimate the balance of direct and indirect activities. For the area teams it appeared that direct time could be seen as approximately 50 per cent of the time to be allocated (if anything this tended to minimise the indirect and overhead costs). This was consistent with the principle that any potential bias in the evaluation should operate against the experimental intervention. For the case management scheme, direct time was estimated as approximately 30 per cent of the total to be allocated, reflecting the higher proportion of indirect time evident in the case management model (Challis and Davies, 1986; Challis et al., 1988, 1990a, 1992).

Unit costs of different types of aids were discounted over periods which reflect their potential useful life.

2.2 The National Health Service

Data collection. This took the same form of weekly costing as described above. Information was obtained from case managers, hospital records and community health service records.

Unit costs. The most significant National Health Service costs were for episodes of in-patient care. These were estimated from regional health authority information. Although this included non-patient-related costs such as maintenance and records, it did not include an allowance for capital elements nor did it discriminate between the costs of different forms of in-patient care within a single hospital. In this area the type of treatment provided generally reflected the kind of hospital to which elderly people were admitted; thus there were no long-stay beds in the acute hospitals. Hence using the average cost for a hospital stay appeared reasonable. An allowance for capital elements was calculated using three different assumptions regarding buildings – improving, upgrading and reconstructing – based on the same assumptions as used by Wright et al. (1981), and discounting these capital elements over a 60-year period. Day hospital costs were calculated in a similar way.

The cost of community nursing was estimated according to the type of nurse undertaking the visit. This cost was made up of a nursing time element, comprising the immediate cost of the nurse calculated from district health authority accounts, together with a fixed charge per visit to cover travelling expenses, materials such as dressings, and administrative overheads. It was assumed that the average visit would take 30 minutes, including travelling in the local area.

The cost of out-patient appointments was estimated from regional health authority accounts by type of specialty. No reasonable data on capital costs associated with out-patient care were available and in any case this was not likely to be a major component of cost.

The costs of National Health Service aids were estimated similarly to those supplied by the social services department.

2.3 The Department of Social Security

Costs to the Department of Social Security included the payment of pensions, attendance allowance, invalid care allowance and other benefits. Tracking the changes in these benefits was undertaken on the same weekly basis as other costs since payments could vary according to whether or not the elderly person or their spouse was in institutional care. Benefits were costed at the rate current in the year for which the price base of the scheme was set.

2.4 Private and voluntary establishments

The most significant private sector cost was that of residential and nursing homes. It was assumed that the weekly average social security payment, less the pocket money allowance, represented the cost to the home. Where voluntary organisations supplied aids these were estimated at the same rate as those provided by the public sector.

2.5 The elderly person

The cost to the elderly person consisted principally of their costs of daily living. This was estimated from the *Family Expenditure Survey* information for older people during the relevant year, based on the income received by each elderly person. While an elderly person was in institutional care their personal consumption or living costs were taken to be equal to the social security allowance made for weekly expenditure in that setting. Housing costs were excluded from these calculations since they were estimated as part of the overall cost to society.

2.6 The principal informal carer

Principal informal carers of elderly people were all visited and interviewed by researchers. At this interview additional costs incurred in caring for the elderly person were discussed and estimates were made of extra expenditure on items such as food, heating and laundry, based on the carers' own estimates. On occasions people had to reduce or give up work or other remunerative activities which could result in substantial amounts of income forgone. For example, one carer had given up professional employment well before retirement age to care for her mother. She received a pension but at a reduced rate. It was therefore necessary to cost the loss of her future pension and of earnings from employment, less the money received from her (reduced rate) pension.

2.7 Society as a whole

The simplest conception of costs to society may commonly be viewed as public expenditure costs. These were calculated by adding service costs and social security benefits together. However, such an approach neglects particularly important areas of cost associated with the provision of community care, namely the costs incurred by the elderly persons and their carers. Our approach to estimating social cost has always focused on this latter approach and consists of: the service costs to health and social services, with capital elements discounted; the costs of private and voluntary care; the costs borne by informal carers; and the costs to the elderly person, both their living expenses and also their housing costs. This latter element is particularly salient to a comparison of extended home care with traditional home care, since one possible effect of enhanced home care services is that people will remain in their own homes for longer. The value of this housing has to be offset against the accommodation (hotel) costs of hospital and residential care for a true comparison (see Chapter 2). In this study, in order to estimate the accommodation costs, housing values were estimated using building society figures for different type and age of house for the period in question. The value of housing was then discounted over a 60-year period. Alternative assumptions were applied according to the circumstances of each elderly person. Thus, if two elderly people were sharing accom- modation then the value of the home was divided between them. Moreover, if an elderly person was living with relatives in accommodation which would not be released for alternative occupation when vacated by the elderly person, then the opportunity cost of that accommodation was taken as zero.

In calculating costs to society, it was important to ensure a particular cost would only be evident under one head, thus avoiding double-counting. An obvious example is the position of pensions and social security entitlements in calculating social opportunity costs. While social security payments can be perceived as a cost to the Department of Social Security, they are normally spent on the personal consumption of the elderly person or paid towards the cost of services. However, there were situations when double-counting of costs was an appropriate representation of the resources consumed. This occurred when, for example, a person entered hospital care but also retained their own home, when the cost of each setting was included in the total social costs.

3 Costing the Darlington Community Care Project

The Darlington Community Care Project was an experimental study designed to provide alternative care at home for frail elderly people who would otherwise require long-stay hospital care. It was a joint health and social services initiative which involved locating case managers in a geriatric multi-disciplinary team. To provide the new long-term care service three case managers and a team of home care assistants were added to the existing geriatric service. The home care assistants were intended to act as multi-purpose care workers undertaking home help tasks and acting as nursing, physiotherapy, occupational therapy and speech therapy aides. During the pilot phase of the project the social services department employed all staff except two health service professionals, an occupational therapist and physio-therapist.

In this study individuals receiving services from the project were compared with a similar group of patients identified in long-stay wards in an adjacent health district, and both groups were followed up after six months. Their informal carers were also interviewed and information on the costs of care was collected over a six-month period (Challis et al., 1989; 1991a; 1991b).

The range of parties identified as potentially bearing costs, from social services and the National Health Service through to society as a whole, were the same as those described in the previous study and shown in Box 1. The costs of residential care and nursing homes provided by the independent sector, housing costs and expenditures by elderly people on daily living costs were calculated in the same way as described for the Gateshead scheme.

3.1 The social services department

The project cost components consisted of a project manager, three case managers, a part-time physiotherapist, a part-time occupational therapist, a number of home care assistants and a care budget. Other social services department costs – such as home help, day care, and residential care – were costed as described in the Gateshead scheme.

Data collection. As in the Gateshead scheme, weekly sheets were maintained by case managers covering the range, frequency and duration of services provided. This covered not only the care inputs of home care assistants and the use of the budget but also episodes of institutional care and the input from other professionals, such as nurses.

Unit costs. The unit costs of the home care assistants, the physiotherapist and the occupational therapist were estimated in a similar way to that described in the Gateshead scheme, allowing for overhead, administrative and travel costs.

The unit costs of the case managers were estimated using project budget information about salary costs, travel expenses, administration and clerical support. As this was a special joint agency project with its own managerial structure outside the normal system, the organisational overheads of central management were not included, although the sensitivity of the results to this extra cost was tested in the analyses. It was not possible to attribute case managers' time precisely to individual cases, proportional to the demands of the workload. Consequently the total case manager time and associated costs, both direct contact and more indirect activities based on a realistic caseload, were divided equally between the cases on a weekly basis.

Home care assistant costs varied according to the times at which services were provided, and four different unit costs were calculated to reflect the different unsociable hours' payments. These variable payments demonstrated the importance of an accurate and reliable information system to identify the care given and the importance of monitoring costs of care through time since the distribution of rates of payment could vary markedly according to changes in patients' health.

3.2 The National Health Service

The long-stay beds from which people were to be discharged to the project were located in a district general hospital which had the status of mainly acute hospital. Such an establishment has a wide range of different medical specialties which vary significantly in the amount of medical, nursing and other services consumed, rendering the average cost per bed day significantly higher than that of purely long-term hospital care for elderly people. An attempt was made to calculate costs in a way that reflected the demand on facilities made in the care of elderly patients. The main component of long-stay care for elderly people is likely to be the nursing care costs, which are lower than those of acutely ill patients. The cost of nursing care for the elderly beds was estimated, taking account of administrative and overhead costs, by weighting the total nursing costs of the hospital proportionately by the number and grade of nurses within the hospital. As a consequence, the unit cost of nursing per in-patient day for the elderly beds was less than 60 per cent of the nursing cost to the hospital as a whole. The costs of medical and dental services, medical and surgical equipment, and pharmacy for the elderly wards were estimated from the district health authority accounts. Non-patient-related costs such as maintenance and records were estimated from the regional health authority accounts. Since the project facilities included both acute and long-stay beds, a feature not always observed in a district general hospital setting, there was a risk of in-patient costs appearing relatively high in this study. In order to render the data comparable with other settings, a second set of cost estimates was prepared, based on the hospital costs of a long-stay geriatric care facility within the same region. Thus, for all analyses, two estimates of hospital costs were provided, presenting the cost consequences of the experimental service in its existing context and also the consequences if it was located in a setting with less costly long-stay beds.

Capital costs were estimated as described in the Gateshead scheme, as were day hospital and out-patient costs.

An allowance was made for medication for patients living at home based on the medication costs of a long-stay geriatric facility. Community health care costs of district nursing, physiotherapy, and similar staff were estimated in the same way as in the Gateshead scheme.

Setting-up costs. There were certain costs incurred in setting up a package of community care for each patient. These consisted of staff involvement in case conferences specially convened for assessment and referral to the project, and additional assessments in hospital and at home. These costs were over and above the usual assessment time received by all patients, which is included in the hospital costs. The concern here is with the *extra* costs incurred by the project clients. The costs to the project of time spent introducing the home care assistants to clients – both with the case manager and other professionals present, and time spent alone with clients – have been estimated, based on observation of staff activities.

Each client was considered twice at case conferences prior to discharge. A cost for the case conference was estimated by assuming a total time spent on each client of fifteen minutes for each person present: a consultant geriatrician, a junior hospital doctor, a ward sister, a physiotherapist, an occupational therapist, a senior ward sister and a social worker. The cost of the additional assessment in hospital was estimated by calculating the cost of the time spent by the professionals involved or closely consulted. The case manager had an overall coordinating role so the calculations included time spent organising and attending meetings, with the client, with their family, collating case notes, as well as that spent at assessment. Fifty per cent of the clients received a home assessment and this was costed according to the time spent by those involved in the visit, travelling and writing up the assessment: on average about two hours. In most cases this assessment involved the case manager, a physiotherapist and an occupational therapist. Finally there was the cost to the project of introducing the home care assistant to the client in hospital, which was calculated by adding together the cost of the time spent by the home care assistant (estimated to be three hours), the case manager (estimated to be one and half hours) and the identified time of other professionals.

Although the setting-up costs of case manager time were calculated, this element was not added to the setting-up cost per case as the case manager costs had already been allocated to the project. This investment cost of an initial assessment was discounted over the six-month monitoring period for each client.

3.3 The Department of Social Security

As in Gateshead, information on pensions and benefits was collected from interviews and client records. Where information was missing, an average level of expenditure was estimated based on national data. In this project patients were discharged from long-stay hospital beds, where some had lived for a considerable time. Some people were entitled to resettlement benefits and one-off grants for household items (such as cookers) to re-establish themselves in the community and these were discounted over an expected period of use.

3.4 The principal informal carer

Costs borne by informal carers of elderly persons who received the Community Care Project services were compared with the corresponding costs for two comparison groups, estimated from interviews with the informal carers. One comparison group consisted of elderly people in long-stay hospital and the other of elderly people living at home, attending day hospital and receiving the usual range of services.

The focus of the evaluation was on the differential costs which carers experienced as a result of the elderly person receiving project services, rather than existing home care services or long-stay hospital care. Therefore other costs incurred equally by all carers prior to the provision of the project service were not available. For example, no one gave up work to care during the evaluation period although some carers in all three groups had earlier given up work or reduced their working hours.

Extra costs to carers which could be attributed to caring for the elderly person either at home or in hospital were calculated in the following areas:

Fuel. This was obviously only applicable to carers of elderly people at home. Using information on the heating bills of some of the carers, an attempt was made to calculate how much higher this was than the average amount spent on fuel, light and power calculated from the *Family Expenditure Survey.* However, this information did not provide regional differences and it appeared that these carers, even when saying they were spending more than usual on fuel due to caring, spent less than the nationally-applicable average. Since these carers identified real additional costs for fuel, the supplementary benefit addition for extra heating at the higher rate was used as an extra weekly cost.

Food. Extra expenditure was noted in this area by all three groups of carers. Many of those carers who lived with the elderly person said that they spent more because of the elderly person's special diet. The supplementary benefit addition for a special diet allowance at the middle rate was used as a weekly extra cost for these carers. For those non-resident carers of elderly people at home who spent extra money on food, a nominal sum was allowed for this based on the frequency and type of provision. A nominal sum was also allowed for carers taking food to the elderly person in hospital, calculated from interview material.

Clothing. Extra costs for clothing for the elderly person were incurred by all three groups of carers. For carers of elderly people in hospital this appeared to be due to the vagaries of the hospital laundry service where much clothing was lost. Accordingly an amount was attributed to the carers who had spent extra, calculated from interview information.

Laundry. Extra laundry costs were incurred by the three groups of carers. For carers of elderly people in hospital, their concerns about the hospital laundry service resulted in some visiting most days and taking laundry on each visit. The supplementary benefit addition for laundry was allowed for these carers. For those caring at home, laundry was obviously a greater burden, and this amount was doubled to allow for heavier washing loads of some items, such as bedclothes.

Travel. Additional travel costs were incurred by the three groups of carers either due to visiting the elderly person in their own home, in hospital, or taking the elderly person out. Calculations were based on interview data on the frequency of these trips and the fares paid. Where fares were not specified, an average was applied.

Other expenditure. Carers in all groups spent extra money on additional items such as toiletries. Carers at home also incurred costs making telephone calls to arrange relief cover, arranging private chiropody and buying extra bedding for the elderly person.

Transfer payments. The cost information collected was not adequate in many cases to specify the extent to which some or all of these costs were offset by transfers of money to the carer from the elderly person. Some carers said that they felt this balanced out overall. It may be assumed that for carers of the hospital group, whom, if they had been in hospital for a year, would only be receiving the social security pocket money allowance, this amount would have been insufficient to recompense them for their extra expenditure. All of the project cases were in receipt of the attendance allowance, provided they lived long enough to receive it, but no firm evidence was available on the extent to which this was used to recompense carers.

These, then, were the ways in which cost information was identified for the two case management schemes. In the next section we examine how this information was deployed in order to judge the relative cost-effectiveness of different ways of providing care.

4 Using the cost information: comparing costs and benefits and cost-effectiveness

There are three levels of activity at which this cost information may be utilised. For the sake of simplicity these could be called the practice level, the agency level, and service evaluation. Although our main focus is on the last of these, it would be inappropriate not to indicate the utility of cost information at the other two levels. Knowledge of the relative costs of different forms of service provision and the possession of decentralised budgets permitted practitioners to use resources more flexibly and appropriately to meet needs. This was markedly different to the more usual situation where practitioners allocate a range of existing services with no knowledge of their costs and no capacity to influence provision. At the agency level, in these schemes, a system of case recording which covered assessments, regular case reviews and costs (Challis and Chesterman, 1985) permitted managers to identify patterns of expenditure by types of case and make projections of future patterns of expenditure with greater exactitude than normal. Hence the availability of cost information, as part of a devolved budgeting system, can have important consequences both for individual practitioners attempting to provide more client-responsive services and for agency managers attempting to ensure that resources are deployed to their best effect.

Having collected information about the relative costs to different parties of alternative modes of care, the first task is to undertake comparisons of the advantages and disadvantages of the two modes. These comparisons were made using measures of effectiveness, such as the level of satisfaction of the elderly person, the adequacy and suitability of the care provided, and the stresses and difficulties experienced by carers, as well as measures of cost. In the first of the studies discussed above (Challis et al., 1988; 1990a; 1992) as well as the earlier Kent Community Care Scheme (Challis and Davies, 1986; Davies and Challis, 1986), the results indicated that the average cost of case management services and existing provision were broadly similar (Table

Table 1
Costs for different parties over one year (1981 prices)
(Gateshead Community Care Scheme)

	Case management scheme	Control group	p-value
Social services department (Revenue net cost)			
Non inner city	1609	1793	ns
Inner city	2008	1535	
National Health Service (Assuming 5 per cent capital allowance)			
Non inner city	1798	1588	ns
Inner city	1505	483	
Social opportunity cost (capital elements discounted at 5 per cent)			
Non inner city	5220	5203	ns
Inner city	5333	3847	

F-test case management v control group. ns = not significant.

1), although the case management service appeared to be considerably more effective. Hence it would be reasonable to conclude that case management would be more efficient than existing provision since it offered greater well-being at a similar cost. It is important to note that in this comparison all the service costs, including case management, were examined. If the costs of case management were excluded and only the services included, the case management service would have appeared less costly. Such an error may occur since the overhead costs of case management and social work are easily overlooked and are difficult to allocate. In fact the overhead costs of case management constitute a significant component of the total: 18 per cent of social services costs and 9 per cent of the joint health and social services agency cost (Challis et al., 1990b). In the study of case management in geriatric care (Challis et al., 1989, 1991a,b) it appeared that the case management service was a less expensive option than the existing pattern of provision (Table 2) and offered a better quality of life to elderly people and their carers. The difference between these two studies is to a large extent explained by the difference in the relative costliness of the institutional care settings which elderly people entered and also the lack of adequate provision for some vulnerable elderly people living at home who receive existing services.

With such findings, it would be possible to leave the comparison process and the evaluation study at this point. However, it is unlikely that the evidence of studies will always permit such clear judgement and, in any case, it is important to explore more subtle factors which are concealed within overall

Table 2

Costs for different parties over six months (1986-87 prices)
(Darlington Community Care Project)

	Case management scheme	Control group	p-value
Community care project	2850	–	–
Other SSD (revenue net cost)	30	115	–
Other NHS (5% capital allowance)			
DMH base[1]	870	9838	–
Geriatric base[2]	659	6205	–
Total agency cost			
DMH base[1]	3750	9953	<.001
Geriatric base[2]	3539	6320	<.001
Total social opportunity cost			
DMH base[1]	4977	10493	<.001
Geriatric base[2]	4766	6859	<.001

F-test case management v control group.
1 Long-stay hospital costs at Darlington Memorial Hospital level.
2 Long-stay hospital costs at geriatric hospital level

averages of cost and well-being. In order to do this it is necessary to explore factors associated with variations in cost. This is particularly important since for many new services it is quite reasonable to assume that one method of provision or some combination of these two will be more effective or less costly for some types of case but have quite different effects for others. Thus, for example, the cost of adequately supporting an elderly person with dementia living alone is likely to be greater than that for a physically disabled but mentally alert elderly person living with their family. For practitioners, policy-makers and managers there is a need to try to identify the characteristics of those individuals for whom one way of providing care is the most appropriate. In order to answer this more complex but crucial question it is necessary to simultaneously estimate the relationship between costs, characteristics of elderly people and the outcomes of care.

In the Kent Community Care Scheme (Challis and Davies, 1986; Davies and Challis, 1986), this process was undertaken in order to identify the characteristics of individuals for whom community care seemed most appropriate. Multiple regression analyses were used to examine the effects of health, dependency, levels of informal care and environmental circumstances on the cost of obtaining different levels of two summary outcome indicators: subjective well-being and quality of care. These resulting equations were then used to predict the cost of achieving different levels of outcomes for different types of elderly person and thereby to calculate the cost of achieving

Table 3
Estimated annual cost to the social services department of varied levels of outcome for different types of case (1977 prices)

Case type	Mode of care	No improve-ment	Some improve-ment	Considerable improve-ment	Substantial improve-ment
Improved subjective well-being		% 0	% 10	% 20	% 30
Improved quality of care		0	20	40	60
		£	£	£	£
Extreme physical frailty with mental impairment. Reliant on spouse for care. Very high dependency.	Case management	363	519	789	1202
	Standard services	1140	1334	1797	2617
Socially isolated, lives alone. Suffers from giddiness and risk of falling. Problems with depressed mood, meal preparation and managing domestic tasks. Moderate dependency.	Case management	296	267	283	404
	Standard services	264	659	851	1635
Very highly dependent suffering mental frailty and incontinence. Considerable degree of informal support. 'Critical interval need' (Isaacs and Neville, 1976).	Case management	510	594	767	1059
	Standard services	156	466	1044	1980
Severe physical frailty. Likely to be bedridden, chairbound or suffering from faecal incontinence.	Case management	11	167	437	850
	Standard services	313	507	970	1790
Mentally impaired, lacking social support. At considerable risk.	Case management	725	809	982	1274
	Standard services	214	524	1102	2038

Source: Challis and Davies, 1986; Davies and Challis, 1986.

combinations of two facets of well-being for elderly clients with different characteristics. Such equations are an approximation to the complexity of the decision-making processes undertaken by care providers where aspects such as health and dependency are crucial determinants of staff decisions about the level of resources required to achieve desired effects in client well-being. The precise equations which indicate the relationships between different determinants of cost can be found in Challis and Davies (1986) and Davies and Challis (1986).

Table 3 provides an example of such analyses. It shows the annual cost to the social services department of case-managed and traditional services for elderly people of achieving different levels of improvement in well-being and quality of care. It is possible to see that there are considerable variations in cost between people with different needs and circumstances. For example, there are two types of individual for whom the case management service appeared particularly cost-effective. The first of these was the extremely dependent elderly person with both mental and physical impairment receiving a considerable degree of informal support. The second group consisted of relatively isolated elderly persons with less severe degrees of dependency who were likely to suffer from affective psychiatric disorder.

These analyses indicate how an exploration of the factors which influence variation in cost can provide a much broader degree of understanding than just a comparison of aggregates and averages.

5 Conclusion

In this chapter we have outlined how, in a series of evaluation studies of case management, cost information has been identified, collected, calculated and deployed. It is clear from this brief discussion that the reliability and validity of cost information is subject to the influence of factors such as the time at which information is collected, the way in which it is collected and the assumptions on which the calculations are based. As much care is required in defining these assumptions to ensure both reliability and validity as is required in measuring apparently more elusive concepts such as depression and cognitive impairment.

References

Carver, V. and Edwards, J.L. (1972) Social Workers and their Workload, National Institute for Social Work, London.

Challis, D. and Chesterman, J. (1985) A system for monitoring social work activity with the elderly, British Journal of Social Work, 15, 115-32.

Challis, D.J. and Davies, B.P. (1986) *Case Management in Community Care,* Gower, Aldershot.

Challis, D.J., Knapp, M.R.J. and Davies, B.P. (1984) Cost effectiveness evaluation in social care, in J. Lishman (ed.) *Research Highlights 8: Evaluation,* Department of Social Work, University of Aberdeen.

Challis, D.J., Chessum, R., Chesterman, J. and Woods, R. (1988) Community care for the frail elderly: An urban experiment, *British Journal of Social Work,* 18 (supplement), 13-42.

Challis, D.J., Darton, R.A., Johnson, L., Stone, M., Traske, K. and Wall, B. (1989) *Supporting Frail Elderly People at Home,* Personal Social Services Research Unit, University of Kent at Canterbury.

Challis, D.J., Chessum, R., Chesterman, J., Luckett, R. and Traske, K. (1990a) *Case Management in Social and Health Care,* Personal Social Services Research Unit, University of Kent at Canterbury.

Challis, D.J., Chesterman, J., Traske, K. and von Abendorff, R. (1990b) Assessment and case management: some cost implications, *Social Work and Social Sciences Review,* 1, 147-62.

Challis, D.J., Darton, R.A., Johnson, L., Stone, M. and Traske, K. (1991a) An evaluation of an alternative to long stay hospital care for frail elderly patients: Part I. The model of care, *Age and Ageing,* 20, 236-44.

Challis, D.J., Darton, R.A., Johnson, L., Stone, M. and Traske, K. (1991b) An evaluation of an alternative to long stay hospital care for frail elderly patients: Part II. Costs and effectiveness. *Age and Ageing,* 20, 245-54.

Challis, D.J., Chessum, R., Chesterman, J., Luckett, R. and Traske, K. (1992) Case management, in F. Laczko and C. Victor (eds) *Social Policy and Eldery People,* Avebury/Gower, Aldershot.

City of Manchester (1981) *Hospital Social Workers: A Study of Patterns of Work and Use of Time,* City of Manchester Social Services Department.

Davies, B.P. and Challis, D.J. (1986) *Matching Resources to Needs in Long Term Care,* Gower, Aldershot.

Kane, R.A., Penrod, J., Davidson, G., Moscovice, I. and Rich, E. (1991) What cost case management in long term care?, *Social Service Review,* 65, 281-303.

Knapp, M.R.J. (1984) *The Economics of Social Care,* Macmillan, Basingstoke.

Wright, K.G., Cairns, J.A. and Snell, M.C. (1981) *Costing Care,* University of Sheffield/Social Services Monographs, London.

11 Costs, Needs and Outcomes in Community Mental Health Care*

Jennifer Beecham, Martin Knapp and Andrew Fenyo

There is a tendency in discussions of mental health policy and psychiatric practice to talk of *the* cost of a treatment, facility or policy – which usually means the average cost – and to ignore variations around the average. These variations can be considerable, which alone suggests they should not be overlooked. Moreover, they can be explored and perhaps exploited to improve the delivery of services. This chapter describes a framework for the examination of cost differences, applies it to data on people with long-term mental health problems who have moved from hospital to community settings, and uses the empirical evidence to address four policy questions. Is there a connection between costs and outcomes? Do people with greater needs get more support or treatment? Is the public sector more or less efficient than the independent sectors in the delivery of mental health services? Finally, how does the type of community residential placement influence cost?

1 Psychiatric reprovision – methodology

The decision was taken in 1983 to close Friern and Claybury hospitals in North London. Friern will close in 1993, and Claybury in the next few years. North East Thames Regional Health Authority, in whose area these hospitals are located, has funded research to examine the psychiatric reprovision services being established to replace them. In association with the Team for the Assessment of Psychiatric Services (TAPS), the PSSRU has been looking at the economics of psychiatric reprovision, including work on the costs of community support. Thus far, the research has concentrated on former in-patients who were in continuous residence for at least a year and, if over 65 years old, do not have a current diagnosis of dementia. This is, therefore, a cost-effectiveness study of different community care arrangements. (In this chapter we use the term *community* to refer to the situation 'not living permanently in hospital'. At the time of the follow-up interview conducted one year after discharge, some members of the sample had returned to hospital, but generally not permanently.)

By August 1989 a total of 355 people who met the study criteria had left the two hospitals, most under the reprovision arrangements which carried financial transfers. Baseline information for all patients meeting the study criteria were collected in hospital. Data ranged over a number of clinical dimensions, including mental health status, patient personal and historical data, patient attitudes, living skills, social networks and living environments. Altogether, including the 'new long-stay' patients who had accumulated in the two hospitals since the study began, TAPS has assembled baseline information on 964 in-patients. The TAPS research design compares aspects of the quality of life for patients discharged from Friern and Claybury Hospitals who have spent one year in the community with similar patients who remained in hospital. (See TAPS 1988, 1990, 1992 for more details on design, method and findings to date.) The present paper on cost variations does not, in fact, compare leavers with stayers in this way; rather, it is focused on the leavers who have not returned 'permanently' to hospital. We are interested here in the variation in community costs.

In costing psychiatric reprovision services we follow the four basic principles of costs research introduced in Chapter 5 (Knapp and Beecham, 1990). We attempted to cost every single service and every appropriate facet of living for the sample of hospital leavers, based on an interview with clients or carers one year after discharge. (A five-year follow-up study is now underway.) Capital as well as revenue costs are included. We use an instrument, the Client Service Receipt Interview (CSRI) developed by the PSSRU (see Beecham and Knapp, 1992) to gather retrospective information on services, service-related issues and income. The costing of client packages of support from the CSRI reflects service utilisation and living arrangements in the twelfth month after leaving hospital, although adjusting for regularly but infrequently-used services.

In this chapter we are concerned with a sample of 216 persons out of 278 who fulfilled the TAPS research criteria and who were discharged from the Friern and Claybury hospitals in a three-year period from September 1985 to August 1988. All were interviewed a year after discharge. Cohort 1 is made up of 40 of the 44 persons who left the hospital during the year ending August 1986; cohort 2, 94 of the 117 who left during the year ending August 1987; and cohort 3, 82 of the 117 who left between September 1987 and August 1988. Of the sample members, 120 were discharged from Friern and 96 from Claybury. Sixty-two people discharged from the two hospitals during the three years of the study were not included in the sample for a variety of reasons. Some had returned to hospital for too long a period to collect reliable community information (15); others refused to be interviewed (13), died (6), left the study (12), or were considered too dangerous to interview and later returned to hospital (4). Full cost information was not available for the remainder.

Half (49 per cent) of the subsample included in the analysis of cost variations were female, and 22 per cent were of non-white ethnic origin; 69 per cent had never married, and 23 per cent were divorced, separated or widowed. Their average age was 56. The average length of stay in hospital since the most recent admission (at the time of the hospital assessments, not at the time of discharge) was thirteen years, and sample members had spent another five years on average in previous hospital in-patient stays (mean number of previous in-patient admissions was 4.4). The primary diagnoses at first presentation to psychiatric services (coded as per the ICD-9; World Health Organization, 1978) were schizophrenia (72 per cent of the people included in the cost analyses which follow), affective disorder (11 per cent), neurosis and personality disorder (11 per cent) and organic disorder (7 per cent).

This group is not representative of the full hospital population of long-stay residents destined for eventual discharge to the community. For example, the people who had already left hospital had less severe psychiatric symptoms and exhibited fewer behaviourial problems (Jones, 1989), and the cost of supporting these future leavers in the community will be higher (Knapp et al., 1990, 1992b). These differences between sample and full population do not cause major problems here, for we are not extrapolating from these findings. We will use statistical results to suggest implications for policy and practice in the broader context.

2 Inexplicable variations?

Cost variations are the norm rather than the exception in community care. Interclient variation in costs is illustrated by the range of costs of maintaining people in the community from £75 per week to £708 (in 1986-87 prices). Table 1 reveals other variations. Former in-patients who left one of the hospitals in the first year of the reprovision programme were receiving packages of community care costing an average of £196, compared to an average of £375 for the third year cohort. For people living in facilities run by the district health authorities, costs were averaging £372 per week, compared to costs of £307 for local authority social services facilities, and £253 for residential settings provided by voluntary organisations.

What do these variations mean? Does the interpersonal cost variation reflect discrimination in the allocation of scarce services to people with mental health problems, or is it an indication of variation in need? If costs and needs are correlated, how tight is the linkage between them? Are those people who are getting more (and more costly) services achieving better outcomes in terms of improvements in their mental health? Are public-voluntary differences to

Table 1
Cost per week for psychiatric reprovision

| | Regression sample[1] | | |
| | Mean[2] | Std dev. | |
	£	£	N
Total sample	303	130	132
Gender			
Male	286	129	67
Female	319	130	65
Hospital of residence			
Friern	291	143	60
Claybury	313	118	72
Cohort year[3]			
First 1985-86	196	57	15
Second 1986-87	278	127	71
Third 1987-88	375	114	46
Managing agency for accommodation			
District health authority	372	132	55
Local authority social services department	307	104	25
Voluntary (non-profit) organisation	253	96	28
Private (for-profit) organisation	195	59	17
Other (mainly rented from local authority)	165	97	6
Accommodation type			
Residential or nursing home	405	111	52
Hostel	284	89	26
Sheltered housing	116	22	4
Staffed group home	229	56	17
Unstaffed group home	224	105	15
Foster care	247	52	8
Independent living	158	82	9

1 The sample of clients included in the cost function regressions reported later in this
  chapter. Some sample members were lost in analysis because of missing values.
2 All costs are expressed as weekly averages, pounds sterling, 1986-87 price levels.
3 Dates refer to discharge from hospital.

be interpreted as evidence of the oft-hypothesised bureaucratic inefficiency
of public authorities? Were those in-patients leaving hospital in the first cohort
less dependent than those in the third cohort, or were they simply dumped

in cheap, low-quality placements? These are baldly-posed questions, but they raise issues which have been rarely addressed in previous studies of psychiatric services.

3 A theoretical basis for exploring cost variations

Cost is just one of the many data elements needed for effective policy-making in the mental health area. It happens to look like a conveniently accessible element in so far as a natural unit for its measurement is readily available, but it is important to remember its context. In previous health and social care research we have found it helpful to employ a conceptual model – the production of welfare approach – as an organising framework within which to locate costs research (see, for example, Davies and Knapp, 1981; Knapp, 1984). The approach distinguishes between final outcomes (changes in client welfare, equivalent to reductions in need) and intermediate outcomes (services delivered, and their quality). In the context of psychiatric and social work practices, the distinction is being made between ends and means. Producing or providing outputs is made possible by employing staff and capital resources, and by fashioning or adapting to the social environments of facilities and agencies, and the personal characteristics and attitudes of key players. The production of welfare perspective is certainly not suggesting that the support of people with mental health problems is mechanistic, nor is it seeking to reduce the many and varied interrelationships between outcomes and inputs to simple summary formulae. The relevance of any one factor for client or other outcomes depends on a combination of factors, the sequence in which they appear or are experienced, and the marginality of the stimulus which they bring to the care setting. We have set out this production of welfare approach to the evaluation of mental health services in slightly more detail elsewhere (Beecham et al., 1991; Knapp and Beecham, 1992).

This approach provides the theoretical grounding for an examination of cost variations. A common approach by economists looking at the costs of producing or delivering goods and services is to estimate a statistical cost function. The cost function is the estimated relationship between the cost of providing a service, the outputs, the prices of resource inputs, and other factors such as the scale and rate of production, product mix, and the arrangements and organisation of care. Chapter 5 discusses the relevance of this tool in analysing social care. The arguments apply equally to the processes of delivering services to people with mental health problems.

The framework also suggests hypotheses for the source of cost variation. At the heart of any evaluation of efficiency or equity is the relationship between outcomes and inputs, or benefits and costs. As noted earlier, outcomes can be measured at two levels: *final outcomes* measure changes in the well-being of clients or patients relative to some control group or baseline, and *intermediate outcomes* are defined in terms of the services themselves – physical care, quantity or quality of accommodation, and so on. The latter are generally more readily obtained, but less informative. The key question is whether higher costs result in better outcomes. Closely associated is the potential effect on cost of client *needs*, their shortfall in health and welfare relative to what they, or their family, or their physician, or society deems to be appropriate. People with greater 'welfare shortfalls' generally need more treatment or support in order to improve, and it is reasonable to hypothesise that greater needs will be associated with higher costs.

The hypothesised determinants of costs are therefore:

- *input prices* – amounts that agencies and facilities pay for the resources they employ, especially staff;
- *outcomes* – changes in individual health and welfare, as well as the intermediate outcome indicators of quality provision;
- *occupancy and throughput* – measures of the 'rate' of service delivery, such as percentage of places occupied or duration of treatment episode;
- *client characteristics* – as well as needs and changes therein (outcomes), a variety of more fundamental or background characteristics may be of influence, such as gender, marital status, and previous mental health care;
- *location* – some areas of the country have higher costs than others;
- *sector of ownership* – public (local or health authority), voluntary or private; and
- *efficiency* – the productive efficiency with which resources are combined to serve people with mental health needs, and the managerial efficiency with which different combinations are used within a fixed budget.

4 Estimated cost functions

A number of differently-specified cost functions were fitted to data on comprehensive weekly cost, and for most of these hypothesised determinants. Altogether over 200 variables were examined. Multiple regression was used, and the results reported in this chapter emerged after approaching the explanation of cost variations from more than one starting perspective. (This implies a linear-in-parameters equation; some variables were also introduced in squared and reciprocal form to test for the presence of non-linearities.) Tests were conducted on several distinct blocks of variables to investigate the separate effects of outcomes, needs, psychiatric history, sector of ownership and residential facility location. At the first stage we included only demographic variables and measures of final outcomes. A quarter of the variation in costs (measured by the adjusted R^2 statistic) could be explained by five variables representing outcomes along several dimensions and three demographic indicators. The next stage was to add measures of need, and this increased the explanatory power to 34 per cent. Multicollinearity between variables meant that the pattern of statistical significance altered as new blocks of variables were tried.

The penultimate step was to add in the quasi-exogenous variables reflecting clients' psychiatric history, extending the proportion of cost variation explained to 50 per cent. Finally, we tested whether there were significant residual variations which could be attributed to either sector of ownership or community residential placement type. This was done by conducting analyses of variance and by attempting to add to the cost function sets of 'dummy' ('zero-one' or 'indicator') variables. These raise the explanatory power to 85 per cent or more, but also introduce problems of interpretation and attribution which we discuss below.

We report two equations in Table 2. The first, which excludes the dummy variables for sector and accommodation type, is statistically robust and parsimonious, and is the 'best' representation of the cost function in that included explanatory variables achieve statistical significance and enter the equation in ways that make sense (that is, we are sensitive to the need to avoid data mining and to produce understandable results). The second equation includes sector and accommodation type as potential explanatory variables.

5 Evidence and implications

In conducting this study of cost variations, we particularly focused on four composite questions. Is there an association between cost and client outcomes? Are client needs related to cost? Are public sector services more costly and/or less efficient than non-public services? What effect does place of community accommodation exert on cost?

5.1 Costs and outcomes

A thoroughly reasonable expectation about mental health services is that the costs of community care service packages respond to or are associated with differences in levels of need and changes in need, the latter being the principal final outcomes of the system. With the accumulation of experience on the needs and preferences of people with long-term mental health problems living outside hospital, the increasing emphasis on efficiency in the utilisation of public resources, and the growing tendency to coordinate services through care management and care programme procedures, there are good reasons for expecting strong associations between costs, client characteristics and outcomes (under the usual *ceteris paribus* conditions).

We measured client outcomes along a variety of dimensions, based on the information gathered by TAPS in hospital (usually before a patient's participation in a hospital-based rehabilitation programme, and certainly before

Table 2
Estimated cost functions

Description	Equation A Coeff.	Sig.[1]	Equation B Coeff.	Sig.[1]
Constant term	37.026		131.224	***
Client never married[2]	54.292	***	53.353	***
Length of stay in hospital (months)	0.211	***	0.118	**
Community skills	18.980	**		
Square of community skills	-1.363	***	-0.385	***
Activity and social relationships	8.592	***	7.822	***
Blunting of affect	59.142	***	53.409	***
Incontinent[2]	72.693	***	71.813	***
Impaired mobility[2]	83.673	**	74.149	**
Social network (patients), squared	1.369	***	1.161	***
Expressed desire to move	54.604	**	44.792	**
Absolute difference in negative symptoms	-22.289	***	-14.309	**
Relative difference in general anxiety, squared	14.040	***	12.261	***
Relative difference in delusions, hallucinations	-0.123	***	-0.083	*
Reduced need for care[2]	150.430	***	116.964	**
Absolute difference in non-professionals network	3.550	**	3.341	***
Relative difference in relatives network	-0.360	***	-0.278	**
Relative difference in patients network	-0.207	**		
Improved helpfulness of medication	72.741	**	70.205	**
Health authority (public sector) accommodation	—[3]		58.847	***
Voluntary or private sector accommodation	—[3]		-44.771	**
Sample size	132		132	
R^2	0.568	***	0.642	***
Adjusted R^2	0.499		0.585	

1 Significance levels from t-tests on individual coefficients are F test on goodness of fit (R^2): *** indicates $p \leq 0.01$; ** indicates $0.01 < p \leq 0.05$; * indicates $0.05 < p \leq 0.10$.
2 Dummy variable taking the value 1 if the condition is satisfied, 0 otherwise.
3 Variable not included in the set of possible regressors.

discharge) and also in the community approximately twelve months after the move. The main instruments relevant to need and outcome are described below.

- The *Present State Examination* (PSE, 9th edition, see Wing et al., 1974) was used to create a dozen subscores, including: general anxiety, specific anxiety syndrome, specific neurotic syndrome, non-specific neurotic syndrome, delusions and hallucinations, blunting of affect, and problems with behaviour, speech and other areas. From the PSE a negative symptoms score is computed (from 0 to 5) that indicates the presence of a number of symptoms: poverty of content of speech, blunting of affect, inattention, apathy, asociability.

- The *Social Behaviour Schedule* (SBS) of Sturt and Wykes (1986) allowed three measures to be calculated: total score, positive symptoms subscore, and anxiety subscore.
- The *Basic Everyday Living Skills* (BELS) schedule, developed by TAPS, gave four constituent measures for self-care, community skills, activity and social relationships, and domestic skills. The BELS was not completed in hospital for the early leavers from the two hospitals and so is not available for the creation of difference scores, although scores from the community assessments are associated with needs.
- The *Social Network Schedule* (SNS), developed by TAPS, provided information on the reported quantity and quality of social contacts such as with acquaintances, relatives, other patients/clients, non-professionals and staff named and seen by patients during a period of one month.
- The *Physical Health Index* (PHI), developed by TAPS, provided data on physical health problems (degree and disability) and levels of care received. One subscore is used to measure daily nursing care requirements. Five disabilities are considered to be of critical importance in the evaluation: incontinence, impaired mobility, dyskinesis, and impairment of vision or hearing. These are scored '1' if any level of disability is present.
- The *Patient Attitude Questionnaire* (PAQ), developed at TAPS, gave a record of patients' attitudes about living in hospital and in the community.

For each scale and subscale we take the difference between hospital and community assessment scores as the basic final outcome measure, either in absolute difference form or relative to the hospital score. For ordinal scales, differences are measured by direction of movement – improvement, no change, deterioration – and included in the regression analyses by creating corresponding sets of dummy variables. Scores at the time of the second (community) assessment are assumed to measure (absence of) need. Information on client background characteristics (gender, age, ethnic group, marital status, in-patient experience including length of stay, original diagnosis, and so on) were gathered using the Personal Data and Psychiatric History (PDPH) instrument developed by TAPS.

Concentrating for the moment on the first regression equation in Table 2, there is evidence that higher costs are associated with better outcomes. A higher score on the various component scales of the PSE indicates worse symptoms of mental illness, so that a negative difference (absolute or relative) between the community and hospital assessments indicates an improvement in health. The influences of the variables measuring changes in negative symptoms and delusions and hallucinations show that improvements are associated with higher costs: more costly community care packages have brought about reductions in symptoms. On the other hand, a third significant effect shows that higher costs are associated with greater anxiety levels. A general broadening of social networks is associated with greater cost. A reduction in the general need for care, assessed through the Physical Health Index and clients' own perceptions of the helpfulness of medications, support the general positive link between cost and outcomes.

When variables for the managing agencies are added to the series of regression equations, one of these outcome variables (for social network) drops out, but the effects of all others remain unaltered.

The overall conclusion that higher community care costs are linked with better outcomes is obviously encouraging at a time when long-stay hospital provision is being replaced with community care. (These findings are consistent with our earlier evaluation of a demonstration programme; see Knapp et al., 1992a.) The results suggest that spending more on community care will bring desirable improvements in clients' health and welfare. (Not all of the outcome dimensions for which we have measures exert an influence on cost, of course, and so this conclusion should be tempered.) It happens that, among the regional health authorities of England, North East Thames has been one of the more generous funders of community care for former long-stay hospital residents. The finding that costs and outcomes are related stems partly from the level and protection of the funding of community care. The funds transferred from hospital to community budgets (the so-called 'dowry' and general joint finance payments), supplemented with regional capital finances, help to ensure that enough resources are available, and that they get spent where intended.

5.2 Cost and needs

We are using the term 'need' in this paper to describe those psychosocial characteristics of individuals that psychiatric and associated services are expected to affect. If costs summarise, albeit imperfectly, the resources expended or services delivered to clients, how well are the services tailored to needs?

The estimated cost functions show that community care costs are clearly sensitive to a variety of client characteristics. Costs are higher for people displaying greater needs in relation to incontinence, mobility, blunted affect, attitude to accommodation, and community living skills (level of dependence in the use of public transport, amenities and budgeting). The effect of the last of these is interesting. Costs are lower for people at either end of the community living skills range: the most dependent and most independent receive less support in the community than others. People who spend more years in hospital before discharge and those who are single require more support services in the community. Low scores on the variables measuring non-participation or withdrawal imply a reduced demand for resource inputs and hence lower cost. Clients who do not live in congregate care settings tend to have few contacts with other clients or patients, and the costs of the community services received by these people are, as expected, lower.

Another positive finding from this examination of cost variations, therefore, is that community care services appear to be responding to the needs of clients. By no means is every facet of need represented in the equation, suggesting that some characteristics do not work through to higher costs. (This could be because they are not recognised as needs, are not within the purview of any agency currently working with these clients, can be met at no noticeable extra cost, or are highly correlated with one or more of the need variables already in the equation. Which of these conditions applies cannot be adduced with the present cost function.)

5.3 Costs and intersectoral differences

One of the central thrusts of the health and social care changes in train in Britain is the promotion of a mixed economy of care (Wistow et al., 1992). Public sector agencies are examining the comparative merits of the different sectors more carefully than before. Among the key questions is whether voluntary and private agencies are more efficient than public agencies. From previous research, if not also from political rhetoric, there are reasons for hypothesising a cost advantage accruing to the non-public sectors: lower management overheads, a greater supply of volunteer staff, subsidisation of fees from charitable income, the ethos of the small business enterprise, and so on.

The services used by people with long-term mental health problems are supplied by many different agencies and sectors, making it difficult to say just where in the mixed economy a client is located. However, many of the people in the present psychiatric reprovision sample have a combination of dependency characteristics and lack informal or familial support, and so the majority live in some form of specialist facility. Accommodation accounts for 80 per cent of total cost. We can therefore usefully examine the impact of ownership of accommodation on cost as a test of the intersectoral cost difference, and the type of accommodation as a limited test of the effect of placement type.

From Table 1 we see that the observed costs for the different sectors support the hypothesis of an intersectoral difference, but these simple cost measures do not take into account the likelihood that clients are not identical across sectors. It is likely – and confirmed by evidence from this study – that people with more severe symptoms of mental illness or greater dependencies in activities of daily living will be accommodated in facilities run by district health authorities. There is a need to standardise the observed costs for differences in client characteristics, and the estimated cost function (equation A in Table 2) is the ideal means for this standardisation. The *residual cost* – the cost not explained statistically by the estimated function – was calculated for each client, and analyses of variance were conducted. The results are given in Table 3, and these in turn led to our inclusion of sectoral dummy variables in a re-estimated series of cost functions. (Equation B in Table 2 is the final one of these cost functions.) Clearly there are cost differences among the sectors, even after standardising for differences in the needs and background characteristics of clients. In fact, we have also standardised for the outcomes achieved, so that the analysis of variance indicates something approaching an intersectoral efficiency difference. The findings suggest that voluntary and private sector facilities are delivering services more cost-effectively than local authority social services departments, which in turn are more cost-effective in service delivery than district health authorities. There is no significant difference between the voluntary and private sectors. Of course, some part of these differences may reflect the influences of client characteristics (needs or outcomes) that have not been adequately measured in the research, despite the battery of indicators employed, and which are systematically associated with sector.

5.4 Costs and type of community residence

As well as indicating intersectoral differences in residual cost, the analysis of variance points to significant differences between accommodation types and yearly cohorts of leavers. These differences are interrelated because the different sectors have specialised to some degree by providing different accommodation types, and later cohorts of leavers were more likely to move into newly-built or converted placements, most of which were commissioned by district health authorities. Ignoring these interactions for the moment, Table 3 shows that, relative to client needs and outcomes, residential homes, nursing homes and hostels (all highly staffed) are more costly than predicted by the cost function, and other facility types less costly.

6 Conclusions

This study has found encouragingly strong positive associations among costs, needs and outcomes. It has also uncovered significant cost-effectiveness differences between the public and non-public sectors and among community accommodation types, although we emphasise that these results should only be the *start* of any discussion of intersectoral and placement effects. The cost function is an insufficiently sensitive tool to explain such differences to the satisfaction of policy makers: it is an excellent tool for sifting through a mass

Table 3

Analysis of residuals from cost function by sector and accommodation type

Sector and accommodation	Total cost (£)		Residual cost (£)	
	Mean	Difference	Mean	N
Managing agency for accommodation				
District health authority	372	+70	+36	55
Local authority social services department	307	+5	+9	25
Voluntary (non-profit) organisation	253	-50	-37	28
Private (for-profit) organisation	195	-108	-66	17
Other (mainly rented from local authority)	165	-137	-9	6
Accommodation type				
Residential or nursing home	405	+103	+47	52
Hostel	284	-19	+18	26
Sheltered housing	116	-187	-97	4
Staffed group home	229	-74	-62	17
Unstaffed group home	224	-79	-63	15
Foster care	247	-55	-41	8
Independent living	158	-145	-20	9
Cohort				
1	196	-106	-51	15
2	278	-24	-1	71
3	375	+72	+19	46
Overall or total	303	0	0	131

Analysis of variance of residuals

Difference between managing agencies (sector)	$F = 7.57$ ***
Difference between accommodation types	$F = 9.64$ ***
Difference between cohort of discharge	$F = 3.94$ **

Two-way analysis of variance: Difference between managing agencies and accommodation types

Main effect – managing agencies	$F = 3.67$ ***
Main effect – accommodation types	$F = 6.87$ ***
Two-way interactions	$F = 2.58$ **

Significance levels: *** indicates $p \leq 0.01$; ** indicates $0.01 < p \leq 0.05$; * indicates $0.05 < p \leq 0.10$.

of evidence and for testing a wide variety of hypotheses about community care provision, but it also needs to be supplemented by other methods for its full relevance to be realised.

These empirical findings have been set within a theoretical framework that both validates the cost function approach and points to its limitations. The signal advantage of that framework is that it helps to move the examination of costs and cost-effectiveness away from sole reliance on averages generated by simple experimental and quasi-experimental designs. For many purposes there is nothing wrong with either those averages or the designs behind them. But they waste a great deal of information: they tell us little about the differences in the circumstances, needs, outcomes and costs of individuals; and they say nothing about the way these are interconnected. Surely this information is fundamental to the delivery of good quality mental health services and the practice of psychiatry.

Note

* This study was funded by North East Thames Regional Health Authority and the Department of Health. We thank the Team for the Assessment of Psychiatric Services, directed by Professor Julian Leff, for allowing us to construct some of the evidence reported in this chapter on their data collections and for their general encouragement and support. This chapter is a shortened version of a paper presented at the First Workshop on the Cost of Schizophrenia, Venice, 29-31 October 1990, and subsequently published in *Schizophrenia Bulletin*, 17, 3, pp.427-439, 1991.

References

Beecham, J.K. and Knapp, M.R.J. (1992) Costing psychiatric options, in G. Thornicroft, C. Brewin and J. Wing (eds) *Measuring Mental Health Needs*, Oxford University Press, Oxford.

Beecham, J.K., Knapp, M.R.J. and Fenyo, A. (1991) Costs, needs and outcomes, *Schizophrenia Bulletin*, 17, 3, 427-439.

Davies, B.P. and Knapp, M.R.J. (1981) *Old People's Homes and the Production of Welfare*, Routledge and Kegan Paul, London.

Jones, D. (1989) The selection of patients for reprovision, in Team for Assessment of Psychiatric Services (eds) *Moving Long-Stay Patients into the Community: First Results*, North East Thames Regional Health Authority, London.

Knapp, M.R.J. (1984) *The Economics of Social Care*, Macmillan, London.

Knapp, M.R.J. and Beecham, J.K. (1990) Costing mental health services, *Psychological Medicine*, 20, 893-908.

Knapp, M.R.J. and Beecham, J.K. (1992) Health economics and psychiatry: the pursuit of efficiency, in J. Leff and D. Bhugra (eds) *Principles of Social Psychiatry*, Blackwell Scientific Publications, Oxford.

Knapp, M.R.J., Beecham, J.K., Anderson, J. Dayson, D., Leff, J., Margolius, O., O'Driscoll, C. and Wills, W. (1990) Predicting the community costs of closing psychiatric hospitals, *British Journal of Psychiatry*, 157, 661-670.

Knapp, M.R.J., Cambridge, P., Thomason, C., Beecham, J.K., Allen, C. and Darton, R.A. (1992a) *Care in the Community: Challenge and Demonstration*, Ashgate, Aldershot.

Knapp, M.R.J., Beecham, J.K. and Gordon, K. (1992b) Predicting the community costs of closing psychiatric hospitals: national extrapolations, Discussion Paper 801, Personal Social Services Research Unit, University of Kent at Canterbury.

Sturt, E. and Wykes, T. (1986) Assessment schedules for chronic psychiatric patients, *Psychological Medicine*, 17, 485-493.

Team for the Assessment of Psychiatric Services (1988) *Preliminary Report of Baseline Data from Friern and Claybury Hospitals*, North East Thames Regional Health Authority, London.

Team for the Assessment of Psychiatric Services (1990) *Better Out Than In?*, North East Thames Regional Health Authority, London.

Team for the Assessment of Psychiatric Services (1992) The TAPS project: evaluation of community placement of long-stay psychiatric patients, *British Journal of Psychiatry*, supplement, forthcoming.

Wing, J.K., Cooper, J. and Satorius, N. (1974) *The Measurement and Classification of Psychiatric Symptoms*, Cambridge University Press, Cambridge.

Wistow, G., Knapp, M.R.J., Hardy, B. and Allen, C. (1992) *Social Care in a Mixed Economy*, Open University Press, Milton Keynes.

World Health Organization (1978) *Mental Disorders: Glossary and Guide to their Classification in Accordance with the Ninth Revision of the International Classification of Diseases*, World Health Organization, Geneva.

12 Intermediate Treatment: User Characteristics and the Prediction of Costs*

Martin Knapp, Paul McCrone, Catherine Drury and Eriko Gould

In so far as any complex piece of legislation can be reduced to slogan summaries, the Government's present criminal justice philosophy and policy is 'punishment in the community', an approach principally rationalised by the expectation that it will achieve more appropriate and effective sentencing. But it is also explicitly acknowledged that a reduction in the 'burden on the taxpayer' would be desirable (Cm 965, para. 9.3). One aim of government policy, therefore, has been to continue the search for community-based alternatives to custody which are simultaneously more effective and less costly than prison. Another is to raise awareness of the outcome and cost implications of decisions made at each stage of the criminal justice process.

These aims were clear in the 1990 White Paper, *Crime, Justice and Protecting the Public*, which proposed legislation which would

place a new duty on the Secretary of State to inform the courts annually of the costs of implementing penalties and to publish information about the costs of the criminal justice system for the attention of those who take decisions in the system (Cm 965, para. 2.21).

The White Paper rightly expressed concern about both the costs of criminal justice – it was estimated that expected total annual expenditure on criminal justice services would be £7 billion in 1990, an increase of 77 per cent in real terms since 1980 – and the social costs of crime.

Gathering evidence on the outcome and cost implications of criminal justice system decisions is far from straightforward, particularly for those alternatives to custody which are provided by a number of different agencies working in concert. Yet it is precisely in these complex circumstances that the need for such information is pressing, for there are dangers of perverse incentives and cost-shunting, leading in turn to inappropriate sentencing (Robertson and Knapp, 1988). For young offenders – who are very likely to be in contact with social services departments as well as the police or the courts, and whose education, employment, accommodation, family ties and social life could all be influenced by both their offending and any action which is taken as a result – the challenge of gathering the information is considerable.

With the exception of two small exercises by the PSSRU (Knapp, 1984; Robertson et al., 1986), work has not yet been published which addresses this research challenge for young offenders. In this chapter, however, we report for the first time the results of a study of *intermediate treatment* in four local authority areas (chosen so as to be representative in England in terms of services for young offenders and certain other aspects). This PSSRU study of the costs and cost-effectiveness of intermediate treatment (IT) was conducted in parallel with (and within the design developed for) research by the Institute of Criminology, University of Cambridge. The two studies followed a sample of young people, sentenced to intermediate treatment, through their sentences and for a twelve month follow-on period. The sentencing process, delivery of intermediate treatment, outcomes and costs were examined. The research also included comparisons of the IT sample with two other samples of young people: one sentenced to custody and the other to supervision orders without intermediate treatment requirements.

In this chapter we concentrate on the intermediate treatment sample. The chapter has three aims:
- to describe the costs of intermediate treatment for individual young people, both during the period of sentence and in the follow-on period;
- to endeavour to explain why these costs vary between individuals, by reference to the characteristics of young offenders at the point at which they come before the courts; and
- to discuss the possible implications of these cost predictions for decision-makers.

These three aims are addressed in turn in sections 3 to 5 below. First, we describe our research method.

1 Principles and methods

The research project on which we base the cost findings was funded by the Department of Health. Five questions were posed by the Department. What are the costs of intermediate treatment? How do these costs compare with alternative sentencing options? Is there a relationship between costs and outcomes? Is intermediate treatment a cost-effective policy option? What policy recommendations or comments emerge from this research? As will have become clear from earlier chapters, these straightforward questions can be difficult to answer. All young people sentenced by the courts in four local authority areas over the research period were identified as potential members of the research samples if their sentences were IT, a supervision order without IT or custody, and if they and their parents consented to the research. In the event, girls were excluded from the study because their numbers were too small. Sample members were included in the study from the point of sentence, when data were collected from the young person, parents and staff. A longitudinal design was adopted which saw a second set of interviews at the end of what we shall refer to as the *intensive period* (generally, this is the end of sentence; see below for full explanation) and a third set of interviews twelve months later. Additional data were collected from other sources, including IT units of provision, the Criminal Records Office, local authority and other service providers.

Given our focus on costs, we sought detailed information on service utilisation over the research period, and conducted interviews with 'principal information holders' (usually the caseholder or the principal IT officer). As with other costs research in the PSSRU, we were guided by the four basic principles set out in Chapter 5 above.

- We sought to define costs comprehensively to include all resource impacts of the policies, practices or decisions under study, wherever they fell. This meant that we needed to adopt consistently comprehensive cost definitions for the three sentencing options.
- The second costing principle follows from the realisation that costs are not identical for every young person, even if the sentence handed down by the court is apparently the same. Some cost differences will be attributable to individual circumstances and offences at the point of sentence – and these we explore below – and some differences will stem from each young person's experiences as they progress through their sentences. In so far as the data allow, we should recognise and explore the reasons for cost variations.
- The immediate corollary and third principle of costing is to make like-with-like comparisons. Interpersonal differences in costs can be expected to be systematically associated with the alternative routes taken by young people after they have been sentenced. The sentencing decision is certainly not random, so adjustments will be needed before costs can be compared between the three study samples.
- The final costing rule requires that cost results should be set alongside or integrated with evidence on outcomes.

All four principles were followed in our study, although in this chapter we report findings which do not illustrate the third and fourth of them.[2] In section 3 we describe the results of applying the first principle – calculating comprehensive costs – and in section 4 we explore cost variations.

We distinguish three time periods. The *intensive period* is the effective sentence: for IT sample members this is the duration of the supervision order over which intermediate treatment is actually received; for members of the custody sample it is the actual time spent in custody (generally shorter than the sentence because of remission for most people); and for members of the supervision order sample, for which there is no distinct phasing, we assumed a four-month intensive period. The *follow-on* period is defined as twelve months after the end of the intensive period for each sample member (a period in which some young people received further sentences for other offences). We use the term *full period* to denote the combined intensive and follow-on periods. For information, the intensive period lasted three months or less for 29 per cent of the IT sample, between three and four months for 39 per cent, and in excess of six months for only one person. We can express costs as the total over each of the periods (we call these the *episode costs*) or as weekly costs.

The study design produced three reasonably-sized samples of people for whom we were able to collect fairly comprehensive cost and other data: 140 young people with an IT sentence, 136 sentenced to custody, and 154 given a supervision order without an IT requirement.

2 The costs of intermediate treatment

In most evaluations of social or public policy, three broad types of cost will be encountered: direct, indirect and non-economic. For the young people receiving intermediate treatment, the *direct costs* would be the IT itself, as recorded in the annual accounts of local authorities, voluntary bodies and other provider agencies, covering all staff and other resources employed in an IT centre or other unit of provision. The *indirect costs* are the necessary complements to IT from other parts of the host agency as well as the inputs from other agencies, such as the costs of field social worker or probation officer time, the amounts spent on residential accommodation, and the involvement of education department staff. These indirect costs may be hidden because they are not immediately identifiable. Nevertheless they are measurable; examples would be the costs associated with volunteers, buildings and other capital costs, and the support of various central functions such as local authority management and clerical services. Finally, there are probably some *non-economic costs*, which are simply impossible to express in monetary terms: stress experienced by families keeping a difficult child at home, for example.

Earlier, we cited the four costing principles which guided this work. In order to abide by the comprehensiveness principle it was clearly necessary to attempt to include all of the measurable costs; and in order to be able to examine possible cost variations it was important to gather data on service use by individual young people. Our interviews with caseholders and others gave us detailed, disaggregated information on service use, to which we were able to attach figures based as far as possible on long-run marginal opportunity costs (see Chapter 3). However, a major component in the package of support for young people in the intermediate treatment sample was IT itself, and two problems arose: first, no two IT units of provision (UOPs) could be assumed to be the same, so that costs would need to be UOP-specific if they were to be accurate; and, second, different young people using the same UOP would be quite likely to receive very different combinations of the component services on offer, so that a single average cost for a UOP would ignore inter-individual variations. The wide inter-UOP variety in relation to scale, scope, objectives, activities, staffing and budget-inclusiveness make it dangerous to rely on a simple overall average cost (say the total UOP spending in the year divided by the number of users during the year).

2.1 Units of provision

The costing of IT was based on the following information for each UOP:
- descriptions of the aims of each UOP, its broad activities (variety, scale, uptake) and sources of funding;
- information on the actual intermediate treatment work of the UOP, covering its core and other activities, such as court work, assessment, group work, one-to-one work and aftercare support;
- estimates or actual figures for the number of young people undertaking each of these activities during the year;
- financial accounts for the UOP for the relevant financial year, with costs reorganised (by us) into a common framework; and
- some additional data from the organisation operating the UOP (such as the local authority) if it was necessary to gain better estimates of staff, capital or overhead costs.

From our other interviews we already knew which of the component intermediate treatment activities on offer within a UOP were being used by each of the people in our sample. In this way, therefore, we were trying to attach precise costs based on actual service use by each young person. This was far from straightforward, for we were endeavouring to get beneath the highly-aggregated financial accounts kept for UOPs and beyond the oversimplified label of 'an IT client', something akin to picking one's way through a sponge cake to separate the flour, sugar and eggs which have got mixed up in the baking. However, this unmixing or disaggregation of the costs of intermediate treatment produced costs which were markedly superior to simple averages. Moreover, for many of the UOPs encountered in this study, there was no other way to attach a cost to the IT itself.

The component costs revealed wide variations between the 37 UOPs covered by this study, giving a measure of differences in intensity of work and service orientation. The tabulated figures describe summary findings from this disaggregation exercise, distinguishing both broad areas of work and specific IT activities (Table 1). Although generally distinct, in some instances there were definitional problems because of blurred boundaries between activities. The most common area of work was referrals (25 of the

Table 1

Cost per client for the activities of intermediate treatment units

Activity	No. of UOPs offering this service	Cost per user (£ 1988/89 prices)			
		Mean	Std dev	Max.	Min.
General prevention	13	560	1142	4435	30
Pre-court work	10	353	258	887	29
Court work	11	346	440	1683	61
Referrals	25	132	238	1213	6
Assessment	16	112	89	343	3
After care					
IT activities					
Offending curriculum	1	445	0	445	445
Home link	2	442	111	553	331
Reparation	2	601	482	1082	119
Befriending	1	48	0	48	48
Personal development	1	48	0	48	48
One-to-one work	13	531	524	2150	74
Group work	9	672	621	2218	52
Activities/leisure	4	650	665	1774	48
Residentials	6	403	237	763	174
Outings	3	144	57	222	88
Above combined[1]	13	786	752	2640	23

1 Not possible to distinguish component activities

37 UOPs operating in this sphere), with cost per referral averaging £132 (at 1988/89 prices), but also showing considerable variation around the mean. One-to-one work was the most commonly-identified individual IT activity, though it should be pointed out that for 13 of the 37 UOPs it was not possible for our interviewees to disaggregate activities or users. The cost of one-to-one work per user averaged £531 across the sample, again with marked variations. All of these UOP costs include capital elements, calculated in the conventional way within applied economics research (see Chapter 3).

One young person in the IT sample did not actually receive any IT, despite the requirement imposed by the juvenile court.

2.2 Indirect costs

Over 60 different services were used by members of the IT sample during the intensive or follow-on periods. These were provided and funded by a number of statutory and non-statutory agencies. For the purposes of exposition we have grouped them by broad service area, and we present summary findings for the intensive, follow-on and full periods in Tables 2, 3 and 4, respectively. The custody cost category was not relevant during the intensive period – by definition no IT client could also be in custody in this period – but was relevant in the follow-on period. The 'family expenses' cost in the tables measures expenditure by each IT user's family (when relevant). Although labelled as costs, these often represent (marginal) savings if young

Table 2
Weekly intensive period costs of intermediate treatments

Service group components	IT sample using the service (%)	Mean weekly cost for full sample (£)
IT itself[1]	99.3	132.58
Residential care, foster care	20.7	61.43
Field social work[2]	55.0	6.96
Day care/activity[3]	17.1	3.75
Education[4]	37.9	4.42
Psychology[5]	27.1	1.14
Work/social security[6]	43.6	4.79
Housing	8.6	0.62
Probation[7]	54.3	4.38
Health care[8]	17.1	13.01
Courts	0.0	0.00
Police, solicitor	25.7	14.69
Custody	2.9	2.88
Volunteers[9]	9.3	1.56
Family expenses	21.4	-3.71
Principal information holder	82.1	4.56
Total IT cost (intensive period)	100.0	£253.06

1 Includes IT (all providing agencies and UOPs), IT juvenile group, link worker, IT officer, IT team leader, IT worker
2 Social worker, child resources panel, family support, family therapist, CIT specialist, principal child care officer, field social work team leader, fostering and adoption officer, legal department SSD, field social worker, NACRO, juvenile liaison officer, social services abuse officer.
3 Social service day centre; probation day centre, training day centre, family centre, youth club, YTS, attendance centre, angling
4 Home tutor, adult literacy, divisional education officer, teacher, head teacher, other educational personnel, year tutor
5 Educational psychologist; EWO, clinical psychologist, senior EWO
6 Careers advice, Job Centre, social security, employment office staff
7 Probation supervisor, senior probation officer, probation assistant, probation student. Excludes probation day centres, probation-run training centres, and probation-run IT UOPs, all of which are included in other categories.
8 GP, hospital, drug therapy, medical day centre, psychiatric consultation, speech therapy, occupational therapy, psychodynamic work, health visitor, hospital inpatient
9 Volunteer inputs are separately costed even if they were provided through one of the other services, such as an IT UOP.

Table 3
Weekly follow-on period costs of intermediate treatment

Service group components	IT sample using the service (%)	Mean weekly cost for full sample (£)
IT itself	0.7	0.04
Residential care, foster care	7.1	8.65
Field social work	0.0	0.00
Day care/activity	2.9	0.34
Education	5.0	0.38
Psychology	0.0	0.00
Work/social security	23.6	0.90
Housing	8.6	0.30
Probation	0.0	0.00
Health care	8.6	0.38
Courts	0.0	0.00
Police, solicitor	0.0	0.00
Custody	1.4	0.91
Volunteers	0.0	0.00
Family expenses	8.6	-0.58
Principal information holder	77.0	7.77
Total IT cost (follow-on period)	82.0	£11.32

1 For service group definitions see Table 2.

people were in residential or foster placements, which accounts for the negative costs in the tables. These family costs/savings were based on *Family Expenditure Survey* data. The principal information holder was generally the caseholder, and the costs of their time are included only if they are not already covered elsewhere.

2.3 The overall costs of IT

It is unnecessary to comment at length on the details reported in Tables 2 to 4 or the summary costs in Table 5, but some key findings need to be emphasised. First and foremost is the large number of agencies, departments and services involved in supporting young people receiving IT. In other words, an IT sentence by the court does not simply impose a cost on the local authority IT unit or service, but has implications for many other budgets. During the intensive period and across the full sample of 140 people, the cost falling to the IT service itself averaged £133 per week (at 1988/89 price levels, as are all figures reported in this chapter), which represents only 52 per cent

Table 4
Weekly full period costs of intermediate treatment

Service group components	IT sample using the service %	Mean weekly cost for full sample £
IT itself	99.0	132.62
Residential care, foster care	23.6	70.08
Field social work	56.0	6.98
Day care/activity	19.3	4.08
Education	40.7	4.80
Psychology	27.1	1.14
Work/social security	53.6	5.69
Housing	15.0	0.93
Probation	55.0	4.40
Health care	20.0	13.39
Courts	1.4	0.05
Police, solicitor	26.4	14.70
Custody	2.9	3.78
Volunteers	9.3	1.56
Family expenses	21.4	-4.29
Principal information holder	96.0	12.33
Total IT cost (intensive period)	100.0	272.24

1 For service group definitions see Table 2.

of the overall cost of £253. Residential and foster care placements account for 24 per cent of overall cost, and the police and the NHS each account for over 5 per cent. Only four service groups were utilised by less than 10 per cent of the sample.

A related finding concerns the follow-on period. Eighteen per cent of people did not receive any services during this period. Although costs in the follow-on period were considerably lower than in the intensive period, they can remain high for some people and some services. Again, cognisance should be taken of the *full* cost ramifications of sentencing decisions. When the intensive and follow-on periods are combined (to produce what we call the full period), we see that IT accounts for only 49 per cent of the total (Table 4).

Overall, we estimate from this study that an IT sentence can be expected to cost over £4,000 (at 1988/89 prices) during the intensive period when the IT required by the court is actually being undertaken, and almost £1,000 in the year which follows.

The variations around these averages are considerable. This can be seen from the standard deviations in Table 5, and is also illustrated by inter-area differences. For example, a full IT package (full period) costs as much as

Table 5
Summary costs of intermediate treatment

		Time period	
	Intensive £	Follow-on £	Full £
Weekly costs			
Mean	253	19	272
Standard deviation	168	48	180
Period costs			
Mean	4062	992	5065
Standard deviation	2920	2477	4050

All costs expressed in £, 1988/89 prices.

£8,907 in one area, compared to £3,296 in another. Area average *weekly* costs (full period) ranged from £388 to £228. One of the questions raised by these variations concerns their predictability. In particular, can the costs of IT be predicted with any accuracy at the point of sentence?

3 Predicting cost variations

3.1 Influences on cost

Intermediate treatment is a community-based service for young offenders offered to the courts as a sentencing option. The objectives, orientation and component activities of any one IT unit or service will be influenced by a number of parties, including the agency which established it in the first place, the agency now running it (if different), the bodies which provide the funding, individual staff, the users, and – directly or indirectly – the juvenile courts. IT services developed rapidly across the country, and so it was inevitable that these various local influences should have been important in shaping what is now a very varied service (Bottoms et al., 1990). Moreover, the non-IT service components of IT will also be dependent on what is available or deemed appropriate locally. These are all supply-side determinants of the service packages which young people receive, and we would therefore expect to find inter-individual and inter-area differences in service use.

There will also probably be demand or need factors influencing service use and therefore cost. It is reasonable to expect of a well-established public service that the service packages offered to members of the population would be responsive to individual needs, and tailored (to a degree) to individual wants. Of course, we know that some social care decision-making has tended to be dominated as much by service availability as need, but the characteristics of the young people given IT, and the characteristics of their families, can be hypothesised to be associated with service use and cost. The most fundamental demand factor, perhaps, will be the offences with which a young person is charged, for – given a choice the court will be likely to choose a longer and/or more intensive sentence for more serious offenders/offences. We should not be too sanguine about the strength or consistency of the links between offences and sentences. As Curtis writes:

> The juvenile justice system has often been compared to a lottery, with the disposal received for an offence differing according to the locality, the temper of the region, or the facilities and services available to the Bench (1989, p.1).

In order to understand and to 'explain' the cost variations revealed in this study, we need to examine these and other hypothesised influences. We do not attempt to try to link costs for individual people to the historical development of the IT services used, or to the characteristics of local authorities and other key agencies, for the collection of the necessary data for such an exercise was some considerable distance outside the remit for the present study. Moreover, these links could well be too tenuous to show up in empirical analyses conducted at the individual level,[3] and we therefore restrict our attention to simple indicator (dummy) variables for the four local authority areas as possible cost correlates.

Our primary concern is the set of characteristics of young people, their families, living circumstances and so on *at the time they come before the courts.* Other potential cost-raising factors would enter the play *after* sentencing; good examples would be key features of the IT programmes on which these young people embark, and post-sentence offending, accommodation, employment and education. In this chapter we are concerned only with the links between the costs of the IT intensive periods and the pre-sentence factors. For this purpose, we examine the data collected by the University of Cambridge team using their Initial Assessment Schedule (IAS). The IAS collected information relating only to the period up to the point of sentence, and covered age, ethnic group, family life, education and/or employment, offending history, accommodation type and arrangements, and relations with parents.

A number of measures or indicators were constructed from the IAS. Some of the characteristics of young people readily lend themselves to quantitative measurement, such as age, number of offences with which charged and (where applicable) the value of property stolen and/or damaged. Other characteristics needed to be converted into indicator or dummy variables which take the value 1 if a young person has a particular characteristic, and the value 0 otherwise. Examples of indicator variables used in this study relate to the place and nature of accommodation, and a young person's relations with their family. Altogether, more than 90 variables were constructed for use in the examination of cost variations.

3.2 Multivariate analyses

We pursued four separate series of analyses: two series take total *episode cost* (over the entire intensive period) as the dependent variable, and the other two take average weekly cost within the intensive period as dependent variable. Within each pair, one series admitted to the analysis *all* possible variables related to the characteristics of the young people and families at the point of sentence, while the other series included only variables defining the characteristics of the young people themselves, and the people with whom they lived (including their criminal records). In fact, in these latter analyses only IT user characteristics remained in the final equations as statistically significant. The latter analyses thus excluded indicators of the nature and quality of relations between young people and families which were based on more subjective responses. We believe these more subjective indicators to be relevant to the explanation of cost differences, although their links with cost may be rather less direct.[4]

For each series we used ordinary least squares multiple regression analysis to explore the simultaneous influences of the hypothesised cost-raising factors, retaining variables in the series (or re-admitting them again later) if they achieved statistical significance and if their impacts on cost made sense.[5] We also wanted the cost equation to be parsimonious without losing predictive power. Multivariate rather than bivariate analyses are needed in order to investigate the influences of different factors simultaneously, so avoiding spurious attribution of causality, and thus also teasing out the individual effects of these factors with the influences of other factors held constant.

The end-stage outcomes of what proved to be four long series of analyses are summarised in Table 6, the first analyses excluding the less objectively measured factors. We will discuss the influences of different groups of factors below. We should first point out that the overall statistical performance of the regression analyses is good. The estimates were robust, in the sense that the removal or addition of one or two variables did not throw the equations into chaos; and the R-square statistics, which measure the proportion of variance in the dependent variable 'attributable to' the included explanatory variables, range from 0.48 to 0.59. As a statistical attribute, a high R-square value is desirable; from a social work or criminal justice practice perspective this may be less so, for it indicates that more than half the observed inter-user variation in service use (cost) can be explained by reference to characteristics *before* the service intervention. Given that there will always be some cost variation which cannot be explained (some of it due to measurement error, for example), this level of pre-sentence explanation leaves less scope for links between costs and outcomes over the intensive and follow-on periods.

To avoid cluttering the tables, we have not included the results of the t-tests of the significance of the individual estimated coefficients in Table 6. Every one of the coefficients in Table 6 is significant at the 90 per cent level,

Table 6
Cost prediction equations, episode and weekly costs

	Episode cost		Weekly cost	
	Series A	Series B	Series C	Series D
Constant term	3503	1687	202.47	72.63
Offences				
No. of charges of arson	2892			
No. of charges of threatening behaviour	1942	2363	100.85	135.98
No. of charges of sexual offences	3189	3629	163.40	176.34
No. of charges of driving offences		−2059		
Value of property stolen/damaged (in £000)		29	2.31	2.89
Background characteristics				
Ethnic group: white British or European			49.15*	
Individual has some (non-trivial) physical illness	1003	994	55.06*	82.50
Individual has attended special school			213.49	55.17*
Individual not in full time education or expelled			61.18	
Pre-sentence accommodation				
Lived alone			−214.44	
Lived in hostel/B&B/local authority accom.	2225	2372	163.57	182.75
Individual lives with friends or girlfriend				−172.20*
Lived in special educational residential estab.		3967		233.00
Area				
Lived in local authority 2			−66.50	
Lived in local authority 3				75.41
Lived in local authority 4	2173	1974		
Relations with parents				
Father hostile or rejective towards individual	exc		exc	127.20
Father has mixed emotions towards individual	exc	1116	exc	76.10
Individual hostile towards mother	exc		exc	194.85
Individual ambivalent towards father	exc	−1820	exc	−88.85*
Two-parent family still together	exc	−769*	exc	−47.24*
Cohabitees and friends				
Cohabitees have no criminal record	exc	888	exc	66.28
Cohabitees have definite criminal record	exc	938*	exc	91.60
Individual mixes mainly with non-delinquents	exc	2433	exc	
R^2	0.51	0.59	0.48	0.54
F-test statistic	18.65	12.45	11.56	8.43

* Coefficients significant at 90% level. All other variables significant at 95% level.
exc = variable excluded *a priori*
Sample size = 133 for all four equations

and most are significant at the 95 per cent level. Only those variables marked with an asterisk in Table 6 attained 90 per cent but not 95 per cent significance.

It can be seen that a range of factors proved to be significantly associated with the costs of the comprehensive IT 'packages' used by members of the sample. We will not discuss the results in great detail here, but instead pick out key findings. We concentrate on the two series of estimates which do not admit the more subjective, less direct factors (series A and C in Table 6). The influences of these other variables (in series B and D) are worthy of consideration for their general and collective influence, but we do not discuss them here.

Offences The length and intensity of an IT sentence are both linked to the offences with which an individual is charged, and it is the more serious offence groups which prove to be quantitatively the more important. The estimated coefficients in the cost equations indicate the *addition* to cost associated with the number of offences *over and above* the costs for people charged with other, including unlisted, offences. (The full list of charges for this sample is given in Table 7.) Clearly, sexual offences and threatening behaviour contribute markedly to the weekly cost of IT, through their influences on the intensity of the IT which is chosen by the juvenile court. These young people are receiving 'heavy end' IT as an alternative to custody. An arson offence pushes up the period cost, but not the weekly cost. Less serious offences,

Table 7
Percentages of clients charged with specific offences

Offence	0	No. of times charged 1	2	3	4
Violence against person	89.4	9.2	1.4	0.0	0.0
Sexual offences	96.5	3.5	0.0	0.0	0.0
Burglary/burglary and theft/attempted burglary/burglary with intent	35.9	38.7	19.0	4.2	2.1
Robbery	99.3	0.7	0.0	0.0	0.0
Theft and handling/shoplifting/handling and receiving	47.2	33.8	14.1	4.2	0.7
Taken without consent	65.5	28.9	5.6	0.0	0.0
Fraud/deception	98.6	1.4	0.0	0.0	0.0
Criminal damage	76.8	21.1	2.1	0.0	0.0
Threatening behaviour/carrying or discharging offensive weapon	93.0	5.6	1.4	0.0	0.0
Arson	97.2	2.8	0.0	0.0	0.0
Driving offences	97.9	1.4	0.7	0.0	0.0
Drug offences	100.0	0.0	0.0	0.0	0.0
Others	87.3	12.0	0.7	0.0	0.0

such as those not listed in Table 6 (for example, theft, driving offences and fraud) do not raise the predicted costs.

The fifth of the offence variables listed in Table 6 measures the value of property stolen or damaged. (For those people whose crimes were not property-related, the value of this variable was set to zero.) As would be expected, the higher the value of the property stolen and/or damaged, the higher the cost of intermediate treatment, although the marginal impact of this factor is low.

Accommodation The places of accommodation immediately prior to the court appearance are summarised in Table 8. Four out of five sample members were living with one or more natural or adoptive parent, and one in ten lived in a hostel, bed and breakfast, or local authority accommodation. The effect of the latter was to push up costs, partly because this accommodation is itself more costly, and partly because non-accommodation costs appeared to be higher for these young people. Not surprisingly, costs were highest for young people previously living in special residential educational establishments, and were lowest for those living alone (see the final equation from series D).

Table 8
Whom the clients live with: percentages in specific settings

Setting	%
Parents/single parent/official or unofficial adoptive parents	83.8
Siblings/grandparents/other relative	3.5
Friends/girlfriend	1.4
Hostel/bed and breakfast/local authority accomodation	9.9
Alone	1.4
No fixed address	0.0

Background characteristics Young people with a recent history of (non-trivial) physical illness needed more services, especially health care, which raised the overall costs of IT, both over the full period and on a weekly basis. There is a small and weak association between cost and ethnic group, and stronger links with educational status. Other things being equal, weekly costs were higher for those young people who were not in full-time education or had been expelled, and considerably higher for those who had attended special schools. As with the effect of physical illness, the higher costs were generally not to be found in relation to the IT service itself but in adjunct services. A community-based service or sentence such as IT obviously cannot generally influence the need for and use of health care and education services, but these needs and services might be dealt with and provided differently (and perhaps not provided at all) in custodial settings. The associated costs therefore need to be taken into account for some public policy discussions.

Area of the country None of the four research areas was in London, so that there were unlikely to be major input price influences on costs. Nevertheless, the four areas are served by different courts and local authorities, and the patterns of voluntary and other activities were not identical. The effects of the area indicator variables on costs therefore reflect both exogenous factors (beyond the control of provider agencies) as well as endogenous efficiency and other differences.

4 Conclusion

We have shown that the costs of intermediate treatment extend some distance and with some impact beyond the budgets of the services to which courts sentence young people. We have concentrated on intermediate treatment, but this finding is likely to be generalisable to all community alternatives to custodial sentences. So too are our other main findings: that the costs of sentences show marked variations between individuals, and that these variations can be explained in part by reference to the pre-sentence characteristics of offenders.

At the national or macro level, no sensible policy can be formulated and discussed without some attention being paid to its cost implications, for resources are almost always scarce relative to the demands placed upon them. Other things being equal, we fervently believe that decision-making informed by costs is better than decision-making without costs data. At the micro level, the impact of costs on those who sentence offenders will be limited but that still does not make costs irrelevant. As the 1990 criminal justice White Paper (Cm 965, 1990, para. 9.1) remarked: 'A price cannot be put on justice, but it is not without its costs'.

Notes

* The work reported here was funded by the Department of Health. The authors would like to express their considerable gratitude to former PSSRU colleagues Dave Bryson and Eileen Robertson who did so much of the groundwork and early field work, and to Tony Bottoms, Bill McWilliams and Brenda McWilliams of the Institute of Criminology, University of Cambridge for support, advice and access to data. All views expressed in the chapter are, however, those of the authors.
1 We are also not aware of similar research outside the UK, though, in the USA, work by Murray and Cox (1979) and Vincent (1980) is of some

relevance. Other PSSRU research on the economics of criminal justice options includes examinations of community service orders (Knapp et al., 1990, 1992a), reparation and mediation (Knapp and Netten, 1992), prisons (Knapp and Fenyo, 1988) and a bail information and accommodation service (work in progress).

2   Further findings from this study are reported in Knapp et al. (1992b; 1992c).

3   In research on community care for adult client groups, the links between the costs of individual care packages and area-level policy or practice indicators were found to be statistically significant but extremely difficult to interpret (see Knapp et al., 1992d, Chap. 14).

4   An added complication is that some of these indicator variables for relations between the young person and his family are strongly correlated with some of the offending and other variables, making it harder to disentangle the underlying causal connections.

5   Statistical significance was usually at the 90 per cent level, although we need to be prepared to relax this criterion when in the kind of exploratory mode of analysis being undertaken here. For an empirical association 'to make sense' it would either need to accord with prior conceptual argument – which is barely a restriction in this study – or we would need to be sure that the association is not masking some other and more fundamental link.

References

Bottoms, A.E., Bown, P., McWilliams, B., McWilliams, W. and Nellis, M. (1990) *Intermediate Treatment and Juvenile Justice*, HMSO, London.

Cm 965 (1990) *Crime, Justice and Protecting the Public*, HMSO, London.

Curtis, S. (1989) *Juvenile Offending: Prevention Through Intermediate Treatment*, Batsford, London.

Knapp, M.R.J. (1984)The relative costs of intermediate treatment and custody, *Home Office Research Bulletin*, 18, 24-7.

Knapp, M.R.J. and Fenyo, A. (1988) Prison costs: why the variation? *Home Office Research Bulletin*, 25, 9-13.

Knapp, M.R.J. and Netten, A. (1992) Reparation, mediation and prosecution: comparative costs, in S. Warner *Making Amends: An Evaluation of the SACRO Reparation and Mediation Project*, Ashgate, Aldershot.

Knapp, M.R.J., Thomas, N. and Hine, J. (1990) The economics of community service orders: a study of costs in five English areas, Discussion Paper 697/2, Personal Social Services Research Unit, University of Kent at Canterbury.

Knapp, M.R.J., Robertson, E. and McIvor, G. (1992a) The comparative costs of community service and custody in Scotland, *The Howard Journal of Criminal Justice*, 31, 1, 8-30.

Knapp, M.R.J., McCrone, P., Drury, C. and Gould, E. (1992b) The comparative costs of sentencing options for young offenders, Discussion Paper 848, PSSRU, University of Kent at Canterbury.

Knapp, M.R.J., McCrone, P., Drury, C. and Gould, E. (1992c) The cost-effectiveness of intermediate treatment as an alternative to custody for young offenders, Discussion Paper 853, PSSRU, University of Kent at Canterbury.

Knapp, M.R.J., Cambridge, P., Thomason, C., Beecham, J., Allen, C. and Darton, R. (1992d) *Care in the Community: Challenge and Demonstration*, Ashgate, Aldershot.

Murray, C.A. and Cox, C.A. (1979) *Beyond Probation: Juvenile Corrections and the Chronic Delinquent*, Sage, London and Beverly Hills.

Robertson, E. and Knapp, M.R.J. (1988) Promoting intermediate treatment: a problem of excess demand or excess supply? *British Journal of Social Work*, 18 (Supplement), 131-47.

Robertson, E., Knapp, M.R.J., Crank, D. and Wood, C. (1986) The comparative costs of intermediate treatment and its alternatives in Tameside, Discussion Paper 374, Personal Social Services Research Unit, University of Kent at Canterbury.

Vincent, J. (1980) *Planning Resources for Community-Based Treatment of Juvenile Offenders*, Social Policy Research Ltd, London.

Part IV:
Epilogue

13 Costs Estimation and Community Care: Why We Must Run Fast To Stand Still

Bleddyn Davies

What are some of the broader principles we should bear in mind when (with sadness or relief) we put down a book like this? There is no danger that we will forget the need for methodological advance, for ensuring that agencies create data systems to answer the essential routine questions for themselves, for finding ways of getting the expensive evidence to tackle non-routine and as yet unanswered (and for that matter, unasked) questions. There is no danger that we will be allowed to forget the importance of sound applications of accepted methodologies. Least of all is there a danger that we will go back to the old days when costs were not central to the thinking of right-minded managers and policy-makers.

The principles which are more likely to be forgotten in our highly-focused all-absorbing lives of intense activity are broader. Their importance is that they can help to put what we know into perspective. They can help to set long-term goals.

But before we speculate more widely, we should remind ourselves of the main aim in putting together this collection. The original intention was to provide examples of the application of principles of costs analysis. There are many textbooks in economics and accounting describing costing principles. There are certainly many descriptive examples of costing in various fields of policy. However, there is a dearth of books compiling examples in British community and long-term care, particularly British analyses of the assumptions which it is now the national agenda to encourage. And there are not many books about the principles written with a sense of proportion, based on actually having applied those principles in this particular area.

But managers and others urgently need to access such examples now. Compared with the Seebohm years, the Griffiths era has given costs an altogether new importance. In the Seebohm years, 'costs' were useful for leaning on the open doors of those controlling buoyant public revenues. In the Griffiths era, 'costs' are uniquely important signals for acting out the new imperative – almost the moral imperative – to be more effective and efficient in the use of public resources in ways which are user-responsive. These signals must be used to define the limits of what can be afforded, to alert managers to impending organisational and personal disaster in a Micawber world in which to spend sixpence in the pound too much spells sorrow. A world in which the responsibility for doing so is increasingly pinned on individuals.

For these reasons, we hope that this collection of essays is useful. This chapter sets the preceding discussion in the context of theoretical approaches developed in the PSSRU and highlights the need for research to reflect local needs and circumstances. In doing this, the chapter focuses on two points: the importance of appropriate interpretive frameworks; and some priorities for continuous re-estimation.

1 Cost estimates as 'facts'

1.1 Cost estimates and interpretive frameworks: POW and SPOW examples

Readers will not have looked at many pages before they appreciate the essential interpretive ambiguity of costs seen as 'facts'.

First, *many of the cost 'facts' of greatest interest can only be estimated within broad limits*. This is illustrated in Chapter 10 on costing in the community care experiments. The chapter summarises the principles and methods for costing for elements of interest in the evaluation of the Thanet ('Kent') Community Care Project, the evaluation design which formed the template for later replications, such as the Gateshead project (also described in that chapter). The narrow cost concepts (such as cost to the social services department) can be estimated far more accurately than the broader concepts (such as social opportunity cost). The more thorough the application of principles to the estimation of costs, the more that has to be imputed on the basis of scant evidence and hypothesis.

There are two problems. One is that information about costs is expensive to get, and what to collect and process should itself be an informed cost-benefit decision. The other is the limits of the precisely knowable: the wide limits within which a 'true' value may lie. (Economists and philosophers are in one respect alike: the cleverer they are, the less they claim they can say with certainty; and so the less use they are to new managerialists - save, of course, for the provision of useful ammunition to produce mighty bangs to impress the opposition.) Chapter 10 illustrates some of this. Davies and Challis (1986, pp.401-42) explore the argument and its implications in greater detail.

Second, *costs as 'facts' gain their meaning from an interpretive framework, loose or tight, explicit and consistent, or implicit and riddled with contradictions born of cognitive dissonance.* The framework which the PSSRU has been developing since the early 1970s we call the production of welfare approach (Davies and Knapp, 1981; Knapp, 1984). No sooner does the reader turn the first few pages of this book than the 'POW approach' is met.

The production of welfare (POW) framework sets cost 'facts' into the context of 'need-related circumstances' and characteristics of service systems (quasi-inputs and non-resource inputs more generally), and outcomes of evaluative significance in their own right (final outputs). The archetypal POW study: estimates costs of individual users to various parties; describes resource flows and the levels and combinations of outcomes; explains *how* these resources needs and outcomes influence one another and so estimates the costs or resources required to achieve outcomes; and explains *why* they have their observed values.

The exact specification of such frameworks as POW matter greatly for the interpretation of the cost estimates produced. Chapter 4 illustrates that well. It was a case drawn from applying a variant of the general production of welfare approach which we call SPOW: the social production of welfare approach (Netten and Davies, 1990). The chapter describes a new way of costing informal care, reflecting the SPOW framework. A comparison of POW and SPOW analyses within the same study illustrates with even greater clarity the influence of the approach on the estimation and interpretation costs as 'facts'. *Community Services and the Social Production of Welfare* (forthcoming) reports the results of SPOW-based modelling of the relations between costs and outcomes. The application of the SPOW ideas leads to the derivation of different variables, different combinations of variables in models, and different cost estimates from those in *Resources Needs and Outcomes in Community-Based Care*, which applied the POW approach (Davies et al., 1990). For example, confidence of relatives in service interventions emerges as an important cost-related outcome using the SPOW approach. More fundamentally, the application of SPOW allows one to see different features of the ways in which services contribute to the production of welfare (Davies and Baines, 1992). There can be no doubt that this research framework would help to suggest policy ideas for the real world.

So a variety of perspectives leads to variety in the formal methods of handling evidence, and to different answers to empirical questions. That is not to argue that some answers are correct and others wrong. The examples above are interesting because they illustrate how differences in paradigm cause differences in estimates in fields where two approaches overlap. The two approaches are different mainly because they have been designed to tackle different questions, but POW and SPOW are in essence complementary. Their estimates of costs as facts are different because they are describing different concepts for different purposes. This is similar in principle to the differences one observes between opportunity cost and (say) revenue cost estimates produced by accountants. Costs as 'facts' estimated from different perspectives can be equally valid, as long as square pegs are not used for round holes.

But that is not the whole truth. The argument context of methodology-embodying paradigms are influenced by judgements about what is important, as it was so fashionable to labour during the 1960s. Paradigms which prosper are those which fit the spirit of the age. What differentiates POW and SPOW is the position from which they view the world. The SPOW vision is a world of persons and primary social networks adapting to the dependency of members. It is a world of emotional interdependence within the networks with likely consequences for the responses of individual members. The form of these responses will pivot on coping with dependence within, of course, histories of relationships and perceptions of rights and obligations (Finch, 1989), but also through time. This is a world in which the network input is important for most dependants for most purposes; a world in which there are, therefore, trade-offs between time uses and benefits over the whole of individual and social life; a world of complex variations between networks creating a vast range of substitution possibilities. Substitutions between inputs in general, and potentially many sources of help in particular, all suggest a world in which the formal services best play their role by fitting around the network, providing support by gap-filling and brokerage (Qureshi et al., 1988). This, of course, must be in a way which makes the most equitable and efficient use of public funds by the criteria embodied in the Community Care White Paper (Cm 849, 1989). (Of course, the only new thing in the SPOW framework is the way the conceptual bits are measured and assembled: the bits themselves have a thoroughly orthodox pedigree.)

POW views the world differently. Its vision was a benevolent state agency, albeit one responsive to consumers needs and values, but ultimately making its prioritisation prevail through its professional judgements and politically-determined allocations. It is the world of top-down democracy, representative and polyarchic, not a world where power is held by enabled consumers. There were contradictions in much of the thinking of the 1960s: the age of Seebohm. They were later made more explicit, for instance in the disagreements expressed over the report of the Barclay Committee (1982) and Robert Pinker's minority report (Pinker, 1982). POW is not the way the Independent Living Movement looks at the world. POW – with its linking of costs, needs and outcomes – quintessentially belongs in the early 1980s. It was not quite a child of its time, but was born prematurely in the 1970s when its first crude statement, in mid-1974, was called the 'needs/production relations approach'.

So there is no denying that if we were forced to choose between POW and SPOW, we would be driven to do so on the basis of assumptions about the rights and obligations of individuals, primary social networks, the more formal of the mediating institutions of society, and the state itself. Faced with such a choice, we would be forced to argue that SPOW is closer to the philosophy of the new community care policy.

Fortunately, we are not faced with such a choice, though perhaps we should, in some cases, make our methodologies for POW cost estimates more SPOW-oriented. We should aim for a balance so more estimates are produced for the areas in which the SPOW approach is best.

1.2 Interpretive frameworks and cost estimates in policy models

In the last section, it was argued that the approach which shapes how costs are estimated should be compatible with the assumptions of the argument in which they are used. That is still more clearly the case when one is considering them in whole 'policy models' which themselves clearly reflect POW assumptions. (Policy models are the policy structures and arrangements designed to induce, or at any rate enable, the achievement of policy goals by the conscious use of data on costs, needs and outcomes.) Several are alluded to in the book. One other model was the system for building compensation for variations in the need-related circumstances of populations and the differences in the prices of inputs into grant formulae embodied in the central grant to local authorities (Davies, 1986).

Drawing on costs estimated using the methodology described in Chapter 6, Bebbington and Kelly (1992) have shown some of the ambiguities in the interpretation of evidence about how well these policies have worked. Over a period long enough for the effects of the contradictions in fundamental structures to work themselves through local political and policy processes, unit costs in Inner London have increased relative to other parts of the country. A spokesperson for the London boroughs could argue that the fall in volume must be accompanied by greater needs, with the effect that unit costs must be higher. The net effect of the grant system, therefore, must have been to increase territorial injustice. However quite a different view could be taken. The authors of the Audit Commission report (1987) on London costs could say that it was because these were the least 'efficient' authorities, that they had been unable to grasp nettles in the way needed to control unit costs, and faced with a constraint on total spending, they have had to deprive their needy populations of service rather than grapple with the management problems of forcing slack out of unit costs. No doubt gross inefficiency is easy to slip into, perhaps not difficult to avoid, but the very devil to escape.

Who is right? Some matters of fact are relevant. The first is whether the gradient of costs by case type over the country as a whole is steep enough to make the reductions in volume drive up London costs sufficiently to justify the supposed claim made by our hypothetical spokesperson for the London boroughs. Chapter 6 has indeed illustrated how types of case affect unit costs in child care and in services for elderly people and does support the case of the spokesperson for the London boroughs. On the other hand, Bebbington and Kelly (1992) also show that political instability is one of the strongest correlates of high unit costs, indicating that the Audit Commission's explanation warrants more attention. These opposing explanations are not entirely contradictory. Indeed, both may be partly true.

The implications, if both were partly true, would be profound. It would quite clearly show circumstances in which the most enlightened POW model for directing the grant could not work to improve equity. If the Audit Commission is more right than the London boroughs' spokesperson, a grant formula which was good on equity grounds – because it allowed (or provided incentives to) authorities of similar efficiency to achieve volumes correlated with relative needs – would be bad on efficiency grounds, since the money would be used to compensate for variations in efficiency at the expense of equity in access and the numbers of units of services received by the needy.

The situation would be worse if vertical target inefficiency were correlated with the inefficiency causing higher unit costs, as well it might be (Bebbington et al., 1991). If this is so, one of the most important forces affecting the overall equity and efficiency in the use of public funds cannot work. We have a recipe for long-run disaster. It may be that is what Bebbington and Kelly's (1992) results describe: the slow slide into increasingly bad outcomes pushed along by a benevolent POW policy model with its compensation for the costs of inputs and the spending needs of populations.

The moral of the story for POW policy models is: it is not enough that the version of POW on which the cost estimates are based must be compatible with values of current policy. The POW logic underlying the policy model itself must be compatible with the major basic structures within which it is being applied.

How then can the problem be overcome in this case? Can we deduce anything from *ad hoc* solutions about solutions generally? One way would be to throw territorial justice to the wolves, and produce a financing system which focused solely on efficiency. A second way would be to throw efficiency to the crocodiles and design the financing system to so overcompensate high-need authorities that they would produce the territorially just volumes while worsening their efficiencies. Neither alternative is attractive, or even viable.

There is another general method: in principle better; in practice, vastly difficult because it is so radical. It would be to change some features of the structure. One variant would be to resolve the Crossman dilemma: to strike a new balance in the trade-off between scale and efficiency and scale and democracy. This is currently considered for Wales.

The proposal is to create smaller unitary authorities. Service commissioners themselves might then be put at arms' length from the political bodies. Local authorities might cover areas smaller than the commissioning authorities. Financing for the commissioning authorities might come largely from a straight central grant, with the local authorities having their own tax-base with a resource equalisation grant for contracting with the commissioners to adapt priorities to local political cultures. In principle, other organisations could do likewise (or commission directly): for example, occupational welfare in a system of Griffiths social care maintenance organisations (Davies and Challis, 1986; Griffiths, 1988). This fits with growing distrust of the capacity of local authorities in several countries to face up to the reduction in public expenditure. If political instability is the problem, then reform of voting systems or boundaries might reduce political instability at the local level. For urban authorities, the most effective solution might be a type of proportional representation designed to enhance stability of control by the political centre for that area.

2 Priorities for continuous re-estimation

Everyone agrees that this is a period of accelerating change in the relations between resources and outcomes in community care. Indeed, it is a time when the policy world may be most affected by the descriptions which are provided. In particular, descriptions of costs and of the costs of outcomes may influence the way in which resources are used, and so costs and the costs of outcomes. The long-run consequence of the policy to create and strengthen mechanisms for monitoring policy achievements and publicising the results will be to make today's costs information affect tomorrow's costs. It will be like the world of macro-economic modelling and forecasting.

Of course, the re-estimation of routine costs will be part of this world. Already directors of social services departments talk proudly of their new financial control systems which give an almost up-to-the minute account of commitments as well as expenditure, and their financial information bases which begin to uncover the variable hidden costs and those other submarine bits of the costs' iceberg described in Chapter 2.

What are some of the things which we must remember?

2.1 Responsiveness of demand to prices given need and income

Chapter 7 on costs, prices and charges reminds us of the potential importance of local charging policies for equity and efficiency in community care. In its review of British policy analysis of the issue, it also reminds us how many issues influence local (and national) policy thinking. American experience suggests that the big financial incentives are best subordinated to one or, at most, a few straightforward goals. For instance, a review of literature in the mid-1980s showed that some American states had successfully designed their methodologies for fixing payments from public funds for nursing homes to provide incentives to keep down costs, but they had used other means to tackle quality and access. Conversely, other American states had been successful in using the design of the payment system as a mechanism to improve quality or access, but only achieved this by using other mechanisms to control costs (Davies, 1986).

By implication, the White Paper sets clear priorities for charging policies. Charges must help to concentrate public funding on those who are in greatest need and who are unable to meet the full service cost themselves, but must do this without preventing priority needs from being met. Whether one can design a charging policy which does both simultaneously depends on how responsive demand is to charges among those most in need.

An analysis of the relationship between charges and consumption of services by elderly people in the mid-1980s showed that the users' degree of need seemed not to affect that responsiveness to the price of the 'marginal unit'. Other things equal, persons of low income and assets were no more responsive to price than those with higher incomes who tended to consume less than poorer persons. Of course, we know the reasons why. The home help organisers and others were able, in effect, to sidestep the strict letter of the policy for cases for whom consumption would have most effect; or there were loopholes thoughtfully built into the book of rules (Davies et al., 1990, pp.40-2, 412).

Recent developments may be changing the relationships between charging and consumption. As higher proportions of income are being recouped from user charges, the pressure of needs on resources may intensify, and field allocators' room for manoeuvre may diminish. (Back to the importance of devolving budgets and discretion in the use of resources – see Chapter 8.) So the earlier results are unlikely to hold in 1994. They may be still less likely to hold by the later 1990s. We can expect quantities consumed to prove much more sensitive to the price of the marginal units. We can expect the sensitivity to be greater for those just above the level at which they would be eligible for free service than for those who are better off, and (depending on the precise nature of the charging policy) perhaps the poorest. This has probably been so for privately-provided residential care (Darton et al., 1987) in which case the two objectives of the White Paper may be less compatible in the future than in the past.

There are two implications.
- We shall have to monitor the demand responsiveness to price and income; that is, estimating the price and income elasticities. But we also must monitor such responsiveness in the context of: needs-related circumstances; the characteristics which make the consequences of lower utilisation seriously reduce the effectiveness of services for preventing deterioration and higher subsequent costs; attitudes and personality; cultural factors; and gender: in short, all the foci of argument about equity.
- Making good quantitative estimates will demand explicitness about the interpretive context, the compatibility of those interpretive assumptions

with the values of the policy itself, their compatibility with knowledge of the workings of the detailed and microscopic processes: the point made in section 1 above. The demands are the same as for costs estimates. So, for example, as for costs estimates, we cannot expect there to be one national picture, but many local pictures.

2.2 *Local variations in relative costs and prices*

Supply prices can differ dramatically with quantities demanded in all but the longest of runs for inputs, particularly for services whose supply takes a long time to adjust. Moreover, they can vary greatly between areas. This point is illustrated in Davies et al. (1990, pp.364-5) and in studies of variations between European countries in the costs of residential care when measured by the number of units of home care inputs that could be bought (Jamieson, 1991).[1]

Therefore, for costs, the national averages of relative prices of service options are just that: national averages concealing big variations. These averages would grossly distort equity and efficiency in individual areas if applied as policy criteria locally. With the variation, the nationally-uniform rates for the *prestation dépendance* proposed by the Schopflin Report would be misguided; but nationally applied criteria for setting the rates would not (Schopflin, 1991). Such prerequisites feed back into the processes required to make estimates of responsiveness to prices.

This local variation is the rule, not the exception. It is the equity-cum-efficiency interpretation of the Benthamite rationale for truly local government: only those from the locality can comprehend local needs well enough to respond to them. Allowance for responding to local factors in making the most equitable and efficient use of resources must be there even for allocations which are inescapably national, such as the formula for allocating central government grant to health and local authorities. And for these, the cost estimates should be made using models which are built around what would be efficient local responses to relative prices in the areas, as well as more exclusively equity logics (Davies and Coles, 1981).

3 Conclusion

Specific costing examples reflect a world in which many important features of the context are already on the move: relative prices, how resources can be combined to produce the desired outcomes, how the desired outcomes are defined. But the preceding chapters have demonstrated things to hold on to. Principles last longer than precise methodologies or the estimates based on them, although how those elementary principles are worked through changes continuously in response to fast-moving ideas and advances in methodologies and theory.

So if we are to make cost estimation fulfil its potential for making the better use of resources, we shall need continuously to revise not just the estimates, but the ways of making them. This book illustrates that such revision requires also the continuous re-estimation of the parameters of the production of welfare to fit changing values and assumptions, as well as the changing economy of welfare. Two decades ago, there was no such work. The effort is still small. It would be a mistake not to invest still more in this work as the pace of change in the real world of community care accelerates. In this game, we have to run fast to stand still.

Note

1   The point applies not only to costs and prices. The same is true for the responsiveness of the demand of areas' populations to different charge levels for services. For instance, the price elasticity of demand for school meals varied massively between areas during the 1960s, and it was established that the demand- and supply-generating circumstances which caused them likewise varied (Davies et al., 1971; Davies, 1978).

References

Audit Commission (1987) The management of London's authorities: preventing the breakdown of services, Occasional Paper 2, Audit Commission, London.

Barclay, P.M. (1982) Social Workers: Their Roles and Tasks, National Institute for Social Work/Bedford Square Press, London.

Bebbington, A.C. and Kelly, A. (1992) Unit costs, policy drift and territorial justice for local authority personal social services, Discussion Paper 799, Personal Social Services Research Unit, University of Kent at Canterbury.

Bebbington, A.C., Davies, B.P., Kheramandia, M. and Moennadin, R. (1991) Target efficiencies revisited: updated estimates incorporating the new policy criteria, Discussion Paper 793, Personal Social Services Research Unit, University of Kent at Canterbury.

Cm 849 (1989) Caring for People: Community Care in the Next Decade and Beyond, HMSO, London.

Darton, R.A., Jefferson, S., Sutcliffe, E. and Wright, K. (1987) The PSSRU/CHE survey of residential and nursing homes: the costs and changes of the surveyed homes, Discussion Paper 563/3, Personal Social Services Research Unit, University of Kent at Canterbury.

Davies, B.P. (1978) *Universality, Selectivity and Effectiveness in Social Policy*, Heinemann, London.

Davies, B.P. (1986) American lessons for British policy and research on long-term care of the elderly, *Quarterly Journal of Social Affairs*, 2, 3, 321-55.

Davies, B.P. and Baines, B. (1992) The SPOW production function, Discussion Paper 856, Personal Social Services Research Unit, University of Kent at Canterbury.

Davies, B.P. and Challis, D.J. (1986) *Matching Resources to Needs in Community Care*, Gower, Aldershot.

Davies, B.P. and Coles, O. (1981) Towards a terrotorial cost function for the home help service, *Social Policy and Administration*, 15, 1, 32-42.

Davies, B.P. and Knapp, M.R.J. (1981) *Old People's Homes and the Production of Welfare*, Routledge and Kegan Paul, London.

Davies, B.P., Reddin, M. and Dales, A. (1971) Some constraints on school meals policy, *Social and Economic Administration*, 5, 1, 34-52.

Davies, B.P., Bebbington, A.C. and Charnley, H. and colleagues (1990) *Resources, Needs and Outcomes in Community-Based Care*, Avebury, Aldershot.

Finch, J. (1989) *Family Obligation and Social Change*, Polity Press, Cambridge.

Griffiths, R. (1988) *Community Care: Agenda for Action*, HMSO, London.

Jamieson, A. (ed.)(1991) *Home Care for Older People in Europe: A Comparison of Policies and Practices*, Commission of the European Communities: Health Services Research Series No. 7, Oxford University Press, Oxford.

Knapp, M.R.J. (1984) *The Economics of Social Care*, Macmillan, London.

Netten, A. and Davies, B.P. (1990) The social production of welfare and consumption of social services, *Journal of Public Policy*, 10, 331-47.

Pinker, R. (1982) The Report: an alternative view, in P. Barclay (ed.) *Social Workers: Their Roles and Tasks*, Bedford Square Press/NCVO, London.

Qureshi, H., Challis, D.J. and Davies, B.P. (1988) *Helpers in Case-Managed Community Care*, Gower, Aldershot.

Schopflin, P. (1991) *Dépendance et solidarités: mieux aider les personnes âgées*, Commissariat Général du Plan, Paris.

Subject Index

Author Index